Knitting
With Bits & Pieces™

Edited by Jeanne Stauffer

HOUSE of
WHITE
BIRCHES
PUBLISHERS
SINCE 1947

Knitting With Bits & Pieces

Editor: Jeanne Stauffer
Associate Editors: Dianne Schmidt, Rachelle Haughn
Design Associate: Vicki Blizzard
Technical Editor: E.J. Slayton
Copy Editors: Mary Martin, Alice Rice
Publications Coordinator: Tanya Turner

Photography: Jeff Chilcote, Tammy Christian, Kelly Heydinger, Chris Kausch, Nancy Sharp
Photography Assistant: Linda Quinlan

Production Coordinator: Brenda Gallmeyer
Book and Cover Design: Jessi Butler
Production Artist: Edith Teegarden
Production Assistants: Janet Bowers, Marj Morgan
Traffic Coordinator: Sandra Beres
Technical Artists: Liz Morgan, Mitch Moss, Travis Spangler, Chad Summers

Publishers: Carl H. Muselman, Arthur K. Muselman
Chief Executive Officer: John Robinson
Publishing Marketing Director: David McKee
Book Marketing Manager: Craig Scott
Product Development Director: Vivian Rothe
Publishing Services Manager: Brenda R. Wendling

Printed in the United States of America
First Printing: 2002
Library of Congress Number: 2001089863
ISBN: 1-882138-86-4

Kelly Sinak, page 108, from Charmaine Model Agency, Fort Wayne, Ind.

Dear Friends,

I love yarn. When I see a new yarn, I want to touch it and knit something from it. I may buy a ball or two, even if I do not have a project in mind. I always like to take advantage of any opportunity to buy yarn and add to my stash.

When I finish a project, I usually have yarn left over, sometimes more than a single odd ball. I know some knitters never buy more yarn than they need, but I am not one of them. If in doubt, I always buy more than I need.

And so, I have a growing stash of yarn. I don't have a lot of any one kind, but small amounts of lots and lots of different yarns.

Some of this yarn has wonderful memories attached to it. I remember the design I made with it and the person who received the project. Other yarn is simply yarn I couldn't resist buying during one of my yarn-shopping trips. It is waiting to be knit into a memory!

Many knitters have told me about their growing stash of yarn, mentioning that they don't have enough of any one kind to do anything with it. So that was our challenge. We looked for designs that used multiple kinds and colors of yarns.

Some of the projects we included in this book are small projects. Others use one main yarn and small amounts of other yarns. Many of our sweater and afghan designs use a combination of yarns of different weights, content and colors.

If you have gorgeous yarns in your stash just waiting to be made into a memory, then you will love this book. You can create wonderful knitted designs from bits and pieces of yarn. So pull out that stash, select the first design you want to make and start knitting! Everyone's stash is different, so every project you make will have your own distinctive look.

Warm regards,

Jeanne Stauffer

Contents

One of a Kind

Odds & Ends

Little Bitties

Yikes! Stripes!

Knitted Samplers

Knitting With Bits & Pieces

One of a Kind

You only need one skein of yarn to create any of these wonderful projects. We've included yardage and/or weight information when possible to help you in selecting yarn from your stash.

Toddler's Happy Hats

Designs by Diane Zangl

*Colorful hats in a variety of patterns are
sure to bring a smile to any child's face.
Choose from three fun styles.*

Skill Level

Intermediate***

Size

Toddlers' 1–2 years (3–4 years) Instructions are given for smaller size, with larger size in parentheses. When only 1 number is given, it applies to both sizes.

Finished Measurements

Fits a head circumference of 17 (19) inches

Materials

- Lamb's Pride Superwash 100 percent wool worsted weight yarn from Brown Sheep Co. (100 yds/50g per ball): 1 ball MC, small amounts each of CC as listed for each hat
- Size 4 (3.5mm) 16-inch circular needles
- Size 6 (4mm) 16-inch circular and double-pointed needles or size needed to obtain gauge
- Tapestry needle

Gauge

19 sts and 24 rows = 4 inches/10cm in St st with larger needles

To save time, take time to check gauge.

Pattern Stitches

1/1 Twisted Rib

All Rnds: *K1b, p1, rep from * around.

2/2 Twisted Rib

All Rnds: *K2b, p2, rep from * around.

Flower Patch Hat

Materials

- Sweeten pink #SW35 (MC), plum crazy #SW55, safron #SW14, sea foam #SW16

With MC and smaller circular needle, cast on 72 (80) sts. Join without twisting, pm between first and last st.

Work even in k1, p1 rib for 1 (1½) inches, inc 8 sts evenly on last rnd. (80, 88 sts)

Change to larger needles and knit 4 (5) rnds.

Referring to Chart A, work 19 rnds in color pat. Work even in MC only until hat measures 6 (7) inches. Change to dpn.

Shape top

Rnd 1: *K1, k2tog, rep from * around, ending with k2 (k1). (54, 59 sts)

Rnds 2–4: Knit.

Rnd 5: *K2tog, k1, rep from * around, ending with k0 (k2tog). (36, 39 sts)

Rnds 6–8: Knit.

Rnd 9: [K1, k2tog] around. (24, 26 sts)

Rnd 10: Knit.

Rnd 11: K2tog around. (12, 13 sts)

Rnd 12: Rep Rnd 11. (6, 7 sts)

Cut yarn, leaving a 12-inch end. Draw end through remaining sts twice. Fasten off securely.

Tassel

Hold all colors tog and [wrap around a 4-inch piece of cardboard] 25–30 times.

Tie 1 end of loops with a separate strand of MC, cut opposite end. Trim ends evenly. Tie tassel securely to top of hat.

Toy Soldiers Hat

Materials

- Navy night #SW58 (MC), red baron #SW81, alabaster #SW10, charcoal heather #SW04

With MC and smaller circular needle, cast on 72 (80) sts. Join without twisting, pm between first and last st.

Work even in 1/1 Twisted Rib for 1 (1½) inches, inc 8 (10) sts on last rnd. (80, 90 sts)

Change to larger needles and knit 4 (5) rnds.

Referring to Chart B, work 24 rnds in color pat. Work even in MC only until hat measures 6 (7) inches. Change to dpn.

Shape top

Mark every 10th st.

Dec rnd: [K to 2 sts before marker, k2tog] 8 (9) times.

Rep dec rnd until 8 (9) sts remain.

Next rnd: [K2tog] 4 times, k0 (1). (4 sts)

Loopy Topknot

Using only 2 dpn, make I-cord: *k4, sl sts back to LH needle. Rep from * until I-cord measures approximately 4 inches.

With separate dpn, pick up 4 sts in top of hat, [k 1 st of cord tog with 1 st of hat] 4 times**. Rep from * to ** for 3 more loops. Bind off remaining 4 sts.

Rainbow Hearts Hat

Materials
- Alabaster #SW10 (MC), red wing #SW01, saffron #SW14, cornflower #SW57, turf green #SW64

With MC and smaller circular needle, cast on 72 (80) sts. Join without twisting, pm between first and last st.

Work even in 2/2 Twisted Rib for 1 (1½) inches, inc 8 (10) sts on last rnd. (80, 90 sts)

Change to larger needles and knit 4 (5) rnds.

Referring to Chart C, work in color pat for 20 rnds.

Sizing note: On Rnds 3–18, motif rep is a multiple of 16 sts for size 1–2, and a multiple of 15 sts on size 3–4.

Work even in MC only until hat measures 6 (7) inches. Change to dpn.

Shape top

Mark every 10th st.

Dec rnd: [K to 2 sts before marker, k2tog] 8 (9) times.

Rep dec rnd until 8 (9) sts remain.

Cut yarn, leaving a 12-inch end. Draw end through remaining sts twice. Fasten off securely.

Braided Tassel

Using CC's of your choice, cut 3 (10-inch) strands of yarn and pull through top of hat. Fold strands in half and braid to end. Tie an overhand knot in end to fasten. Make 4 more braided strands in same manner. ❖

COLOR KEY A
- ☐ Sweeten pink
- ▨ Sea foam
- ■ Plum crazy
- ▧ Safron

COLOR KEY B
- ☐ Alabaster
- ■ Red baron
- ■ Navy nite
- ■ Charcoal heather

COLOR KEY C
- ☐ Alabaster
- ■ Red wing
- ▧ Safron
- ▨ Turf green
- ■ Cornflower

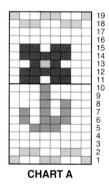

CHART A

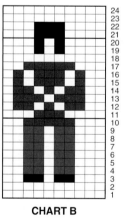

CHART B

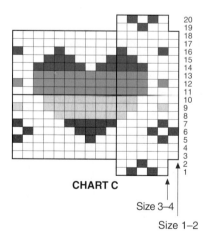

CHART C

Size 3–4

Size 1–2

Mock Cable Purse

Design by Kathie Ballard

This easy and fast mock cable purse features an easy pattern and is a good take-along project. It would make a great gift!

Skill Level

Easy**

Finished Size

Approximately 8 inches square (excluding strap)

Materials

- Worsted Weight 100 percent acrylic yarn (180 yds/3.5 oz per skein): 1 skein light blue
- Size 7 (4.5mm) needles or size needed to obtain gauge
- Tapestry needle

Gauge

Approximately 24 sts and 26 rows = 4 inches/10cm in pat

To save time, take time to check gauge.

Border

Cast on 45 sts.

Row 1: K1, *p1, k1, rep from * across.

Row 2: P1, *k1, p1, rep from * across.

Rows 3–10: Rep Rows 1 and 2.

Body

Rows 1, 3 and 5 (WS): K3, *p3, k3, rep from * across.

Row 2: P3, *k3, p3, rep from * across.

Row 4: P3, *sl 1 knitwise, k1 in st in row below next st, k2, pass sl st over 3 sts, p3, rep from * across.

Row 6: Rep Row 2.

Rep Rows 1–6 until 14 mock cables have been completed, ending with Row 6.

Border

Work 10 rows of ribbing as for beg. Bind off in pat.

Strap

Cast on 8 sts.

Work in k1, p1 ribbing until piece measures 30 inches. Bind off in rib, leaving a 12-inch end for sewing up.

Fold purse in half with RS tog, matching beg and end ribbing sections. Sew 1 end of strap to edge, centering on fold, sew edges of purse to sides of strap, matching rows. Rep on other side, being sure strap is not twisted. ❖

Baby's Car Seat Blanket

Design by Sue Childress

Tuck your little one into his or her car seat with love and lace. This easy-to-knit blanket will quickly become a favorite.

Skill Level

Easy**

Finished Size

Approximately 19 x 23 (38 x 48) inches Instructions are given for smaller size, with larger size in parentheses. When only 1 number is given, it applies to both sizes.

Materials

- DK weight acrylic blend yarn (260 yds/100g per ball): 2 (3) balls pink
- Size 7 (4.5mm) 24-inch circular needle or size needed to obtain gauge
- Tapestry needle

Gauge

16 sts = 4 inches/10cm in pat

To save time, take time to check gauge.

Blanket

Cast on 93 (191) sts.

Knit 3 (6) rows.

Border

Row 1: P2, *k5, p2, rep from * across.

Row 2: K2, *p5, k2, rep from * across.

Row 3: P2, *k2tog, yo, k1, yo, ssk, p2, rep from * across.

Row 4: K2, *p5, k2, rep from * across.

Knit 2 (4) rows, dec 1 st at beg of each row. (91, 187 sts)

Body

Row 1 (RS): P2, k5, p2, k4, [k2tog, yo, k1, yo, ssk, k7] 5 (13) times, end k2tog, yo, k1, yo, ssk, k4, p2, k5, p2.

Row 2 and remaining WS rows: K2, p5, k2, p across to last 9 sts, end k2, p5, k2.

Row 3: P2, k2tog, yo, k1, yo, ssk, p2, k3, [k2tog, yo, k3, yo, ssk, k5] 5 (13) times, end k2tog, yo, k3, yo, ssk, k3, p2, k2tog, yo, k1, yo, ssk, p2.

Row 5: P2, k5, p2, k2, [k2tog, yo, k5, yo, ssk, k3] 5 (13) times, end k2tog, yo, k5, yo, ssk, k2, p2, k5, p2.

Row 7: P2, k2tog, yo, k1, yo, ssk, p2, k1, [k2tog, yo, k7, yo, ssk, k1] 6 (14) times, end p2, k2tog, yo, k1, yo, ssk, p2.

Row 9: P2, k5, p2, k2tog, yo, k9, [yo, sl 1, k2tog, psso, yo, k9] 5 (13) times, end yo, ssk, p2, k5, p2.

Row 11: P2, k2tog, yo, k1, yo, ssk, p2, k4, [k2tog, yo, k1, yo, ssk, k7] 5 (13) times, end k2tog, yo, k1, yo, ssk, k4, p2, k2tog, yo, k1, yo, ssk, p2.

Row 13: P2, k5, p2, k3, [k2tog, yo, k3, yo, ssk, k5] 5 (13) times, end k2tog, yo, k3, yo, ssk, k3, p2, k5, p2.

Row 15: P2, k2tog, yo, k1, yo, ssk, p2, k2, [k2tog, yo, k5, yo, ssk, k3] 5 (13) times, end k2tog, yo, k5, yo, ssk, k2, p2, k2tog, yo, k1, yo, ssk, p2.

Row 17: P2, k5, p2, k1, [k2tog, yo, k7, yo, ssk, k1] 6 (14) times, p2, k5, p2.

Row 19: P2, k2tog, yo, k1, yo, ssk, p2, k2tog, yo, k9, [yo, sl 1, k2tog, psso, yo, k9] 5 (13) times, end yo, ssk, p2, k2tog, yo, k1, yo, ssk, p2.

Row 20: Rep Row 2.

Rep [Rows 1–20] a total of 6 (12) times.

Knit 2 (4) rows, inc 1 st at beg of each row. (93, 191 sts)

Rep border [Rows 1–4] 2 (4) times, knit 3 (6) rows and bind off in purl. ❖

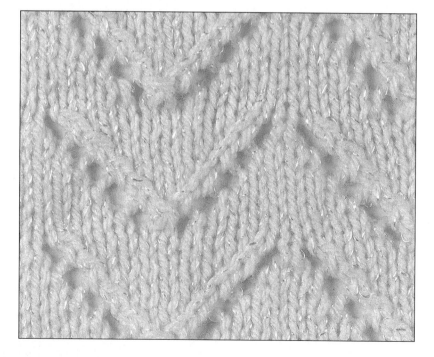

Tie-Dye Cap

Design by Laura Polley

One four-ounce skein of yarn will make two of these colorful and fun-to-knit hats. Your children will love them!

Skill Level

Easy**

Size

Child's 1–3 (4–7) years
Instructions are given for smaller size, with larger size in parentheses. When only 1 number is given, it applies to both sizes.

Finished Measurements

Head circumference: 20 (22) inches

Length to crown: 4½ (6) inches

Materials

- Red Heart Kids 100 percent acrylic worsted weight yarn from Coats & Clark Inc. (242 yds/ 4 oz per skein): 1 skein bikini variegated #2945
- Size 8 (5mm) straight needle (both sizes)
- 1-3 year size: Size 10 (6mm) double-pointed needles and 16-inch circular needles or size needed to obtain gauge
- 4-7 year size: Size 11 (8mm) double-pointed needles and 16-inch circular needles or size needed to obtain gauge
- Tapestry needle

Gauge

1–3 year size: 12 sts = 4 inches/10cm in St st with size 10 needles

4–7 year size: 11 sts = 4 inches/10cm in St st with size 11 needles

To save time, take time to check gauge.

Pattern Notes

One 4 oz skein will make a minimum of 2 hats in either size.

A yarn with a color sequence length of approximately 60 inches will give best color swirl effect.

Instructions

With appropriate circular needle for desired size, cast on 60 sts. Pm and join without twisting.

Work in rnds of St st (knit every rnd) until hat measures approximately 4½ (6) inches from beg.

Shape Top

Note: Switch to dpns as needed.

Rnd 1: *K8, k2tog, rep from * around. (54 sts)

Rnd 2: *K7, k2tog, rep from * around. (48 sts)

Rnd 3: *K6, k2tog, rep from * around (42 sts)

Rnd 4: *K5, k2tog, rep from * around. (36 sts)

Rnd 5: *K4, k2tog, rep from * around. (30 sts)

Rnd 6: *K3, k2tog, rep from * around. (24 sts)

Rnd 7: *K2, k2tog, rep from * around. (18 sts)

Rnd 8: *K1, k2tog, rep from * around. (12 sts)

Rnd 9: *K2 tog, rep from * around. (6 sts)

Cut yarn, leaving a 5-inch tail. With tapestry needle, weave tail through remaining sts and draw up tightly to close top.

Finishing

Hold hat so cast-on edge is at top. With size 8 needle, RS facing, loosely pick up and k 2 sts from first rnd worked after cast on. *With left forefinger or extra size 8 needle, pass first picked up st over 2nd picked up st. Loosely pick up and k 1 st to left of st on needle. Rep from * until 1 loop remains on needle. Cut yarn and draw through loop. ❖

Lacy Baby Bibs

Designs by Diane Zangl

Lacy openwork stitches define these delicate bibs for baby. You'll want to make several sets to give as baby shower gifts.

STITCH KEY
- ☐ K on RS, p on WS.
- ○ Yo
- ◿ K2tog
- ◺ Ssk
- ◮ Sl 2 tog knitwise, k1, p2sso
- ⋂ Sl 1 knitwise wyib
- ⋀ Sl 1 purlwise wyif
- ⊠ Make clockwise loop and place on RH ndl.
- ⊡ Make counterclockwise loop and place on RH ndl.

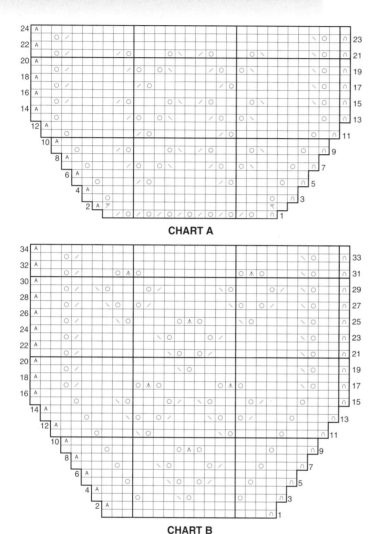

CHART A

CHART B

Referring to Chart A, work [Rows 1–22] once. (31 sts)

Rep [Rows 17–22] once, then work [Rows 23 and 24] 3 times.

Shape left neck (RS): Ssk, k1, yo, ssk, k4, k2tog, sl remaining sts to holder.

Rows 2, 4, 6 and 8: Sl 1, purl across.

Row 3: Ssk, k1, yo, ssk, k2, k2tog.

Row 5: Ssk, k1, yo, ssk, k2tog.

Row 7: K3, k2tog.

Row 9: K2, k2tog. (3sts)

I-cord tie

*K3, sl sts back to LH needle. Rep from * until tie measures 6 inches. K3tog, fasten off last st.

Shape right neck (RS): Sl sts from holder to needle. With RS facing, join yarn at left neck edge. Bind off next 9 sts, sl last st back to LH needle, ssk, k4, k2tog, yo, k1, k2tog.

Rows 2, 4, 6 and 8: Sl 1, purl across.

Row 3: Ssk, k2, k2tog, yo, k1, k2tog.

Row 5: Ssk, k2tog, yo, k1, k2tog.

Row 7: Ssk, k3.

Row 9: Ssk, k2. (3 sts)

Rep I-cord tie as above.

White Bib

Materials
- Plymouth Wildflower DK 51 percent cotton/49 percent acrylic DK weight yarn (137 yds/50g per ball): 1 ball white #41

Skill Level

Easy**

Size

Infant, 1 size fits most

Finished Size

Approximately 7 x 6 inches

Yellow Bib

Materials
- DK weight 100 percent cotton yarn (50g per ball): 1 ball yellow

- Size 5 (3.75mm) needles or size needed to obtain gauge
- Stitch holder
- Tapestry needle

Gauge

19 sts and 24 rows = 4 inches/ 10cm in pat

To save time, take time to check gauge.

Instructions

Cast on 17 sts. Knit 2 rows, purl 1 row.

One of a Kind

- Size 5 (3.75mm) needles or size needed to obtain gauge
- Stitch holder
- Tapestry needle

Gauge

18 sts and 26 rows = 4 inches/ 10cm in pat

To save time, take time to check gauge.

Instructions

Cast on 17 sts. Work [Rows 1–34] from Chart B. [Rep Rows 33 and 34] twice.

Shape left side of neck (RS): Ssk, k1, yo, ssk, k4, k2tog, sl remaining sts to holder.

Rows 2, 4, 6 and 8: Sl 1, purl across.

Row 3: Ssk, k1, yo, ssk, k2, k2tog.

Row 5: Ssk, k1, yo, ssk, k2tog.

Row 7: K3, k2tog.

Row 9: K2, k2tog. (3sts)

I-cord tie

*K3, sl sts back to LH needle. Rep from * until tie measures 6 inches. K3tog, fasten off last st.

Shape right neck (RS): Sl sts from holder to needle. With RS facing, join yarn at left neck edge. Bind off next 9 sts, sl last st back to LH needle, ssk, k4, k2tog, yo, k1, k2tog.

Rows 2, 4, 6 and 8: Sl 1, purl across.

Row 3: Ssk, k2, k2tog, yo, k1, k2tog.

Row 5: Ssk, k2tog, yo, k1, k2tog.

Row 7: Ssk, k3.

Row 9: Ssk, k2. (3 sts)

Rep I-cord tie as above. ❖

Smocked Ribbons Hat

Design by Frances Hughes

Every little girl looks cute in smocking—especially in this little hat. An I-cord trim bow adds the finishing touch.

Skill Level

Intermediate***

Finished Measurement

Circumference: Approximately 18 inches

Materials

- Reynolds Saucy 100 percent cotton worsted weight yarn from JCA/Reynolds Inc. (185 yds/50g per skein): 1 skein pink #601
- Size 7 (4.5mm) 16-inch circular needle
- Size 9 (5.5mm) 16-inch circular and double-pointed needles or size needed to obtain gauge
- Cable needle
- Tapestry needle

Gauge

16 sts and 24 rows = 4 inches/10cm in St st with larger needles

To save time, take time to check gauge.

Special Abbreviation

C6 (cluster 6): K2, p2, k2, sl these 6 sts to cable needle, wrap yarn counterclockwise around sts, sl sts back to RH needle.

Hat

With smaller needles, cast on 82 sts. Join without twisting and work 14 rnds of k1, p1 ribbing.

Inc rnd: Purl, inc 6 sts evenly spaced around. (88 sts)

Rnds 1 and 2: Change to larger needles, *p2, k2, rep from * around.

Rnd 3: *P2, C6, rep from * around.

Rnds 4–6: Rep Rnd 1.

Rnd 7: P2, k2, [p2, C6] 11 times. *Note: Last cluster st will use first 4 sts of next rnd.*

Rnd 8: Rep Rnd 1.

Rnds 9–22: Rep Rnds 1–8, ending with Rnd 4.

Shape top

Rnd 1: *K6, k2tog, rep from * around.

Rnd 2 and remaining even rnds: Knit.

Rnd 3: *K5, k2tog, rep from * around.

Rnd 5: *K4, k2tog, rep from * around.

Rnd 7: *K3, k2tog, rep from * around.

Rnd 9: *K2, k2tog, rep from * around.

Rnd 11: *K1, k2tog, rep from * around.

Rnd 13: K2tog around. Cut yarn, leaving a 6-inch tail. Thread tail through remaining sts, pull tight and fasten off.

I-Cord Trim

Using 2 dpns, cast on 3 sts. *Do not turn. Sl sts to other end of needle, pull yarn across back, k3. Rep from * until cord measures 15 inches. Fasten off sts. Tie cord in a bow and attach to side of hat. ❖

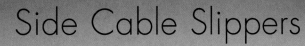

Side Cable Slippers

Design by Dixie L. Butler

Quick and easy, these slippers are great gifts for family and friends. The simple cable on each side adds a touch of style.

Skill Level

Easy**

Size

1 size fits most. Sample shown measures approximately 9 inches long.

Materials

- Red Heart Fiesta 100 percent acrylic worsted weight yarn from Coats & Clark (330 yds/ 6 oz per skein): 1 skein light periwinkle #6347
- Red Heart Super Saver 100 percent acrylic worsted weight yarn from Coats & Clark (170 yds/3 oz per skein): 1 skein light blue #381
- Size 13 (9mm) needles
- Cable needle
- Tapestry needle

Gauge

Approximately 4 sts and 6 rows = 2 inches/5cm in St st with 3 strands of yarn held tog

Gauge is not critical to this project.

Pattern Note

Sample shown used 3 strands (about 3½ oz) of yarn. They may also be worked with 4 strands for a slightly larger size.

Slippers

Cast on 22 sts with either 3 or 4 strands of yarn.

Row 1 (RS): P1, k4, p1, k10, p1, k4, p1.

Row 2: K1, p4, k1, p10, k1, p4, k1.

Row 3 (cable row): P1, sl 2 sts to cn, hold in back, k2, k2 from cn, p1, k10, p1, sl 2 sts to cn, hold in front, k2, k2 from cn, p1.

Row 4: Rep Row 2.

Rows 5–8: Rep Rows 1 and 2.

Rep Rows 1–8 for pat until piece measures about 8 inches or desired length. Work [k2tog] across row.

Cut yarn, leaving a 14-inch end. Run through sts on needle, then seam top (approximately ⅔ of length). Sew back heel seam. ❖

Peek-a-Boo Holes Place Mat

Design by Thelma Jean Young

Use extra skeins of yarn to knit place mats for everyone. Make them in holiday colors or in a variety of colors for a unique look.

Skill Level

Beginner*

Finished Size

12 x 18 inches (30 x 45 cm)

Materials

- Sirdar Tropicana Cotton Effect DK 100 percent acrylic DK weight yarn (262 yds/100g per ball): 1 ball gold #736
- Size 3 (3mm) needles or size needed to obtain gauge
- Size 5 (3.75mm) needles (to cast on)
- 40 T pins (for blocking—optional)
- Tapestry needle

Gauge

12 sts and 16 rows = 2 inches/5cm in pat with smaller needles

To save time, take time to check gauge.

Pattern Note

Review all abbreviations, diagrams and instructions before beginning.

Special Abbreviation

Up-1: K1 in top of st in row below (1 new st).

Place Mat

With larger needles, cast on 107 sts. Change to smaller needles.

Rows 1–4: K1, *p1, k1, rep from * across.

Row 5 (RS): [K1, p1] twice, k2tog, k across, end [p1, k1] twice. (106 sts)

Row 6: [K1, p1] twice, p across to last 4 sts, end [p1, k1] twice.

Row 7 (beg pat): [K1, p1] twice, k4, *p2, k6, rep from * to last 10 sts, end p2, k4, [p1, k1] twice.

Row 8: [K1, p1] twice, p4, *k2, p6, rep from * to last 10 sts, end k2, p4, [p1, k1] twice.

Rows 9 and 10: Rep Rows 7 and 8.

Row 11: [K1, p1] twice, k4, *p2, k2, rep from * to last 10 sts, end p2, k4, [p1, k1] twice.

Row 12: [K1, p1] twice, p2, k1, *k2tog, yo, k2tog tbl, k4, rep from * to last 10 sts, end k2tog, yo, k2tog tbl, k1, p2, [p1, k1] twice. (95 sts)

Row 13: [K1, p1] twice, k4, *[p1,

k1] in yo, k2, p2, k2, rep from * to last 10 sts, end [p1, k1] in yo, k4, [p1, k1] twice. (107 sts)

Row 14: [K1, p1] twice, p4, *k2, p6, rep from * to last 10 sts, end k2, p4, [p1, k1] twice.

Row 15: [K1, p1] twice, k4, *p2, k6, rep from * to last 10 sts, end p2, k4, [p1, k1] twice.

Row 16: Rep Row 14.

[Rep Rows 7–16] 7 more times.

Top Border

Rows 1 and 2: Rep Rows 15 and 16.

Row 3: [K1, p1] twice, up-1, k across, end [p1, k1] twice. (107 sts)

Rows 4–6: K1, *p1, k1, rep from * across.

Bind off all sts in pat.

Finishing

Pin, block and steam mat to shape. ❖

Art Deco Place Mat

Design by Lois S. Young

Retro 1930s-style art deco mats will add a sharp, crisp look to your table. It only takes one skein of yarn.

Skill Level

Beginner*

Finished Measurements

18 x 12½ inches

Materials

- Lion Brand Kitchen Cotton 100 percent cotton worsted weight yarn (236 yds/5 oz per skein): 1 skein natural #98
- Size 6 (4mm) needles or size needed to obtain gauge
- Tapestry needle

Gauge

19 sts and 28 rows = 4 inches/10cm in St st

To save time, take time to check gauge.

Pattern Notes

Sl first st of each row purlwise.

Place mat is reversible if ends are worked neatly into selvages.

Pattern Stitches

Pattern A

Row 1 (RS): Sl 1, k22, p13, k23.

Row 2: Sl 1, k4, p18, k13, p18, k5.

Pattern B

Row 1 (RS): Sl 1, k13, p10, k11, p10, k14.

Row 2: Sl 1, k4, p9, k10, p11, k10, p9, k5.

Pattern C

Row 1 (RS): Sl 1, k9, p5, k8, p1, k11, p1, k8, p5, k10.

Row 2: Sl 1, k4, p5, k5, p29, k5, p5, k5.

Pattern D

Row 1 (RS): Sl 1, k9, p1, k3, p1, k8, p1, k11, p1, k8, p1, k3, p1, k10.

Row 2: Sl 1, k4, p49, k5.

Place Mat

Cast on 59 sts.

Border

Row 1: Sl 1, k58.

Rows 2–10: Rep Row 1.

Body

Row 1 (RS): Sl 1, k58.

Row 2: Sl 1, k4, p49, k5.

Rows 3–8: Rep Rows 1 and 2.

Rows 9–22: [Work Rows 1 and 2 of pat A] 7 times.

Rows 23–30: [Work Rows 1 and 2 of pat B] 4 times.

Rows 31–34: [Work Rows 1 and 2 of pat C] twice.

Rows 35–72: [Work Rows 1 and 2 of pat D] 19 times.

Rows 73–76: Rep Rows 31–34.

Rows 77–84: Rep Rows 23–30.

Rows 85–98: Rep Rows 9–22.

Rows 99–106: Rep Rows 1–8.

Border

Rep border Rows 1–10.

Bind off knitwise on WS, working last 2 sts as k2tog before binding off last st. Block. ❖

Skill Level

Easy**

Finished Size

Approximately 12 inches square

Materials

- Red Heart Super Saver 100 percent acrylic worsted weight yarn from Coats & Clark (452 yds/8 oz per skein): 1 skein soft white #316
- Size 10 (6mm) needles or size needed to obtain gauge
- 12-inch square pillow form
- Tapestry needle

Gauge

16 sts and 26 rows = 4 inches/10cm in pat

To save time, take time to check gauge.

Pattern Notes

Front and back of pillow are made alike.

St count is constant throughout pat.

One Skein Textured Pillow

Design by Carolyn Pfeifer

This slip-stitch project is very portable. You'll want to make several pillows to decorate your living room. They also make great gifts.

Pillow

Cast on 50 sts.

Row 1 (RS): *K1, p1, rep from * across row.

Row 2 and all WS rows: Purl across.

Row 3: K1, sl 2 wyif, yarn back, k2 (this creates yarn loop used in next RS row), *sl 2 wyif, yarn back, k2, rep from * across row, end k3.

Row 5: K1, *k2tog, k1 in yarn loop, sl 2 wyif, yarn back, rep from * across row to last st, k1.

Row 7: K1, *sl 2 wyif, yarn back, k1 in yarn loop, ssk, rep from * across row, end k1.

Row 8: Rep Row 2.

Rows 9–84: [Rep Rows 5–8] 19 times.

Row 85: K1, *k2tog, k1 in yarn loop, k2, rep from * across row, end k1.

Bind off all sts knitwise.

Rep for 2nd piece.

Finishing

Seam 3 sides of pillow. Insert pillow form, seam remaining edge. ❖

Face Cloth Quartet

Designs by Frances Hughes

*Knit up four textured face cloths, each quite
unique, for gift giving or for your own use.
Each uses only one ball of cotton yarn.*

Leafy Green Ladders Cloth

Skill Level

Easy**

Finished Size

Approximately 8½ inches square

Materials

- Reynolds Saucy 100 percent cotton worsted weight yarn from JCA/Reynolds Inc. (185 yds/100g per ball): 1 ball green #11
- Size 8 (5mm) needles or size needed to obtain gauge
- Tapestry needle

Gauge

9 sts and 10 rows = 2 inches/5cm in pat

To save time, take time to check gauge.

Pattern Note

Slip all sts purlwise with yarn on WS of fabric.

Instructions

Cast on 41 sts.

Border

Row 1: *K2tog, yo, rep from * to last st, end k1.

Rows 2–4: K1, yo, *k2tog, yo, rep from * across.

Body

Foundation row: [K2tog, yo] twice, k1, p across to last 5 sts, end k1, [yo, k2tog] twice.

Row 1 (RS): K1, [yo, k2tog] twice, k3, *sl 1, k3, rep from * to last 5 sts, end k1, [yo, k2tog] twice.

Row 2: K1, [yo, k2tog] twice, *k3, sl 1, k3, rep from * across to last 5 sts, end k1, [yo, k2tog] twice.

Row 3: K1, [yo, k2tog] twice, k1, sl 1, *k3, sl 1, rep from * to last 6 sts, end k2, [yo, k2tog] twice.

Row 4: K1, [yo, k2tog] twice, p1, sl 1, *p3, sl 1, rep from * across to last 6 sts, end p1, k1, [yo, k2tog] twice.

Work [Rows 1–4] 7 times, then rep Rows 1–4 of border. Bind off all sts.

Cherry Red Boxes Cloth

Skill Level

Beginner*

Finished Size

Approximately 9 inches square

Materials

- Reynolds Saucy 100 percent cotton worsted weight yarn from JCA/Reynolds Inc. (185 yds/100g per ball): 1 ball red #361
- Size 8 (5mm) needles or size needed to obtain gauge
- Tapestry needle

Gauge

9 sts and 12 rows = 2 inches/5cm in pat

To save time, take time to check gauge.

Instructions

Cast on 41 sts

Border

Knit 4 rows.

Body

Row 1 (RS): K4, p3, *k3, p3, rep from * to last 4 sts, end k4.

Row 2: K3, p1, k3, *p3, k3, rep from * to last 4 sts, end p1, k3.

Row 3: K4, yo, k3tog, yo, *k3, yo, k3tog, yo, rep from * to last 4 sts, end k4.

Row 4: K3, purl across to last 3 sts, end k3.

Row 5: K7, p3, *k3, p3, rep from * to last 7 sts, end k7.

Row 6: K3, p4, k3, *p3, k3, rep from * to last 7 sts, end p4, k3.

Row 7: K7, yo, k3tog, yo, *k3, yo, k3tog, yo, rep from * to last 7 sts, end k7.

Row 8: Rep Row 4.

Work [Rows 1–8] 6 times.

Knit 4 rows. Bind off all sts.

Golden Acorns Cloth

Skill Level

Easy**

Finished Size

Approximately 8½ inches

Materials

- Reynolds Saucy 100 percent cotton worsted weight yarn from JCA/Reynolds Inc. (185 yds/100g per ball): 1 ball pale gold #901
- Size 8 (5mm) needles
- Tapestry needle

Gauge

9 sts and 12 rows = 2 inches/5cm in seed st

To save time, take time to check gauge.

Special Abbreviation

M3 (make 3): [K1, p1, k1] in next st.

Instructions

Cast on 41 sts.

Border

Rows 1–5: *K1, p1, rep from * across.

Body

Row 1 (RS): [K1, p1] twice, p3, *k3, p3, rep from * to last 4 sts, end [p1, k1] twice.

Row 2: [K1, p1] twice, k3, *p3, k3, rep from * to last 4 sts, end [p1, k1] twice.

Row 3: [K1, p1] twice, p1, M3, p1, *sl 1, k2tog, psso, p1, M3, p1, rep from * to last 4 sts, end [p1, k1] twice.

Row 4: [K1, p1] twice, k1, p3, *k3, p3, rep from * to last 5 sts, end k1, [p1, k1] twice.

Row 5: [K1, p1] twice, p1, k3, *p3, k3, rep from* to last 5 sts, end p1, [p1, k1] twice.

Row 6: Rep Row 4.

Row 7: [K1, p1] twice, p1, sl 1, k2tog, psso, p1, *M3, p1, sl 1, k2tog, psso, p1, rep from * to last 4 sts, [p1, k1] twice.

Row 8: Rep Row 2.

Work [Rows 1–8] 5 times.

Rep border Rows 1–5. Bind off all sts.

Diamonds Raspberry Cloth

Finished Size

Approximately 9 inches square

Materials

- Reynolds Saucy 100 percent cotton worsted weight yarn from JCA/Reynolds Inc. (185 yds/100g per ball): 1 ball raspberry #624
- Size 8 (5mm) needles
- Tapestry needle

Gauge

8 sts and 6 rows = 2 inches/5cm in pat

To save time, take time to check gauge.

Instructions

Cast on 43 sts.

Border

Rows 1–3: *K1, p1, rep from * across.

Body

Row 1 (RS): K1, p1, k1, *[k3, p1] twice, k1, p1, rep from * to last 10 sts, end k3, p1, k4, p1, k1.

Row 2: K1, p1, k1, *[p3, k1] twice, p1, k1, rep from * to last 10 sts, p3, k1, p3, k1, p1, k1.

Row 3: K1, p1, k3, p1, k1, p1, *[k3, p1] twice, k1, p1, rep from * to last 5 sts, end k3, p1, k1.

Row 4: K1, p1, k1, p2, k1, p1, k1, *[p3, kl] twice, p1, k1, rep from * to last 5 sts, end p2, k1, p1, k1.

Row 5: K1, p1, k1, [k1, p1] 3 times, *[k2, p1] twice, [k1, p1] twice, rep from * to last 4 sts, end k2, p1, k1.

Row 6: K1, p1, k1, [p1, k1] 3 times, *[p2, k1] twice, [p1, k1] twice, rep from * to last 4 sts, [p1, k1) twice.

Row 7: Rep Row 3.

Row 8: Rep Row 4.

Row 9: Rep Row 1.

Row 10: Rep Row 2.

Row 11: K1, p1, k4, p1, *k2, [p1, k1] twice, p1, k2, p1, rep from * to last 6 sts, end k4, p1, k1.

Row 12: K1, p1, k1, p3, k1, *p2, [k1, p1] twice, k1, p2, k1, rep from * to last 6 sts, end p3, k1, p1, k1.

Work [Rows 1–12] 4 times.

Border

Rep border Rows 1–3. Bind off all sts. ❖

Cherry Red Boxes Cloth

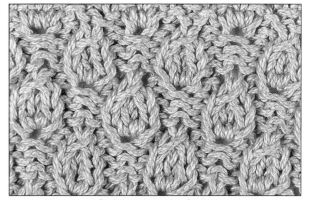
Golden Acorns Cloth

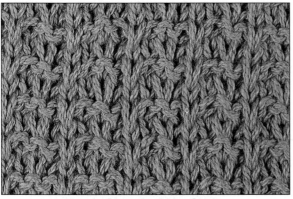
Leafy Green Ladders Cloth

Diamonds Raspberry Cloth

Rainbow Eyeglass Case

Design by Edie Eckman

You'll never lose your glasses in this colorful buttoned case. Single crochet adds the finishing touch to this beginner-level project.

Skill Level

Beginner*

Finished Size

4 x 7 inches

Materials

- Lorna's Laces Bullfrogs & Butterflies 85 percent wool/15 percent mohair worsted weight yarn (219 yds/100g per skein): partial skein child's play #62
- Size 9 (5.5mm) needles
- Size I/9 (5.5mm) crochet hook
- Novelty button or bead

Gauge

20 sts = 4 inches/10cm in pat

To save time, take time to check gauge.

Pattern Stitch

Granite St (multiple of 2 sts)

Row 1 (RS): Knit.

Row 2: *K2tog, rep from * across.

Row 3: [K1, p1] into same st, rep from * across.

Row 4: Purl.

Rep Rows 1–4 for pat.

Case

Cast on 20 sts. Work even in pat until piece measures approximately 15½ inches from beg, ending with Row 2. Bind off loosely. Cut yarn.

Finishing

Referring to Fig.1, fold case along A–B and pin. Starting at B, sc through both layers to C, then around flap only to D. Sc 3 in corner st at D, sc to E. Ch 8, or number needed to go around button, sc in same st, sc to F, 3 sc in corner st at F, sc to G, then through both layers to A. Fasten off. ❖

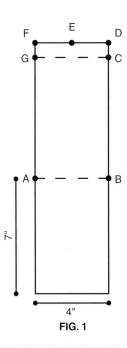

FIG. 1

7"

4"

Glitzy Clutch & Shoulder Bag

Designs by Edie Eckman

You will be set for the evening with these fun-to-knit bags. If you have extra skeins from a sweater, knit a matching purse.

Clutch

Skill Level

Intermediate***

Finished Measurements

Approximately 6 x 4 inches

Materials

- Berroco Metallica 85 percent rayon/15 percent metallic worsted weight yarn (85 yds/25g per skein), 1 skein gold #1001
- Size 7 (4.5mm) needles or size needed to obtain gauge
- Tapestry needle
- Size G/6 (4mm) crochet hook
- 2 snaps
- Fabric for lining (optional)

Gauge

25 sts and 42 rows = 4 inches/10cm in pat

Gauge is not crucial in this project.

Pattern Stitch

(Multiple of 4 sts +2)

Row 1 (RS): P2, *sl 2 purlwise wyif, p2, rep from * across.

Row 2: K2, *p2, k2, rep from * across.

Rep Rows 1 and 2 for pat.

Instructions

Cast on 38 sts. Knit 1 row. Work even in pat until piece measures 8 inches from beg, ending with a WS row.

Flap

Rows 1–8: K2, work in established pat to last 2 sts, k2.

Row 9: K1, ssk, work in established pat to last 3 sts, k2tog, k1.

Row 10: K2, work in established pat to last 2 sts, k2.

Rows 11–16: Rep Rows 9 and 10. (30 sts)

Row 17: Rep Row 1.

Knit 3 rows. Bind off remaining sts.

Finishing

Referring to Fig. 1, fold bag along lines A and B. Line with fabric if desired. Single crochet side seams tog. Sew snaps invisibly under flap.

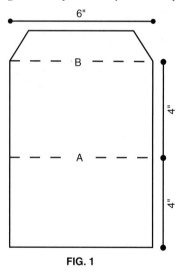

FIG. 1

Shoulder Bag

Skill Level

Intermediate***

Finished Measurements

Approximately 7 x 5 inches

Materials

- Berroco Metallica 85 percent rayon/15 percent metallic worsted weight yarn (85 yds/25g per skein), 2 skeins black/gold #1003
- Size 7 (4.5mm) straight and 2 double-pointed needles or size needed to obtain gauge
- Tapestry needle
- 1 button (any size)
- Fabric for lining (optional)

Gauge

23 sts and 44 rows = 4 inches/10cm in moss st

Gauge is not crucial in this project.

Pattern Note

Make button loop shorter or longer to fit chosen button.

Pattern Stitch

Moss Stitch (odd number of sts)

Row 1: K1, *p1, k1, rep from * across.

Rep this row for pat.

Instructions

Cast on 39 sts. Work in pat until piece measures 5 inches from beg, ending with a RS row. Knit 1 row (turning ridge). Work in pat until piece measures 10 inches from beg, ending with a RS row. Knit 1 row (turning ridge). Work 4 rows in pat.

Dec row: K1, ssk, work in established pat to last 3 sts, k2tog, k1.

Next row: K2, work in established pat to last 2 sts, k2.

Rep these 2 rows until 23 sts remain. Bind off all sts.

Finishing

Attached I-cord: With dpn, cast on 3 sts. Beg at right edge of flap, with RS facing, pull up a loop through edge of fabric. (4 sts)

*Do not turn. Sl sts to other end of needle. K3, sl 1 knitwise, pull up a loop through fabric, psso, rep from * to corner of flap.

Unattached I-cord: [Do not turn. Sl sts to other end of needle, k4] twice.

Continue working attached I-cord along straight edge to center of flap. Work 12 rows unattached I-cord (or needed length) for buttonhole loop. Continue working attached I-cord

along straight edge, 2 rows unattached I-cord at corner of flap, and attached I-cord along remaining edge of flap. [K2tog] twice. Bind off sts.

Fold bag along turning ridges and pin. With back of bag facing, beg at lower RH corner, knit attached I-cord as for flap, picking up loop through both layers of fabric. Work 2 layers tog to top of bag. Knit unattached I-cord for approximately 34 inches. Beg at top left edge, work attached I-cord through both layers to lower corner. [K2tog] twice. Bind off sts. Sew button opposite buttonhole. Line with fabric if desired. ❖

Silky Pink Evening Bag With Coin Purse

Design by Kennita Tully

Use your extra skein of yarn to knit a matching evening bag and its clever little zipped coin purse.

Skill Level

Advanced****

Finished Size

Bag: Approximately 6½ x 4 inches

Coin purse: Approximately
3 x 2 inches

Materials

- Avignon 85 percent pima cotton/
  15 percent tussah silk worsted
  weight yarn from Classic Elite
  (115 yds/50g per skein): 1 skein
  pink stucco farmhouse #3189
- Size 5 (3.75mm) needles or size
  needed to obtain gauge
- Tapestry needle
- 1 (⅝ x ¹⁵⁄₁₆-inch) button classic wave
  #7023 from JHB International, Inc.
- 3-inch metal zipper

Gauge

26 sts and 54 rows = 4 inches/10cm
in pat

To save time, take time to check
gauge.

Pattern Notes

Sl all sts purlwise with yarn on WS
of fabric.

When working short row shaping
on purse flap, always knit last st
before wrap and turn.

If unable to find a 3-inch zipper,
shorten a longer one as directed
on package.

Special Abbreviation

W/t (wrap and turn): Wrap yarn
around next st and turn.

Pattern Stitch

(multiple of 4 sts + 3)

Row 1 (RS): K3, *sl 1, k3, rep
from * across.

Row 2: K3, *sl 1, k3, rep from *
across.

Row 3: K1, *sl 1, k3, rep from *,
end sl 1, k1.

Row 4: K1, *sl 1, k3, rep from *,
end sl 1, k1.

Rep Rows 1–4 for pat.

Evening Bag

Cast on 43 sts.

Work in pat until piece measures
8 inches, ending with a WS row.

Shape flap

Row 1 (RS): Work in pat across
42 sts, w/t.

Row 2: Work 41 sts, w/t.

Row 3: Work 40 sts, w/t.

Row 4: Work 39 sts, w/t.

Row 5: Work 38 sts, w/t.

Row 6: Work 37 sts, w/t.

Row 7: Work 36 sts, w/t.

Row 8: Work 35 sts, w/t.

Row 9: Work 34 sts, w/t.

Row 10: Work 33 sts, w/t.

Row 11: Work 32 sts, w/t and *at
the same time*, work a buttonhole
over center 3 sts.

Rows 12–19: Continue to work in
established pat as above, having 1
less st before turning on each row.

Row 20: Work 17 sts, w/t.

Cut yarn and attach at beg of RS row.
Knit across all sts. Bind off on next row.

Finishing

Fold cast on edge up to beg of flap
shaping, sew side seams. Sew button opposite buttonhole.

Coin Purse

Cast on 19 sts and work 2 rows in
garter st.

Beg st pat and work until piece
measures approximately 4 inches.

Work 2 rows garter st. Bind off on
next row.

Finishing

Sew zipper in coin purse and sew
side seams.

Make twisted cord to attach coin
purse to bag by tightly twisting 2
strands of yarn approximately 18
inches long. Slide zipper tab to
center, then let cords twist back on
themselves. Secure end and sew
into purse. ❖

Stretchy Headbands

Designs by Elizabeth Mattfield

Use the chart below to make headbands that always fit. Make them in school colors or to match a special outfit.

Skill Level

Intermediate***

Finished Size

Children–adults small (medium, large, extra-large) Refer to Fig. 1.

Materials

- Worsted weight yarn: ½–1 oz OR Bulky weight yarn: 1–2 oz
- Size 5 (3.75mm) 16-inch circular or double-pointed needles or size needed to obtain gauge with worsted weight yarn OR Size 9 (5.5mm) 16-inch circular or double-pointed needles or size needed to obtain gauge with bulky weight yarn
- Tapestry needle

Gauge

Worsted weight yarn: Approximately 12 sts = 2 inches/5cm in k2, p2 ribbing (relaxed)

Bulky weight yarn: Approximately 10 sts = 2 inches/5cm in k2, p2 ribbing (relaxed)

Gauge is not critical for this project.

Pattern Notes

Designer has made these headbands in many yarns and sizes, so she developed a table to plug in any yarn that works to the gauges listed above. Because k2, p2 rib is so stretchy, size doesn't have to be exact, but headbands fit better if wearer's head size is about midway between stretched and relaxed measurements.

Instructions

Referring to Fig.1, cast on number of sts given for desired yarn weight and head size (W). Join without twisting and work in k2, p2 ribbing until piece measures Y inches.

Bind off X sts, centered so that remaining sts beg and end with k2. Maintaining rib pat throughout, [work across, k2tog at beg of each row] 4 times, 2 rows even, [work across, k2tog at beg of each row] twice, 2 rows even.

Continue in pat, k2tog at beg of each row until piece measures Z inches (See table). Bind off all sts in pat. ❖

Size	Finished Size (worsted)	Finished Size (bulky)	W	X	Y	Z
small (blue)	10"–17"	12"–20"	60 sts	22 sts	1½"	2½"
medium (red)	12"–20"	14"–24"	72 sts	26 sts	1¾"	3"
large (yellow)	15"–25"	17"–29"	88 sts	30 sts	2"	3½"
extra-large (variegated)	18"–30"	21"–36"	108 sts	38 sts	2½"	4"

FIG. 1

Odds & Ends

Use one main yarn and small amounts of other yarns to knit these delightful projects. After you select the main yarn, the fun begins when you search your stash for the right combination of odds and ends.

It's a Dog's Day!

Design by Svetlana Avrakh

Your dog will look jaunty walking down the street in a warm and cozy sweater. He'll love taking winter walks. Instructions are given for five sizes.

Zebra Dog Coat

Skill Level

Intermediate***

Size

To fit 10- (13-, 16-, 24-, 30-) inch chest Instructions are given for smallest size, with larger sizes in parentheses. When only 1 number is given, it applies to all sizes.

Materials

- Patons Canadiana worsted weight yarn from Spinrite Yarns (241 yds/100g per skein): 1 (1, 1, 1, 2) balls white #1 (MC), 1 ball each black #3 (A) and old Christmas green #56 (B)
- Size 6 (4mm) straight, circular and double-pointed needles
- Size 7 (4.5mm) needles or size needed to obtain gauge
- Stitch holder
- Tapestry needle
- Size F/5 (3.75mm) crochet hook (optional for fringe)

Gauge

20 sts and 26 rows = 4 inches/10cm with larger needles in St st

Pattern Notes

When working pat from chart, wind a separate small ball for each area of color in design.

When changing colors, pick up new color under old to avoid holes.

Zebra Coat

With smaller needles and B, cast on 39 (47, 61, 85, 101) sts.

Row 1 (RS): K1, *p1, k1, rep from * across.

Row 2: P1, *k1, p1, rep from * across.

Rep Rows 1 and 2 until ribbing measures 1 (1½, 1½, 2, 2) inches, ending with Row 2 and inc 1 st in center of last row. Cut B. (40, 48, 62, 86, 102 sts)

Change to larger needles and work pat from chart, beg and ending as

Odds & Ends

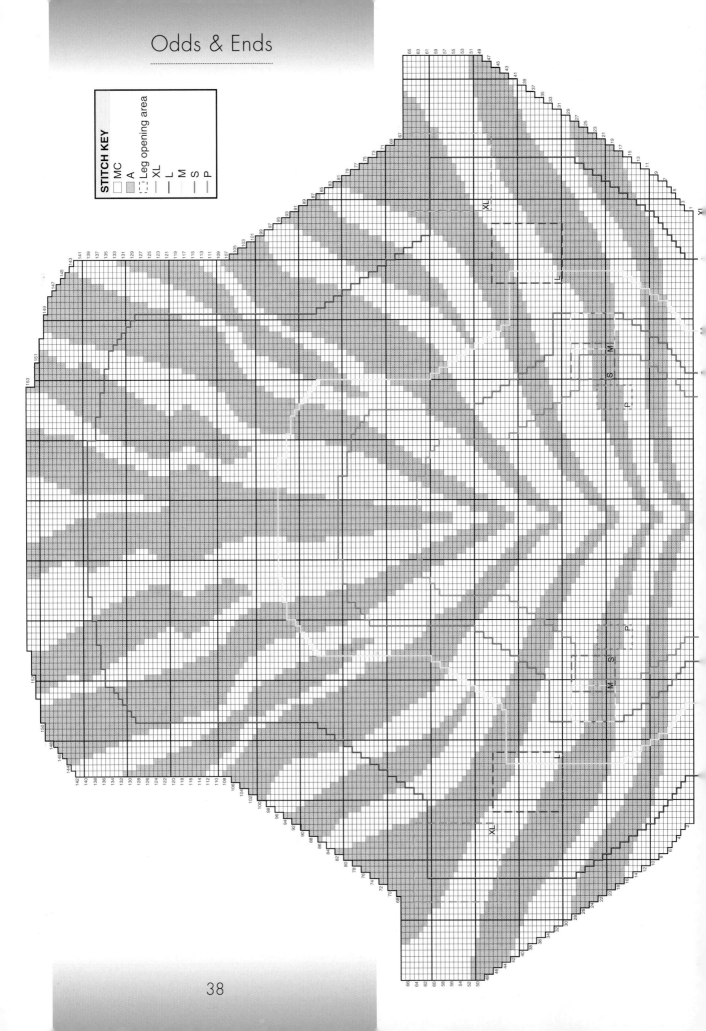

STITCH KEY
MC
A
Leg opening area
XL
L
M
S
P

indicated for size. *At the same time, beg on Row 3, inc 1 st at each end of needle as indicated until Row 14 (18, 18, 30, 46) of chart is completed. (54, 68, 82, 120, 150 sts)*

Leg Openings

Note: All sections are worked at the same time, using separate balls of yarn for each section.

Row 1 (RS): Work in pat across 5 (5, 7, 11, 12) sts; bind off next 4 (6, 6, 10, 13) sts; work across 36 (46, 56, 78, 102) sts (including st on needle after bind off); bind off next 4 (6, 6, 10, 13) sts; complete row in pat.

Beg with a purl row, continue pat and shaping until chart Row 22 (28, 28, 46, 64) is completed.

Next row (RS): Work in pat across 5 (5, 7, 11, 13) sts; cast on 4 (6, 6, 10, 13) sts; work across 36 (46, 56, 78, 102) sts; cast on 4 (6, 6, 10, 13) sts; complete row in pat. (54, 68, 82, 120, 154 sts)

Continue to work even in pat until Row 26 (32, 42, 60, 66) of chart is completed. Place a marker at each end of row.

Back Shaping

Maintaining pat, bind off 6 (7, 9, 13, 14) sts at beg of next 2 rows. (42, 54, 64, 94, 126 sts)

Beg on next row and continuing in pat, dec 1 st at each end every other row until 26 (36, 46, 68, 86) sts remain.

Work even in pat for 16 (24, 26, 42, 36) rows, then follow chart to complete shaping. Place remaining 14 (14, 20, 26, 44) sts on a holder.

Finishing

Back edging

With B and circular needle, RS facing, pick up and k 42 (51, 67, 92, 99) sts along edge of body from marker to back, k14 (14, 20, 26, 44) from holder, dec 1 st at center, pick up and k 42 (51, 67, 92, 99) sts along opposite edge of body to marker. (97, 115, 153, 209, 241 sts)

Work in k1, p1 ribbing for 1 (1, 1½, 1½, 2) inches, ending with a WS row. Bind off in ribbing.

Sew neck and body seam.

Leg ribbing

With dpn and A, pick up and k 22 (26, 30, 36, 42) sts around leg opening. Pm, join and work in rnds of k1, p1 ribbing for 1 (1½, 2, 2, 3) inches. Bind off loosely in ribbing. Rep for other leg.

Fringe (optional)

Cut 3-inch strands of MC and A. Working along center back and matching fringe to stripes, *fold 1 strand in half, insert crochet hook under strand between sts, pull loop through, pull ends through loop. Rep from * along back. ❖

Tiger Dog Coat

Skill Level

Intermediate***

Size

To fit 10- (13-, 16-, 24-, 30-) inch chest Instructions are given for smallest size, with larger sizes in parentheses. When only 1 number is given, it applies to all sizes.

Materials

- Patons Canadiana worsted weight yarn from Spinrite Yarns (241 yds/100g per skein): 1 (1, 1, 2, 2) balls black #3 (MC), 1 ball carrot top #431 (A)
- Size 6 (4mm) straight, circular and double-pointed needles
- Size 7 (4.5mm) needles or size needed to obtain gauge
- Stitch holder
- Tapestry needle

Gauge

20 sts and 26 rows = 4 inches/10cm with larger needles in St st

Pattern Notes

When working pat from chart, wind a separate small ball for each area of color in design.

When changing colors, pick up new color under old to avoid holes.

Tiger Coat

With smaller needles and MC, cast on 39 (47, 61, 85, 101) sts.

Row 1 (RS): K1, *p1, k1, rep from * across.

Row 2: P1, *k1, p1, rep from * across.

Rep Rows 1 and 2 until ribbing measures 1 (1½, 1½, 2, 2) inches, ending with Row 2 and inc 1 st in center of last row. (40, 48, 62, 86, 102 sts)

Change to larger needles and work pat from chart, beg and ending as indicated for size. *At the same time, beg on Row 3, inc 1 st at each end of needle as indicated until Row 14 (18, 18, 30, 46) of chart is completed. (54, 68, 82, 120, 150 sts)*

Leg Openings

Note: All sections are worked at the same time, using separate balls of yarn for each section.

Row 1 (RS): Work in pat across 5 (5, 7, 11, 12) sts; bind off next 4 (6, 6, 10, 13) sts; work across 36 (46, 56, 78, 102) sts (including st on needle after bind off); bind off next 4 (6, 6, 10, 13) sts; complete row in pat.

Beg with a purl row, continue pat and shaping until chart Row 22 (28, 28, 46, 64) is completed.

Next row (RS): Work in pat across 5 (5, 7, 11, 13) sts; cast on 4 (6, 6, 10, 13) sts; work across 36 (46, 56, 78, 102) sts; cast on 4 (6, 6, 10, 13) sts; complete row in pat. (54, 68, 82, 120, 154 sts)

Continue to work even in pat until Row 26 (32, 42, 60, 66) of chart is completed. Place a marker at each end of row.

Back Shaping

Maintaining pat, bind off 6 (7, 9, 13, 14) sts at beg of next 2 rows. (42, 54, 64, 94, 126 sts)

Beg on next row and continuing in pat, dec 1 st at each end every other row until 26 (36, 46, 68, 86) sts remain.

Odds & Ends

STITCH KEY
- ☐ MC
- ■ A
- ⬚ Leg opening area
- — XL
- — L
- — M
- — S
- — P

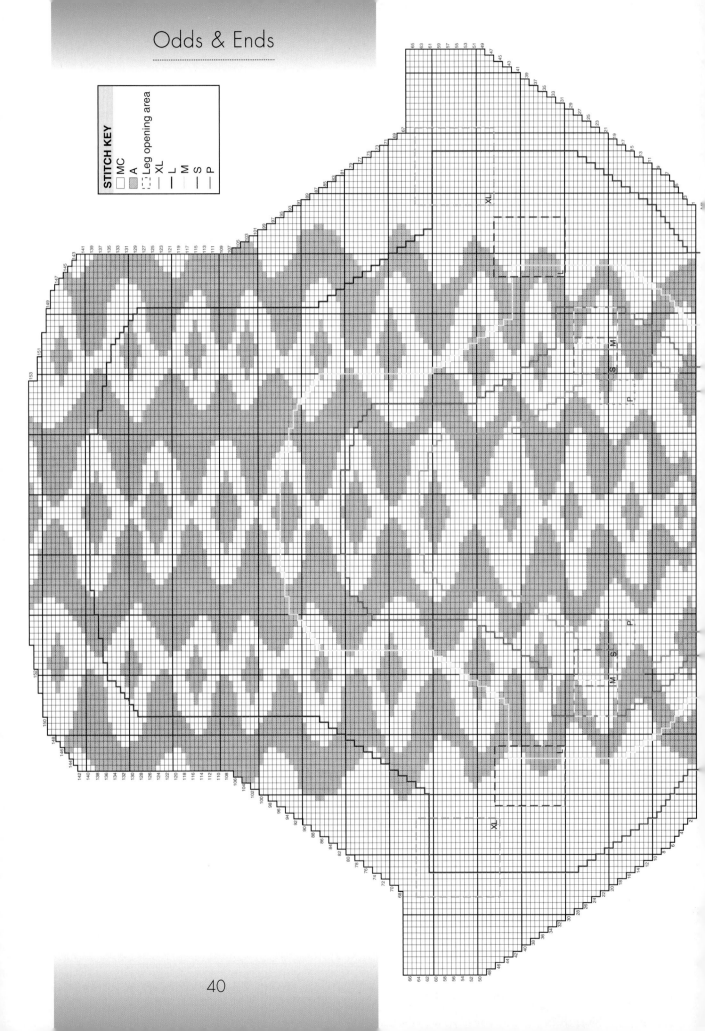

Work even in pat for 16 (24, 26, 42, 36) rows, then follow chart to complete shaping. Place remaining 14 (14, 20, 26, 44) sts on a holder.

Finishing

Back edging

With MC and circular needle, RS facing, pick up and k 42 (51, 67, 92, 99) sts along edge of body from marker to back, k14 (14, 20, 26, 44) from holder, dec 1 st at center, pick up and k 42 (51, 67, 92, 99) sts along opposite edge of body to marker. (97, 115, 153, 209, 241 sts)

Work in garter st for 1 (1, 1½, 1½, 2) inches, ending with a RS row. Bind off knitwise.

Sew neck and body seam.

Leg ribbing

With dpn and MC, pick up and k 22 (26, 30, 36, 42) sts around leg opening. Pm, join and work in rnds of k1, p1 ribbing for 1 (1½, 2, 2, 3) inches. Bind off loosely in ribbing. Rep for other leg. ❖

Dalmatian Dog Coat

Skill Level

Intermediate***

Size

To fit 10- (13-, 16-, 24-, 30-) inch chest Instructions are given for smallest size, with larger sizes in parentheses. When only 1 number is given, it applies to all sizes.

Materials

- Patons Canadiana worsted weight yarn from Spinrite Yarns (241 yds/ 100g per skein): 1 (1, 1, 1, 2) balls white #1 (MC), 1 ball each black #3 (A) and cardinal #5 (B)
- Size 6 (4mm) straight, circular and double-pointed needles
- Size 7 (4.5mm) needles or size needed to obtain gauge

- Stitch holder
- Tapestry needle

Gauge

20 sts and 26 rows = 4 inches/10cm with larger needles in St st

Pattern Notes

When working pat from chart, wind a separate small ball for each area of color in design.

When changing colors, pick up new color under old to avoid holes.

Dalmatian Coat

With smaller needles and B, cast on 39 (47, 61, 85, 101) sts.

Row 1 (RS): K1, *p1, k1, rep from * across.

Row 2: P1, *k1, p1, rep from * across.

Rep Rows 1 and 2 until ribbing measures 1 (1½, 1½, 2, 2) inches, ending with Row 2 and inc 1 st in center of last row. Cut B. (40, 48, 62, 86, 102 sts)

Change to larger needles and work pat from Chart A, beg and ending as indicated for size. *At the same time,* beg on Row 3, inc 1 st at each end of needle as indicated until Row 14 (18, 18, 30, 46) of Chart A is completed. (54, 68, 82, 120, 150 sts)

Leg Openings

Note: All sections are worked at same time, using separate balls of yarn for each section.

Row 1 (RS): Work in pat across 5 (5, 7, 11, 12) sts; bind off next 4 (6, 6, 10, 13) sts; work across 36 (46, 56, 78, 102) sts (including st on needle after bind off); bind off next 4 (6, 6, 10, 13) sts; complete row in pat.

Beg with a purl row, continue pat and shaping until Row 22 (28, 28, 46, 64) of Chart A is completed.

Next row (RS): Work in pat across 5 (5, 7, 11, 13) sts; cast on 4 (6, 6, 10, 13) sts; work across 36 (46, 56, 78, 102) sts; cast on 4 (6, 6, 10, 13) sts; complete row in pat. (54, 68, 82, 120, 154 sts)

Continue to work even in pat until Row 26 (32, 42, 60, 66) of Chart A is completed. Place a marker at each end of row.

Back Shaping

Maintaining pat, bind off 6 (7, 9, 13, 14) sts at beg of next 2 rows. (42, 54, 64, 94, 126 sts)

Beg on next row and continuing in pat, dec 1 st at each end every other row until 26 (36, 46, 68, 86) sts remain.

Work even in pat for 16 (24, 26, 42, 36) rows, then follow Chart A to complete shaping. Place remaining 14 (14, 20, 26, 44) sts on a holder.

Finishing

Back edging

With B and circular needle, RS facing, pick up and k 42 (51, 67, 92, 99) sts along edge of body from marker to back, k 14 (14, 20, 26, 44) sts from holder, dec 1 st at center, pick up and k 42 (51, 67, 92, 99) sts along opposite edge of body to marker. (97, 115, 153, 209, 241 sts)

Work in garter st for 1 (1, 1½, 1½, 2) inches, ending with a RS row. Bind off knitwise.

Sew neck and body seam.

Leg ribbing

With dpn and A, pick up and k 22 (26, 30, 36, 42) sts around leg opening. Pm, join and work in rnds of k1, p1 ribbing for 1 (1½, 2, 2, 3) inches. Bind off loosely in ribbing. Rep for other leg.

Referring to Chart B, randomly embroider spots on coat. ❖

Odds & Ends

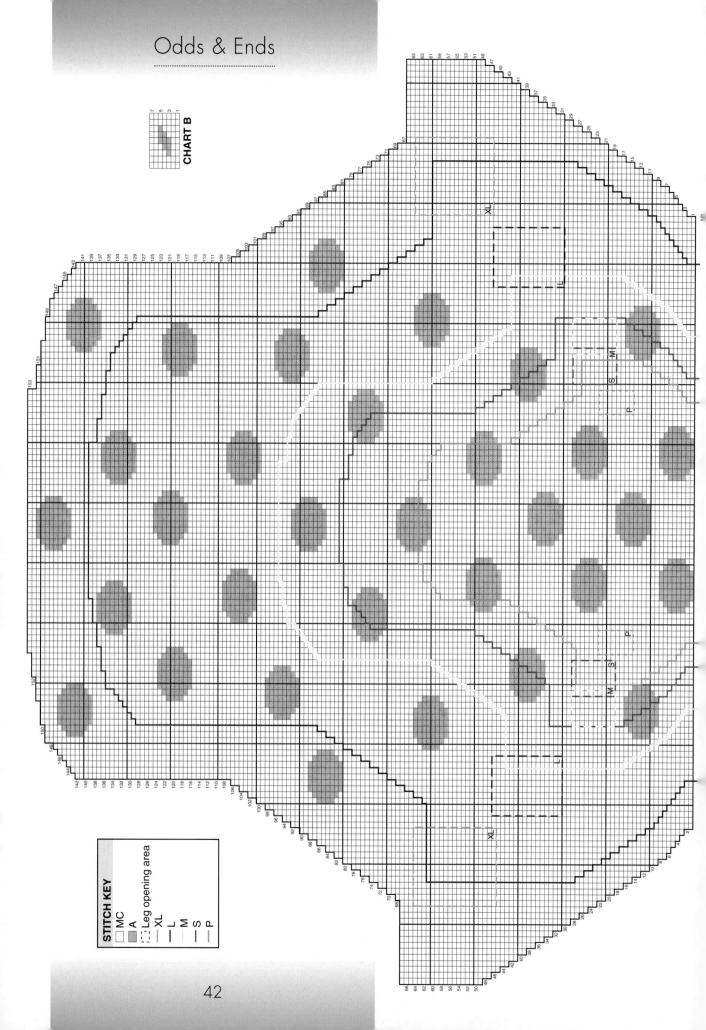

CHART B

STITCH KEY
- ☐ MC
- ▨ A
- ⌐⌐ Leg opening area
- — XL
- — L
- — M
- — S
- — P

Skill Level

Easy**

Finished Size

Approximately 12 x 13 inches

Materials

- Reynold's Saucy 100 percent cotton worsted weight yarn from JCA Inc. (185 yds/50g per skein): 1 skein tan (MC), approximately 50 yds each of 5 CC's
- Size 7 (4.5mm) needles or size needed to obtain gauge
- Tapestry needle
- 12 x 30-inch piece of lining fabric
- Sewing needle and thread
- 1 button

Gauge

16 sts = 4 inches/10cm in pat

To save time, take time to check gauge.

Front and Back

Make 1 each

With MC, cast on 47 sts.

Knit 8 rows.

Pattern

Row 1 (WS): With CC, knit.

Row 2: K1, p1, *yo, p2tog, rep from * to last st, end k1.

Rows 3 and 4: Knit. Cut CC.

Row 5: With MC, purl.

Row 6: K1, *k4, yo, ssk, rep from * to last 4 sts, end k4.

Row 7: Purl.

Row 8: K3, *k2tog, yo, k1, yo, ssk, k1, rep from * to last 2 sts, end k2.

Row 9: Purl.

Row 10: K2, k2tog, yo, *k3, yo, sl 1, k2tog, psso, yo, rep from * to last 7 sts, end k3, yo, ssk, k2.

Row 11: Purl.

Row 12: K4, *yo, sl 1, k2tog, psso, yo, k3, rep from * to last st, k1.

Row 13: Purl.

Row 14: K1, *k4, yo, ssk, rep from * to last 4 sts, end k4.

Row 15: Purl.

Row 16: Knit.

[Rep Rows 1–16] 4 times, using a different CC on Rows 1–4 each time, rep [Rows 1–5] once, then knit 4 more rows. Bind off all sts.

Finishing

Sew side and lower seams. Sew side seams of lining and turn under a hem at top edge. Place inside front and back and sew to top of purse.

Using CC yarns, make a twisted cord long enough to go around top and along sides and bottom, making a loop at center back for closure, sew in place. Make a 2nd twisted cord twice the weight of first, tie ends leaving a tassel effect and sew at sides for strap. Sew button at center front. ❖

Diamond Eyelet Purse

Design by Sue Childress

Knit this lovely eyelet purse for yourself or to give as a gift. Small bits of yarn add flavor to the design.

Catarina Kitt, Figure-Skating Gold Medalist

Design by Rita Garrity Knudson

Sock knitting experience and a good understanding of short row shaping, Kitchener stitch and raglan shoulder shaping is helpful when stitching this challenging project.

Skill Level

Advanced****

Finished Size

Approximately 16 inches tall

Materials

- Sport weight angora blend yarn (126 yds/25g per ball): 2 balls charcoal (MC), 1 ball white, 1 yd green, small amount pink
- Size 2 (2.75mm) double-pointed needles or size needed to obtain gauge
- Iridescent lurex-type thread for whiskers
- Plastic filler beads for weighting body
- Fiberfill stuffing
- Sewing needle and thread
- Tapestry needle
- 1 pair doll skates

Gauge

16 sts and 19 rows = 2 inches/5cm in St st

To save time, take time to check gauge.

Pattern Notes

Catarina is worked almost entirely in rounds. It is helpful to have sock knitting experience as well as a good understanding of short row shaping, Kitchener st, and Elizabeth Zimmermann's raglan shoulder-shaping for attaching paws.

Use smaller needles and tighter gauge than usual for a firm fabric to keep stuffing and filler beads from poking through. Filler beads may be enclosed in a bit of nylon stocking to prevent them from poking through fabric.

Special Abbreviations

Cdd (central double decrease): Sl next 2 sts as if to k2tog, k1, p2sso.

Wrap: Sl next st to RH needle, take yarn to other side of work, return st to LH needle.

Catarina

Legs

Using waste yarn, cast on 20 sts. With MC, knit 1 row then join without twisting. Work in MC and St st in rnds until piece measures 4 inches.

Arrange sts so there are 9 sts on 1 needle for heel flap, divide remaining 11 sts on 2 needles and leave them for instep. Working back and forth on heel sts only, work 6 rows of St st, ending with a WS row.

Shape heel

Row 1: K2, ssk, k1, k2tog, k2.

Rows 2 and 4: Purl.

Row 3: K1, ssk, k1, k2tog, k1.

Row 5: K5. With needle containing heel sts, pick up and k 6 sts along side of heel (Needle 1), k 11 instep sts (Needle 2), pick up and k 6 sts along other side of heel flap, k2 heel sts from Needle 1 (Needle 3). (28 sts)

Knit 1 rnd.

Shape instep

Dec rnd: K to 2 sts from end of Needle 1, k2tog; k11 (Needle 2); ssk, k to end of Needle 3.

Rep dec rnd until 18 sts remain, then work even in St st for 2 inches. Sl 1 st from each end of Needle 2 to adjoining needle.

Shape toe

Dec rnd: K to 2 sts from end of Needle 1, k2tog; ssk, k to 2 sts

from end, k2tog (Needle 2); ssk, k to end of Needle 3.

Rep dec rnd until 6 sts remain. Weave sts tog.

Stuff legs

Place about 3 teaspoons of filler beads in each foot. Generously stuff remainder of leg with fiberfill. Remove waste yarn at tops of legs and place legs on spare needles or st holders. Set aside.

Paws

Using waste yarn, cast on 16 sts. With MC, knit 1 row, then join without twisting. Work in MC and St st in rnds until piece measures 3¼ inches.

Shape paw

Rnd 1: [K7, pm, k1, pm] twice.

Rnd 2: K6, cdd, k5, cdd. (12 sts)

Rnd 3: K2, cdd, k3, cdd. (8 sts)

Rnd 4: K2, cdd, k1, cdd. (4 sts)

Rnd 5: Sl 2, k1, p2sso, pass last st over first st and pull through.

Stuff paws

Place about a teaspoonful of filler beads in bottom of each paw. Generously stuff each paw with fiberfill. Set paws aside.

Body

Using left leg made earlier, divide 20 sts evenly on 2 needles, making certain that foot is squarely centered. With heel toward you, k front and back sts tog across top of leg. (10 sts remain)

On same needle, cast on 6 sts for crotch. Divide 20 sts of other leg as above, [k2tog] across. (26 sts total)

To make seat flap, beg and ending with a purl row, work in St st in rows on these 26 sts for 2¼ inches.

After flap is completed, shape seat like a sock heel.

Row 1: K17, k2tog tbl, k1, turn.

Row 2: Sl 1, p9, p2tog, p1, turn.

Row 3: Sl 1, k10, k2tog tbl, k1, turn.

Row 4: Sl 1, p11, p2tog, p1, turn.

Continue to work in this manner, having 1 st more before dec until all sts have been worked.

Next row: Sl 1, k across, dec 1 st in center of last row. (17 sts remain)

With RS facing, pick up and k 12 sts along edge of flap, 26 sts across front of legs and crotch and 12 sts across other edge of flap. Join and k 1 rnd, dec 10 sts evenly across front. (57 sts remain)

K in rnds until body measures 3½ inches.

Attach paws

Note: Body sts are divided so paws are closer to front instead of centered at sides. This prevents them from sticking out directly from sides when stuffed.

Divide sts as follows: 31 sts for back, 3 sts on a holder (underarm), 20 sts for front, 3 sts on a holder (underarm).

Remove waste yarn from tops of paws and sl sts onto needles. Place 3 underarm sts from each paw on a holder.

K 13 sts of first paw, 20 front sts, 13 sts of 2nd paw, pm for beg of rnd, k 31 back sts. (77 sts total)

K 2 rnds, ending at marker.

Shape shoulders

Rnd 1: Beg with back sts, k30, cdd, k9 (paw), cdd, k18 (front), cdd, k9 (paw), cdd. (69 sts)

Rnd 2 and all even rnds: Knit.

Rnd 3: K28, cdd, k8, cdd, k17, cdd, k8, cdd. (61 sts)

Rnd 5: K26, cdd, k6, cdd, k15, cdd, k6, cdd. (53 sts)

Rnd 7: K24, cdd, k4, cdd, k13, cdd, k4, cdd. (45 sts)

Rnd 9: K22, cdd, k2, cdd, k11, cdd, k2, cdd. (37 sts)

Rnd 10: Knit.

Weave underarm sts tog.

Place 5–10 teaspoonsful of plastic filler beads into seat (more if desired). Stuff body with fiberfill.

Fill paw with stuffing, being sure to place stuffing around areas where paws join body so that there are no gaps and body looks evenly stuffed (not creased) at underarm join.

Divide sts among 3 dpn as follows: Needle 1, 20 sts beg at center back; Needle 2, 17 sts (front); Needle 3, 20 sts ending at center back.

K 5 rnds of St st (neck) over 37 sts.

Inc rnd: Needle 1, inc 5 sts evenly (25 sts); Needle 2, inc 1 st at center (18 sts); Needle 3, inc 5 sts evenly (25 sts). (68 sts total)

K 2 rnds.

Work short row shaping on back of head (50 sts on Needles 1 + 3): K to last st on Needle 1, wrap and turn.

Row 1: P to last st on Needle 3, wrap and turn.

Row 2: K to 2 sts from previous wrap on Needle 1, wrap and turn.

Row 3: P to 2 sts from previous wrap on Needle 3, wrap and turn.

Rep Rows 2 and 3 until 6 sts remain between wraps (3 sts each on Needles 1 and 3).

Turn and k across Needle 1,

working each wrap and st tog so wrap is on WS of fabric; k 18 sts on Needle 2; k across Needle 3, working each wrap and st tog so wrap is on WS of fabric. (68 sts)

K 2 rnds.

Next rnd: K, dec 14 sts evenly spaced over Needles 1 and 3. (54 sts; 18 sts on each needle)

K 1 rnd.

Next rnd: Inc 9 evenly sts on Needle 1; k 18 sts on Needle 2; inc 9 evenly sts on Needle 3. (72 sts)

K 3 rnds.

Next rnd: On Needle 1, [k2, k2tog] 4 times, k11; k18; on Needle 3, k11, [k2tog, k2] 4 times. (64 sts)

Note: Concentration of decs on each side creates fullness in cheeks.

K 1 rnd.

Next rnd: On Needle 1, dec 5 sts evenly (18 sts); on Needle 2, dec 6 sts evenly (12 sts); on Needle 3, dec 5 sts evenly (18 sts). (48 sts total)

K 1 rnd.

Working in rows with MC on Needle 2 only, create bottom of muzzle.

Row 1: K1, ssk, k6, k2tog, k1.

Row 2 and even rows: Purl.

Row 3: K1, ssk, k4, k2tog, k1.

Row 5: K1, ssk, k2, k2tog, k1.

Row 9: Ssk, k2tog, pass 1 st over other st and pull thread through.

Divide 36 sts that remain on Needles 1 and 3 onto 3 needles as follows: top of muzzle, center 14 sts, sides of muzzle, 11 sts on each side.

With white, k11; with MC, k14 (top of muzzle); attach 2nd ball of white, k11. Do not join.

Using intarsia method, p back over 36 sts.

Dec as follows: k1, ssk, k6, k2tog; ssk, k10, k2tog; ssk, k6, k2tog, k1. (30 sts)

Continue to dec in this manner on RS rows until 4 sts remain. Fasten off.

Stuff head and neck. Sew bottom of muzzle to sides.

Beaded Red Lace Skating Dress

Materials
- Sport weight 100 percent nylon ribbon yarn (82 yds/50g per ball): 1 ball red
- Size 5 (3.75mm) double-pointed needles or size needed to obtain gauge
- Size E red gold-lined beads: approximately 600 beads
- Tapestry needle

Gauge
22 sts and 32 rows = 4 inches/10cm in St st

To save time, take time to check gauge.

Pattern Note
Dress is begun at hem, skirt is worked in rnds, then halter top is worked back and forth in rows.

Special Abbreviation
Bead: Slide 1 bead up to needle, sl next st with yarn and bead in front. Bead will lay on top of sl st.

Dress
Using tapestry needle that will pass easily through hole in beads, pre-string all beads onto ribbon yarn.

Cast on 320 sts, join without twisting.

Rnd 1: [K2tog] around. (160 sts)

Rnd 2: [K2tog] around. (80 sts)

Rnd 3: *Yo, k2tog, rep from * around.

Rnd 4 and remaining even rnds: K1, *bead, k1, rep from * around.

Rnd 5: Rep Rnd 3.

Rnd 7: *K1, yo, cdd, rep from * around. (60 sts)

Rnd 9: *[Yo, cdd] twice, yo, k2tog, rep from * to last 2 sts, end yo, k2tog. (44 sts)

Rnds 11, 13 and 15: Rep Rnd 3.

Rnd 16: Rep Rnd 4.

Beg working in rows.

Row 1 (RS): Pm, k2, *bead, k1, rep from * to last 2 sts, end k2, turn and remove marker.

Row 2: Purl.

Row 3: and 4: Rep Rows 1 and 2.

Row 5: [K2, bead] 4 times, k1, cdd, k1, bead, [k2, bead] 3 times, k1, cdd, k1, [bead, k2] 4 times. (40 sts)

Continue to work in this manner until 4 sets of double decs have been completed. (28 sts)

Shape armholes

Row 1 (RS): K1, ssk, [bead, k2] 7 times, bead, k2tog, k1. (26 sts)

Rows 2: Purl.

Row 3: K1, ssk, k2, [bead, k2] 6 times, k2tog, k1. (24 sts)

Row 4: P across, dec 1 st at each edge. (22 sts)

Divide for halter straps

Row 1: Working on first 11 sts, k1, ssk, k1, bead, k2, bead, k2tog, k1. (9 sts)

Row 2: P2tog, p across. (8 sts)

Row 3: K1, ssk, [bead, k1] twice. (7 sts)

Row 4: Rep Row 2. (6 sts)

Row 5: Ssk, [bead, k1] twice. (5 sts)

Row 6: P across.

Row 7: K1, [bead, k1] twice.

[Rep Rows 6 and 7] 6 times, or until strap will reach back neck. Leave sts on holder.

Rep for right strap, reversing shaping. Weave ends tog.

Hair Bow

Cast on 6 sts.

Rows 1 and 2: Knit.

Row 3: K2tog, k2, ssk.

Row 4: K2tog, ssk. (2 sts)

Rows 5 and 6: K, inc 1 st at each edge. (6 sts)

Rows 7 and 8: Knit.

Bind off all sts. Sew beads as desired. Attach to top of head. ❖

Paparazzi Hat

Design by Virginia Vaughn

Whimsical hats are riding a wave of popularity today. Use novelty yarn to add pizzazz to a simple stockinette stitch hat.

Skill Level

Easy**

Size

Woman's medium (large) Instructions are given for smaller size, with larger size in parentheses. When only 1 number is given, it applies to both sizes.

Materials

- Paparazzi 25 percent wool, 75 percent acrylic bulky weight novelty yarn from Tahki/Stacy Charles Inc.

(55 yds/100g per skein): 1 skein variegated #5259 (A)
- Lamb's Pride 100 percent wool Superwash Bulky yarn from Brown Sheep Co. (110 yds/100g per skein): 1 skein midnight pine #SW63 (B)
- Size 11 (8mm) double-pointed and 16-inch circular needles or size needed to obtain gauge
- Size 13 (9mm) 16-inch circular needle
- Tapestry needle
- 6-inch-wide piece of cardboard

Gauge

7 sts = 4 inches/10cm in St st with larger needles and A

12 sts = 4 inches/10cm in St st with smaller needles and B

To save time, take time to check gauge.

Hat

With A and larger needles, cast on 35 (40) sts. Join without twisting and work in St st until piece measures 3 inches from beg. Cut A.

Change to smaller needles, attach B and inc 25 sts evenly around. (60, 65 sts)

Work in B for 4 inches.

Shape top

Rnd 1: [K10 (11), k2tog] 5 times.

Rnd 2: [K9 (10), k2tog] 5 times.

Rnd 3: [K8 (9), k2tog] 5 times.

Continue to dec in this manner, having 1 less st between dec every rnd until 10 sts remain.

Next rnd: K2tog around.

Cut yarn, leaving a 12-inch end. Thread yarn through sts, pull snug and fasten off securely. Leave end to attach tassel.

Tassel

Wrap A 6 times around cardboard. Pinch center, wrap tightly with yarn and fasten securely to top of hat. ❖

Checkered Socks

Design by Virginia Vaughn

Checks, a simple form of Fair Isle, make these two-color socks outstanding. Knit them from worsted weight wool and size 5 needles.

Skill Level

Intermediate***

Size

Adult's medium/large

Materials

- Galway 100 percent wool worsted weight yarn from Plymouth Yarn Co. (230 yds/100g per ball): 1 ball each charcoal #704 (A), medium gray #702 (B)
- Size 5 (3.75mm) double-pointed needles or size needed to obtain gauge
- Stitch markers
- Tapestry needle

Gauge

20 sts and 26 rnds = 4 inches/10cm in St st

To save time, take time to check gauge.

Sock

With A, cast on 44 sts and join without twisting, pm at beg of rnd. Work in k2, p2 rib until piece measures 1 inch from beg.

Beg pat

Rnds 1 and 2: *K2 A, k2 B, rep from * around.

Rnds 3 and 4: *K2 B, k2 A, rep from * around.

Rnds 5–10: Rep Rnds 1–4, ending with Rnd 2.

Rnd 11: With A, knit.

Rnd 12: With A, purl.

Rnd 13: With A, knit.

Rnds 14–21: Rep Rnds 1–4.

Rnds 22–24: Rep Rnds 11–13.

Rnds 25–30: Rep Rnds 1–4.

Rnds 31–33: Rep Rnds 11–13.

Sock top should now measure approximately 7 inches.

Work 5 rnds with A.

Heel

Centering pat, divide sts so there are 22 heel sts on 1 needle, and 11 sts on each of 2 needles (22 instep sts).

Work heel flap back and forth in rows on 22 heel sts, working checked pat over center 14 sts, and keeping sides in seed st. Pick up new color under old to avoid holes at edges of checked pat.

Row 1 (RS): With A, sl 1, k1, p1, k1, pm, [k2 B, k2A] 3 times, k2 B, pm, with A, k1, p1, k2.

Row 2: With A, sl 1, k1, p1, k1, [p2 B, p2 A] 3 times, p2 B, with A, [k1, p1] twice.

Row 3: With A, sl 1, k1, p1, k1, [k2 A, k2 B] 3 times, k2 A, with A, k1, p1, k2.

Row 4: With A, sl 1, k1, p1, k1, [p2 A, p2 B] 3 times, p2 A, with A, [k1, p1] twice.

Rows 5–14: Rep Rows 1–4, ending with Row 2. Cut B and work with A.

Row 15: With A, sl 1, knit across.

Turn heel

Row 1 (WS): Sl 1, p12, p2tog, p1, turn.

Row 2: Sl 1, k5, ssk, k1, turn.

Row 3: Sl 1, p6, p2tog, p1, turn.

Row 4: Sl 1, k7, ssk, k1, turn.

Continue to work in this manner, having 1 more st before dec each row until all sts have been worked, ending with a RS row. (14 sts remain)

Instep

With A and needle containing remaining heel sts, pick up and k 9 or 10 sts along edge of heel flap (Needle 1); k 22 sts from both instep needles onto Needle 2; pick up and k 9 or 10 sts along edge of heel flap, then k7 heel sts (Needle

3), leaving remaining 7 heel sts on Needle 1. (54 or 56 sts total)

Rnd 1: Knit with A.

Rnd 2: *K1 A, k1 B, rep from * around. Cut A and work with B.

Rnd 3: On Needle 1, k to last 3 sts, k2tog, k1; on Needle 2, knit; on Needle 3, k1, ssk, k to end.

Rnd 4: Knit.

Rep Rnds 3 and 4 until 44 sts remain.

Work even in B until foot measures approximately 2 inches less than desired length.

Toe

Rnd 1: *K1 A, k1 B, rep from * around. Cut B and work with A.

Rnd 2: On Needle 1, k to last 3 sts, k2tog, k1; on Needle 2, k1, ssk, k to last 3 sts, k2tog, k1; on Needle 3, k1, ssk, k to end.

Rnd 3: Knit.

Rep Rnds 2 and 3 until 24 sts remain (6 sts each on Needles 1 and 3, 12 sts on Needle 2), ending with Rnd 3.

Rep Rnd 2 only until 8 sts remain.

Sl 2 sts from Needle 2 onto Needle 1, sl remaining 2 sts from Needle 2 onto Needle 3 (4 sts on each needle).

Note: You will be weaving sides of toe tog, not top to bottom.

Weave toe

Cut yarn, leaving an 18-inch end. Thread yarn in tapestry needle, hold needles holding sts parallel, *insert needle in first st on front needle as if to purl, leave st on needle, go into first st on back needle as if to knit, sl st off needle, go into next st on back needle as if to purl, leave st on needle, go into first st on front needle as if to knit, sl st off needle, rep from * until all sts have been worked. Fasten off. ❖

Yarn Painting Cardigan

Design by Laura Polley

Get that expensive, hand-painted look using up leftover yarns of similar colors! You'll enjoy using this technique for other projects.

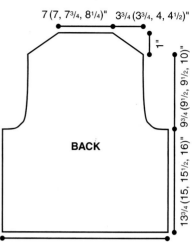

7 (7, 7¾, 8¼)"   3¾ (3¾, 4, 4½)"

1"

9¾ (9½, 9½, 10)"

13¾ (15, 15½, 16)"

BACK

20½ (22½, 24¾, 27½)"

Skill Level

Easy**

Size

Woman's small (medium, large, extra-large) Instructions are given for smallest size, with larger sizes in parentheses. When only 1 number is given, it applies to all sizes.

Finished Measurements

Chest (buttoned): 41½ (46, 50¼, 56) inches

Length: 24½ (25½, 26, 27) inches

Materials

• Cotton Fleece 80 percent pima cotton/20 percent merino wool worsted weight yarn from Brown Sheep Co. (215 yds/100g per skein): 6 (6, 7, 7) skeins goldenrod #CW340 (MC)
• Cotton or cotton-blend yarns, DK to heavy worsted weight, in coordinating colors, lighter than MC: 10–20 partial skeins for CC's, approximately 1,075 (1,200, 1,300, 1,425) yards total
• DK weight cotton or cotton-blend yarn (50g per skein): 1 (1, 2, 2) skeins for edgings (CC1)
• Size 10 (6mm) needles
• Size 10½ (6.5mm) needles or size needed to obtain gauge
• Stitch holders
• Tapestry needle
• 7 (7, 8, 8) ⅞-inch buttons

Gauge

14½ sts and 20 rows = 4 inches/10cm in St st with larger needles and 1 strand each of MC and CC held tog

To save time, take time to check gauge.

Pattern Notes

Pocket lining serves as gauge swatch. Use a CC of equal or lighter weight than MC.

Take care to vary yarn weights used as evenly as possible to avoid large variations in gauge.

Measure each piece by inches rather than by counting rows. Differences in gauge should be slight and easily corrected by blocking.

CC's should be used randomly; however, you may choose to match colors (roughly) across both fronts of cardigan, and/or both sleeves, if desired.

Yarn Painting Pat

Holding 1 strand of MC and 1 strand of chosen CC tog throughout, work in St st, changing CC's at random.

To change CC (on RS or WS row): *Cut CC strand, leaving an 8-inch tail attached to work. Hold new CC next to WS of work, approximately 2 inches from end of strand. Work next few sts by holding MC, first CC, and new CC strands tog until about 2 inches of first CC strand remains. Drop first CC and continue with MC and new CC. When new CC is desired, rep from *.

Back

With MC, CC1 and smaller needles, cast on 66 (74, 82, 90) sts.

Row 1 (RS): K2, *p2, k2, rep from * across.

Row 2: P2, *k2, p2, rep from * across.

Rows 3–12: Rep Rows 1 and 2.

Change to larger needles and knit 1 row, inc 8 (8, 8, 10) sts evenly across row. (74, 82, 90, 100 sts)

Work in pat, changing CC's as desired, until back measures 13¾

(15, 15½, 16) inches from beg, ending with a WS row.

Shape armholes

Bind off 5 (7, 8, 9) sts at beg of next 2 rows, then dec 1 st at each edge [every other row] 5 (7, 8, 9) times. (54, 54, 58, 64 sts)

Work even in pat until back measures 23½ (24½, 25, 26) inches from beg, ending with a WS row.

Shape shoulders

At beg of row, bind off [4 (4, 4, 5) sts] twice, and [5 (5, 5, 6) sts] 4 times. Place remaining 26 (26, 30, 30) sts on holder for back neck.

Pocket Linings

Make 2

Using MC, a CC of equal or lighter weight, and smaller needles, cast on 18 sts. Work 24 rows in St st (do not change CC). Place all sts on a holder for pocket.

Left Front

With MC, CC1 and smaller needles, cast on 34 (38, 40, 46) sts. Work 12 rows in k2, p2 rib as for back.

Change to larger needles and knit 1 row, inc 3 (3, 5, 4) sts evenly across row. (37, 41, 45, 50 sts)

Work 23 rows even in yarn painting pat.

Insert pocket

Next row (RS): K across first 9

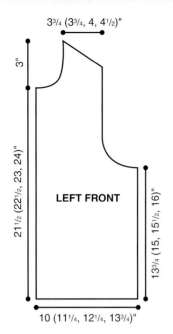

3¾ (3¾, 4, 4½)"

3"

21½ (22½, 23, 24)"

LEFT FRONT

13¾ (15, 15½, 16)"

10 (11¼, 12¼, 13¾)"

(13, 15, 18) sts, place next 18 sts on a holder for pocket edging, k across 18 sts of pocket lining, keeping lining on WS of work, k remaining 10 (10, 12, 14) sts.

Work even in pat until piece measures same as back to armhole, ending with a WS row.

Shape armhole

Next row (RS): Bind off 5 (7, 8, 9) sts at beg of row, work to end. Dec 1 st at armhole edge [every other row] 5 (7, 8, 9) times. (27, 27, 29, 32 sts)

Work even in pat until piece measures 21½ (22½, 23, 24) inches from beg, ending with a RS row.

Shape neck

Next row (WS): Bind off 8 (8, 10, 10) sts at beg of of row, work to end.

Work 1 row even.

Bind off 3 sts at beg of next row, then dec 1 st [every 4th row] twice. (14, 14, 14, 17 sts remain)

Work even in pat until piece measures same as back to shoulder, ending with a WS row.

Shape shoulder

Bind off 4 (4, 4, 5) sts at beg of next row. Work 1 row even.

Bind off 5 (5, 5, 6) sts at beg of next row. Work 1 row even. Bind off remaining 5 (5, 5, 6) sts.

Right Front

Work as for left front, reversing shaping and pocket placement.

Sleeves

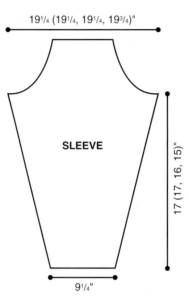

19¼ (19¼, 19¼, 19¾)"

SLEEVE

17 (17, 16, 15)"

9¼"

With MC, CC1 and smaller needles, cast on 34 sts. Work 12 rows k2, p2 rib as for back.

Change to larger needles and knit 1 row, inc 0 (0, 4, 4) sts evenly across row. (34, 34, 38, 38 sts)

Work in pat, inc 1 st at each end [every 4th (4th, 4th, 2nd) row] 18 (18, 14, 3) times, then [every 5th row] 0 (0, 2, 0) times, then [every 4th row] 0, (0, 0, 14) times. (70, 70, 70, 72 sts)

Work even in pat until sleeve measures 17 (17, 16, 15) inches from beg, ending with a WS row.

Shape cap

Bind off 5 (7, 8, 9) sts at beg of next 2 rows, then dec 1 st at each side [every row] 7 (8, 5, 2) times, then [every other row] 11 (8, 10, 13) times. Bind off remaining 24 sts.

Finishing

Block pieces. Sew shoulder seams.

Neck band

With MC, CC1 and smaller needles, pick up and k 24 sts along neck edge of right front, k 26 (26, 30, 30) sts from back neck holder, then pick up and k 24 sts along neck edge of left front. (74, 74, 78, 78 sts)

Row 1 (WS): P2, *k2, p2, rep from * across.

Rows 2–7: Work in established rib.

Bind off all sts in rib.

Button band

With MC, CC1 and smaller needles, beg at upper edge of left front neck band, pick up and k 82 (86, 90, 94) sts evenly along left front to lower edge.

Row 1 (WS): P2, *k2, p2, rep from * across.

Rows 2–7: Work in established rib.

Bind off all sts in rib.

Buttonhole band

With MC, CC1 and smaller needles, beg at lower edge of right front, pick up and k 82 (86, 90, 94) sts evenly along right front edge to top of neck band.

Row 1 (WS): P2, *k2, p2, rep from * across.

Rows 2 and 3: Work in established rib.

Buttonhole row

Size S (RS): K2, p2, k2, [yo, p2tog, {k2, p2} twice, k2] 6 times, yo, p2tog, k2.

Size M (RS): [K2, p2] twice, k2, [yo, p2tog, {k2, p2} twice, k2] 6 times, yo, p2tog, k2.

Size L (RS): K2, [yo, p2tog, {k2, p2} twice, k2] 7 times, yo, p2tog, k2.

Size XL (RS): K2, p2, k2, [yo, p2tog, {k2, p2} twice, k2] 7 times, yo, p2tog, k2.

All sizes: Work 3 rows more in established rib.

Bind off all sts in rib.

Mark left front for 7 (7, 8, 8) buttons opposite buttonholes. Sew on buttons.

Pocket edging

Place 18 sts of pocket holder on smaller needle.

Row 1: With MC and CC to match front, using 2nd smaller needle, k2, *p2, k2, rep from * across.

Rows 2–6: Work in established rib.

Bind off all sts loosely in rib.

Sew side edges of pocket tops to RS of fronts and pocket linings to WS of fronts.

Set in sleeves. Sew sleeve and side seams.

To finish yarn ends, pull each end to tighten. Trim ends to approximately ½ inch on WS. For cotton yarns, apply a dab of fray preventive before washing, if desired. ❖

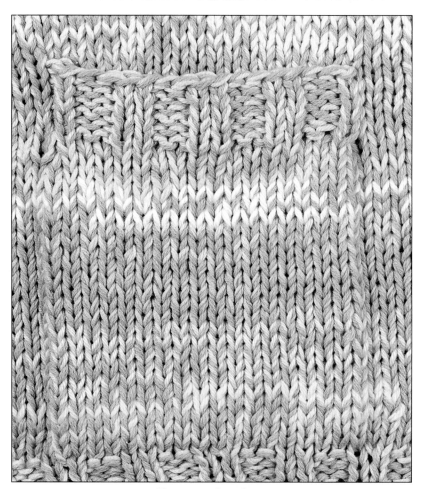

Close-up of pocket.

Funky Hemmed Hat

Design by Virginia Vaughn

This hat is sized to be a loose fit so it won't crush your hair! The hemmed bottom provides extra warmth around the ears.

Skill Level

Easy**

Size

Woman's medium

Materials

- Lamb's Pride Superwash Bulky 100 percent wool yarn from Brown Sheep Co. (110 yds/100g per skein): 1 skein onyx #SW05 (A)
- Filatura di Crosa Adhoe 50 percent wool, 30 percent polyester, 20 percent acrylic bulky weight novelty yarn from Tahki/Stacy Charles Inc. (44 yds/50gm per skein): 1 skein variegated #2 (B)
- Size 10½ (6.5mm) double-pointed and 16-inch circular needles or size needed to obtain gauge
- Stitch markers
- Tapestry needle

Gauge

12 sts = 4 inches/10cm in St st with A

To save time, take time to check gauge.

Pattern Notes

Hat has a hemmed bottom for extra warmth and comfort around ears. For less bulk at hem, use open or provisional cast on, then knit hem and hat sts tog. If you are not familiar with this technique, you may use any cast on and loosely sew hem in place when hat is completed.

To join hem when using open cast on, sl sts from auxiliary yarn to spare needle. Fold cuff in half with WS of fabric tog, *k first st on front and back needles tog, rep from * around.

It is not necessary to cut strands between rnds. Carry colors loosely up inside of hat.

Hat can be made smaller by using a smaller needle. A gauge of 14 sts = 4 inches will make a hat circumference of approximately 20½ inches.

Hat

Using circular needle and A, cast on 72 sts. Join without twisting and work in St st for 5 inches. If using open cast on, join hem at this point, do not cut A.

Beg pat

Rnds 1 and 2: With B, purl.

Rnds 3 and 4: With A, knit.

Rep Rnds 1–4 until hat measures 6 inches from fold, or 8½ inches from beg.

Shape top

Maintain established pat, and change to dpn as needed.

Rnd 1: [K10, k2tog, pm] 6 times.

Rnd 2: [K to 2 sts before marker, k2tog] 6 times.

Rep Rnd 2 until 6 sts remain. Cut yarn and thread end through remaining sts. Pull snug and fasten off securely.

Sew hem loosely in place if needed. ❖

Kid's Color Pair

Design by Diane Zangl

With its alternating loops and buttons, this vest can be worn by little boys and girls alike. Bound-off braid edges, accent pockets, and twisted stitches add textural interest.

Skill Level

Intermediate***

Size

Child's 2 (4, 6) Instructions are given for smallest size, with larger sizes in parentheses. When only 1 number is given, it applies to all sizes.

Finished Measurements

Chest (buttoned): 24 (26, 29) inches

Side to underarm: 6 (7, 8) inches

Armhole depth: 5 (6, 7) inches

Materials

- Wildflower 51 percent cotton/49 percent acrylic DK weight yarn from Plymouth Yarn Co. (137 yds/50g per ball): 2 balls each red #46 and blue #57, 1 ball each yellow #48 and green #49
- Size 4 (3.5mm) 16-inch circular needle
- Size 6 (4.25mm) straight and 16-inch circular needles or size needed to obtain gauge
- Stitch holders
- 3 (⅝-inch) round buttons, JHB International #43383
- 3-inch-wide piece of cardboard

Gauge

23 sts and 30 rows = 4 inches/10cm with larger needles in twisted st pat

To save time, take time to check gauge.

Pattern Note

To avoid holes when changing colors, always pick up new color from under old.

Pattern Stitches

1/1 Twisted Rib (worked in rnds)

All rnds: *K1b, p1, rep from * around.

Twisted Stitch Pat

Row 1 (RS): Knit all sts tbl.

Row 2: Purl all sts tbl.

Rep Rows 1 and 2 for pat.

Color Sequence

Work 2 rows each red, yellow, green, then blue.

Hat

With red and smaller circular needle, cast on 90 (94, 100) sts. Join without twisting, pm between first and last st.

Work even in 1/1 twisted rib for 1 (1, 1½) inches, inc 8 (10, 10) sts evenly on last rnd. (98, 104, 110 sts)

Change to larger needles and twisted st pat. Work even in color sequence until hat measures 7 (8, 8) inches.

Finishing

Sl 49 (52, 55) sts to 2nd needle. Holding both needles parallel with WS facing, bind off sts tog as follows: With 3rd needle, k first st on front and back needles tog, *k next st on both needles tog, bind off 1 st, rep from * until all sts are worked, fasten off.

Tassels
Make 2

Wrap red around a 3-inch piece of cardboard approximately 15 times. With separate strand, tie one end firmly. Cut opposite end.

With another strand, wrap tassel about ½ inch below first knot. Tie firmly. Trim tassel evenly.

Attach one tassel to each corner of hat.

Vest

With larger needles, cast on 29 (32, 37) sts yellow, 34 (37, 42) sts red, 34 (37, 42) sts blue, and 29 (32, 37) sts green. (126, 138, 158 sts)

Working in established colors and twisted st pat, inc 1 st at each end [every other row] 5 times. (136, 148, 168 sts)

Work even until vest measures 6 (7, 8) inches, ending with a WS row.

Divide for fronts and back

Work 25 (27, 29) sts of right front and sl to holder, bind off 18 (20, 26) sts for underarm, work 50 (54, 58) sts of back, bind off 18 (20, 26) for left underarm, k to end of row and sl sts of left front to holder.

Back

Work even in established color pats until armhole measures 5 (6, 7) inches. Bind off all sts.

Right Front

With WS facing, join yellow at underarm. Work even until

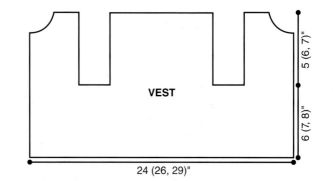

VEST

5 (6, 7)"

6 (7, 8)"

24 (26, 29)"

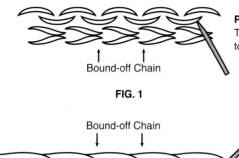

PICK UP IN K:
Tip work forward slightly, pick up in top bar behind bound off chain.

FIG. 1

Bound-off Chain

PICK UP IN P:
Insert needle under top bar of st, yarn rnd needle as if to p, pull loop through st.

FIG. 2

armhole measures 3 (4, 5) inches, ending with a WS row.

Shape neck

Bind off 7 sts at beg of next RS row. Dec 1 st at neck edge [every other row] 3 times. (15, 17, 19 sts)

Work even until armhole measures same as for back. Bind off all sts.

Left Front

With WS facing, join green at front edge. Work as for right front, reversing shaping.

Sew shoulder seams.

Bound-off Braid Edging

Right half

With RS facing, beg at lower center back with blue and smaller circular needle, pick up and k 3 sts for every 4 rows or sts along lower edge, right front, and neck, ending at center back neck.

Turn and bind off all sts purlwise. Do not cut yarn.

Mark front edge for 2 button loops, having top loop at neck edge and 2nd loop 6 (6, 7) inches below first.

Pick up and k 1 st in p bump of each st on previous row. (see Fig.1)

Button loop row: *Bind off in p to marked st, p marked st, [sl 2 sts just worked back to LH needle, k2] 10 times.* (twisted button loop made) Rep from * to * once. Bind off remaining sts.

Left half

With WS facing, beg at lower center back with red and smaller circular needle, pick up and p (see Fig. 2) at same ratio as for right edging. Turn, bind off all sts knitwise.

Pick up and p 1 st in p bump of each st of previous row. Mark left front for 1 button loop, halfway between loops of right front. Bind off all sts knitwise to marked st, make twisted button loop as above, bind off to end of row.

Arm edging

Note: Right edging is worked in green, left in yellow.

Beg at underarm, pick up and k 3 sts for every 4 rows or sts.

Next rnd: *Bind off all sts knitwise*. Pick up and k 1 st in each p bump of previous rnd. Rep from * to * once.

Pockets

With red and larger needles, cast on 11 (13, 15) sts. Working in twisted st pat, inc 1 st at each end [every other row] 3 times. (17, 19, 21 sts)

Work even until pocket measures 1¾ (1¾, 2) inches, ending with a WS row.

Trim

Change to yellow and knit 1 row. Bind off purlwise. Pick up and k 1 st in p bump of each st of previous row. Bind off purlwise.

Make 2nd pocket as above, using blue for pocket and green for trim.

Finishing

Referring to photo, sew pockets to front of vest. Sew buttons opposite button loops. ❖

Skill Level

Intermediate***

Finished Size

Runner: Approximately 13 x 26 inches

Coasters: 5 inches square

Materials

- Saucy Sport, 100 percent mercerized cotton yarn from JCA Inc. (123 yds/50g per skein): 4 skeins white #800, 1 skein green #604, approximately 15 yds each of red #361, gold #143, rose #417, purple #640, approximately 2 yds of black #899
- Size 5 (3.75mm) needle or size needed to obtain gauge
- Tapestry needle

Gauge

22 sts and 32 rows = 4 inches/10cm in St st and color pat

To save time, take time to check gauge.

Coasters & Floral Squares

Make 3 of each flower block from Charts A, B, C and D

With white, cast on 31 sts and work Rows 1–45 from charts. Bind off all sts knitwise on WS.

For coasters (1 of each), steam block lightly. Set aside remaining blocks for runner.

Plain Rectangles

For each rectangle, cast on given number of sts.

Border

Rows 1–4: Beg with a RS row, sl 1 purlwise, knit across.

Body

Work given number of rows in St st, beg every row sl 1 purlwise, k2, work to last 3 sts, end k3.

Border

Beg with a RS row, work 5 border rows as above. Bind off all sts knitwise on WS.

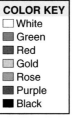

COLOR KEY
- □ White
- ▨ Green
- ▧ Red
- ▨ Gold
- ▨ Rose
- ▨ Purple
- ■ Black

STITCH KEY
- □ K on RS, p on WS
- ⊟ P on RS, k on WS
- ⋒ Sl as if to p

Floral Table Runner & Coasters

Design by Lois S. Young

Coneflowers, asters, roses and goldenrod will grace your table with the beauty of spring with this lovely knitted table set.

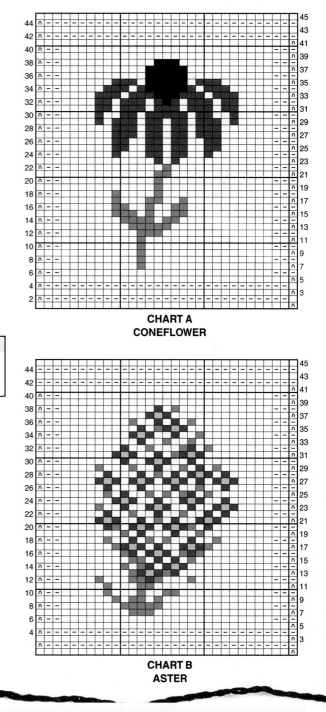

CHART A
CONEFLOWER

CHART B
ASTER

Rectangle A
Make 6

Cast on 11 sts. Referring to instructions above, work border, 36 rows in St st, then border. Bind off all sts.

Rectangle B
Make 4

Cast on 31 sts. Referring to instructions above, work border, 18 rows in St st, then border. Bind off all sts.

Rectangle C
Make 3

Cast on 11 sts. Referring to instructions above, work border, 18 rows in St st, then border. Bind off all sts.

Finishing

Referring to Fig. 1, beg and ending with B, sew B and C rectangles into a strip by overcasting chained sts of selvages tog. Sew A rectangles between floral squares, then sew B and C strip between floral strips with tops of flowers toward center of runner.

Steam block lightly. ❖

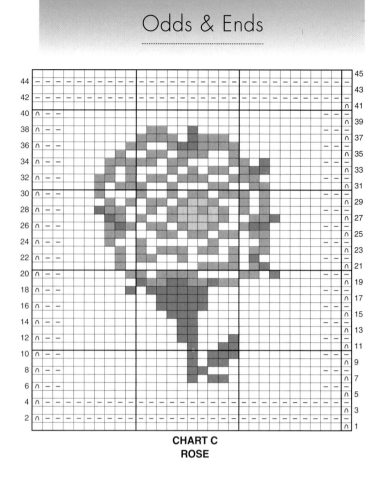

CHART C
ROSE

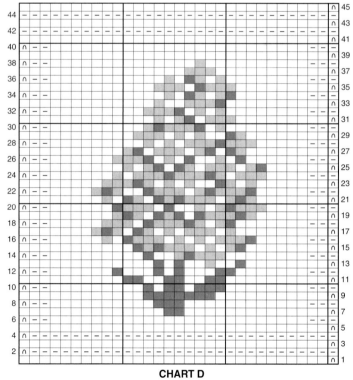

CHART D
GOLDENROD

Golden-rod	A	Rose	A	Aster	A	Cone-flower
B	C	B	C	B	C	B
Cone-flower	A	Aster	A	Rose	A	Golden-rod

FIG. 1

Picnic Blanket & Pillow

Designs by Kennita Tully

This fun, modular technique, recently popularized by Horst Schulz, may be habit-forming. It's a great way to use up small amounts of yarn.

Skill Level

Easy**

Finished Size

Blanket: Approximately 47 inches square

Pillow: 18 inches square

Materials

- Cotton Fleece 80 percent pima cotton/20 percent merino wool worsted weight yarn from Brown Sheep Co. (215 yds/100g per skein): 10 skeins blue slate #CW575 (MC), 3 skeins rue #CW375 (CC1), 3 skeins dusty sage #CW380 (CC2), 1 skein alpine lilac #CW690 (CC3), 1 skein lilac haze #CW695 (CC4), 1 skein nymph #CW610 (CC5)
- Size 6 (4mm) needle or size needed to obtain gauge.
- 18-inch square pillow form
- Tapestry needle

Gauge

18 sts and 18 rows = 4 inches/10cm in garter st.

To save time, take time to check gauge.

Pattern Notes

Each square block is knit individually, but joined while knitting. Ends may be worked in as you knit, minimizing finishing.

Blanket is worked in a counterclockwise manner, beg with center top right square and working outward to edges in rings.

First st of each row is sl as if to knit, last st of each row is purled.

Special Abbreviation

Dd (double decrease): Sl 1 as if to knit, k2 tog, psso.

Basic Square

Row 1 (RS): Cast on 23 sts.

Row 2 and all WS rows: Sl first st, k to last st, p1.

Row 3: Sl 1, k9, dd, k9, p1.

Row 5: Sl 1, k8, dd, k8, p1.

Row 7: Sl 1, k7, dd, k7, p1.

Row 9: Sl 1, k6, dd, k6, p1.

Row 11: Sl 1, k5, dd, k5, p1.

Row 13: Sl 1, k4, dd, k4, p1.

Row 15: Sl 1, k3, dd, k3, p1.

Row 17: Sl 1, k2, dd, k2, p1.

Row 19: Sl 1, k1, dd, k1, p1.

Row 21: Sl 1, dd , p1.

Row 23: Dd, pull yarn through remaining st.

To join a square to left edge: With RS facing and diagonal line running from lower left to upper right (cast on edges along left edge and bottom), pick up and k 11 sts along left side of square, cast on 12 sts. Follow basic square pat beg with Row 2.

To join a square to bottom edge: Holding square upside down, pick up and k 11 sts along bottom edge, cast on 12 more sts. Follow basic square pat, beg with Row 2.

To join a square to right side edge: Cast on 12 sts, then pick up and k 11 sts along right side edge. Follow basic square pat, beg with Row 2.

To join a square to top edge: Pick up and k 11 sts along top of square, cast on 12 more sts. Follow basic square pat, beg with Row 2.

To join last square in a ring: Pick up and k along edge of first square, pick up center st from corner of opposite square, pick up 11 sts along next square. Follow basic square pat, beg with Row 2.

Blanket

Following instructions for basic square and referring to Fig. 1 for placement, work blocks in colors as follows:

Block A: Work with MC.

Block B: Work with CC1, working Rows 11 and 12 only with MC.

Block C: Work Rows 1–12 in CC2 and Rows 13–23 in MC.

Block D: Work with CC3.

Block E: Work with CC4.

Block F: Work with CC5.

Work each square in sequence until blanket is completed.

B	A	C	A	B	A	C	A	B	A	C	A	B	A	C	A	B	A	C	A
A	C	A	B	A	C	A	B	A	C	A	B	A	C	A	B	A	C	A	B
C	A	F	A	C	A	F	A	C	A	E	A	C	A	E	A	C	A	B	A
A	B	A	C	A	B	A	C	A	B	A	C	A	B	A	C	A	F	A	C
B	A	C	A	D	A	C	A	E	A	C	A	F	A	C	A	B	A	C	A
A	C	A	B	A	C	A	B	A	C	A	B	A	C	A	D	A	C	A	B
C	A	E	A	C	A	B	A	C	A	B	A	↗ C 37	A	B	A	C	A	B	A
A	B	A	C	A	B	A	D 21 ↖	A 20 ↖	C 19 ↖	A 18 ↖	↗ D 17	↗ A 36	B	A	C	A	E	A	C
B	A	C	A	F	A	C	A ↙ 22	C 7 ↖	A 6 ↖	↗ C 5	↗ A 16	↗ C 35	A	C	A	B	A	C	A
A	C	A	B	A	C	A	C ↙ 23	A ↙ 8	B 2 ↖	↗ A 1	↗ C 15	↗ A 34	C	A	F	A	C	A	B
C	A	D	A	C	A	B	A ↙ 24	C ↙ 9	A ↙ 3	↘ B 4	↗ A 14	↗ E 33	A	B	A	C	A	B	A
A	B	A	C	A	B	A	F ↙ 25	A ↙ 10	↘ C 11	↘ A 12	↘ C 13	↗ A 32	B	A	C	A	D	A	C
B	A	C	A	D	A	C	A ↙ 26	↘ C 27	↘ A 28	↘ F 29	↘ A 30	↘ C 31	A	C	A	B	A	C	A
A	C	A	B	A	C	A	B	A	C	A	B	A	C	A	F	A	C	A	B
C	A	E	A	C	A	B	A	C	A	B	A	C	A	B	A	C	A	B	A
A	B	A	C	A	D	A	C	A	D	A	C	A	F	A	C	A	E	A	C
B	A	C	A	B	A	C	A	B	A	C	A	B	A	C	A	B	A	C	A
A	C	A	F	A	C	A	E	A	C	A	F	A	C	A	D	A	C	A	B
C	A	B	A	C	A	B	A	C	A	B	A	C	A	B	A	C	A	B	A
A	B	A	C	A	B	A	C	A	B	A	C	A	B	A	C	A	B	A	C

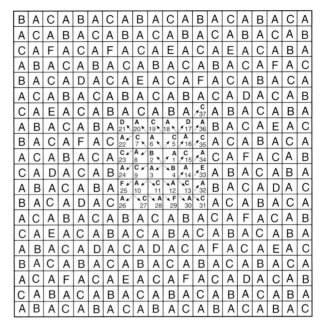

Squares 1–37 are marked to give an idea of sequence.
Arrows indicate diagonals from cast on edge outward.
Letters indicate blocks.

FIG. 1

Pillow

Front

Refer to Fig. 2.

H	G
G	H

FIG. 2

Block G: With MC, cast on 79 sts.

Row 2 and all WS rows: Sl first st, k to last st, p1.

Row 3: Sl 1, k38, dd, k38, p1.

Row 5: Sl 1, k37, dd, k37, p1.

Row 7: Sl 1, k36, dd, k36, p1.

Row 9: Sl 1, k35, dd, k35, p1.

Continue in this manner, working dd on center 3 sts every RS row until 3 sts remain, ending with dd on RS row.

Block H: With CC1, pick up and k 39 sts along left side of Block G, cast on 40 sts and work as for block G. Beg with Row 2, dd center on 3 sts every RS row for 36 rows, work 6 rows MC, then complete square with CC1.

Block G: With MC, pick up and k 39 sts along bottom of block H, pick up 1 st from corner of G and H, cast on 39 more sts. Continue with Row 2 as for block A.

Block H: With CC1, pick up and k 39 sts along top edge previous block G, pick up and k corner sts of blocks G and H, pick up and k 39 sts along left side edge of block H. Work as above, beg with Row 2.

Back

Referring to Fig. 3, work as above, using CC2 instead of CC1. Work Rows 1–40 with CC2 and complete square with MC for Block I.

I	G
G	I

FIG. 3

Seam 3 sides, insert pillow form and sew remaining side. ❖

Patchwork Squares Afghan

Design by Carolyn Pfeifer

Create an afghan that looks like a patch-work quilt by using one main color and odds and ends of yarn in random colors, worked in the intarsia method.

Skill Level
Easy**

Finished Size
Approximately 52 x 66 inches

Materials
- Red Heart Super Saver 100 percent acrylic worsted weight yarn from Coats & Clark (452 yds/8 oz per skein): 5 skeins Aran #313 (MC)
- Small amounts of yarn: 5 yds each of colors 1–12 for each of 14 outside edge blocks (approximately 840 yds total), 20 yds each for 6 center blocks (approximately 120 yds total)
- Size 6 (4mm) needles or size needed to obtain gauge
- Tapestry needle
- Size F/5 (3.75mm) crochet hook (optional)

Gauge
20 sts and 28 rows = 4 inches/10cm in pat

To save time, take time to check gauge.

Pattern Notes
Some worsted weight yarns will vary in gauge. If you use thinner yarns, you will need to knit with a looser tension with those yarns. Variegated yarns add a little more dimension to color of afghan.

Afghan is made in 4 strips of 5 blocks each. Top and bottom blocks have an additional 2-inch border. Outside strips have an additional 1-inch border.

Use separate balls for each area of color in pat.

When changing colors, pick up new color from under old to avoid holes.

Right Strip
With MC, cast on 65 sts.

Border

Rows 1 and 2: Purl across.

Row 3 (RS): K1, *p1, k1, rep from * across row.

Row 4: Purl across.

Rows 5–14: [Rep Rows 3 and 4] 5 times.

First Block

Rows 1–14: Rep [Rows 3 and 4 of border] 7 times.

Row 15 (beg patchwork): With MC, [k1, p1] 7 times, k1, attach color 1, k10, attach color 2, k10, attach color 3, k10, attach color 4, k10, attach another ball of MC, [p1, k1] 5 times.

Row 16: P10 MC, p10 color 4, p10 color 3, p10 color 2, p10 color 1, p15 MC.

Row 17: With MC, [k1, p1] 7 times, k1, k10 color 1, k10 color 2, k10 color 3, k10 color 4, with MC [p1, k1] 5 times.

Rows 18–27: Rep [Rows 16 and 17] 5 times.

Row 28: Rep Row 16, breaking colors 1, 2, 3 and 4.

Row 29: With MC, [k1, p1] 7 times, k1, attach color 5, k10, attach another ball of MC, k20, attach color 6, k10, with MC [p1, k1] 5 times.

Row 30: P10 MC, p10 color 6, p20 MC, p10 color 5, p15 MC.

Row 31: With MC, [k1, p1] 7 times, k1, k10 color 5, with MC [p1, k1] 10 times, k10 color 6, with MC [p1, k1] 5 times.

Rows 32–41: Rep [Rows 30 and 31] 5 times.

Row 42: Rep Row 30, breaking colors 5 and 6.

Rows 43–56: Rep [Rows 29–42],

using colors 7 and 8 instead of 5 and 6. At end of row 56, break off colors 7 and 8 and center MC strand.

Rows 57–70: Rep [Rows 15–28], using colors 9, 10, 11 and 12 instead of 1, 2, 3 and 4. At end of row 70, break off all strands except 1 MC.

Row 71: With MC, [k1, p1] 7 times, k41, [p1, k1] 5 times.

Row 72: Purl across.

Rows 73–84: Rep [Rows 3 and 4] 6 times.

Rows 85 and 86: Purl across.

Rows 87–422: [Rep Rows 3–86] 4 times, ending last rep with Row 84. (a total of 5 blocks)

Border

Rep [Rows 3 and 4] 7 times for border. Bind off all sts knitwise at end of last row.

Center Strip
Make 2

With MC, cast on 60 sts.

Border

Rows 1 and 2: Purl across.

Row 3 (RS): *K1, p1, rep from * across.

Row 4: Purl across.

Rows 5–14: Rep [Rows 3 and 4] 5 times.

First Block

Rows 1–14: Rep [Rows 3 and 4 of border] 7 times.

Row 15 (beg patchwork): With MC, [k1, p1] 5 times, attach color 1, k10, attach color 2, k10, attach color 3, k10, attach color 4, k10, attach another ball of MC, [k1, p1] 5 times.

Row 16: P10 MC, p10 color 4, p10 color 3, p10 color 2, p10 color 1, p10 MC.

Row 17: With MC, [k1, p1] 5 times, k10 color 1, k10 color 2, k10 color 3, k10 color 4, with MC [k1, p1] 5 times.

Rows 18–27: Rep [Rows 16 and 17] 5 times.

Row 28: Rep Row 16, breaking colors 1, 2, 3 and 4.

Row 29: With MC, [k1, p1] 5 times, attach color 5, k10, attach another ball of MC, k20, attach color 6, k10, with MC [k1, p1] 5 times.

Row 30: P10 MC, p10 color 6, p20 MC, p10 color 5, p10 MC.

Row 31: With MC, [k1, p1] 5 times, k10 color 5, with MC [p1, k1] 10 times, k10 color 6, with MC [k1, p1] 5 times.

Rows 32–41: Rep [Rows 30 and 31] 5 times.

Row 42: Rep Row 30, breaking colors 5 and 6.

Rows 43–56: Rep [Rows 29–42], using colors 7 and 8 instead of 5 and 6. At end of row 56, break off colors 7 and 8 and center MC strand.

Rows 57–70: Rep [Rows 15–28], using colors 9, 10, 11 and 12 instead of 1, 2, 3 and 4. At end of row 70, break off all strands except 1 MC.

Row 71: With MC, [k1, p1] 5 times, k40, [k1, p1] 5 times.

Row 72: Purl across.

Rows 73–84: Rep [Rows 3 and 4] 6 times.

Rows 85 and 86: Purl across.

2nd Block

Rows 1–26: Rep [Rows 3 and 4 of border] 13 times.

Row 27: With MC, [k1, p1] 10 times, attach color 1, k20, attach another ball of MC, [k1, p1] 10 times.

Row 28: P20 MC, p20 color 1, p20 MC.

Row 29: With MC [k1, p1] 10 times, k20 color 1, with MC [k1, p1] 10 times.

Rows 30–53: Rep [Rows 28 and 29] 12 times.

Row 54: Rep Row 28, breaking off color 1 and 1 strand of MC.

Row 55: With MC [k1, p1] 10 times, k20, [k1, p1] 10 times.

Row 56: Purl across.

Rows 57–82: Rep [Rows 3 and 4 of border] 13 times.

Rows 83 and 84: Purl across.

3rd and 4th Blocks

Rep Rows 1–84 of 2nd block.

5th Block

Rep Rows 3–84 of first block.

Border

Rep border [Rows 3 and 4] 7 times. Bind off all sts knitwise at end of last row.

Left Strip

Cast on 65 sts. Work border and Rows 1–14 as for right strip.

First block

Row 15: With MC [k1, p1] 5 times, attach color 1, k10, attach color 2, k10, attach color 3, k10, attach color 4, k10, attach another ball of MC [k1, p1] 7 times, k1.

Row 16: P15 MC, p10 color 4, p10 color 3, p10 color 2, p10 color 1, p10 MC.

Row 17: With MC [k1, p1] 5 times, k10 color 1, k10 color 2, k10 color 3, k10 color 4, with MC [k1, p1] 7 times, k1.

Rows 18–27: Rep [Rows 16 and 17] 5 times.

Row 28: Rep Row 16, breaking off colors 1, 2, 3 and 4.

Row 29: With MC [k1, p1] 5 times, attach color 5, k10, attach another ball of MC, k20, attach color 6, k10, with MC [k1, p1] 7 times, k1.

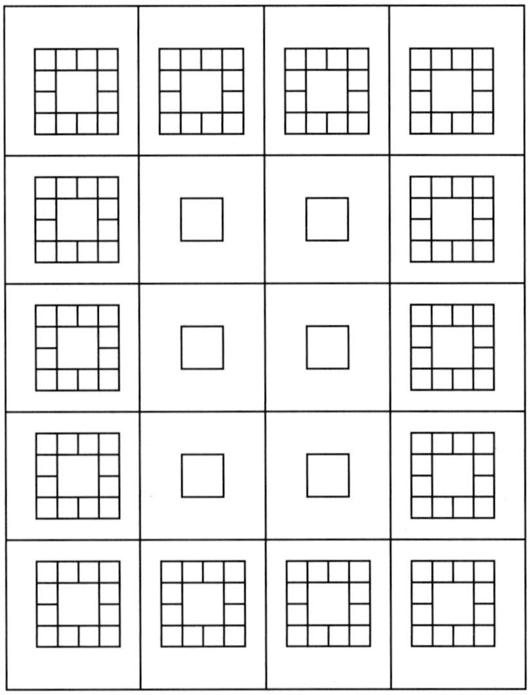

FIG. 1

Row 30: P15 MC, p10 color 6, p20 MC, p10 color 5, p10 MC.

Row 31: With MC [k1, p1] 5 times, k10 color 5, with MC [k1, p1] 10 times, k10 color 6, with MC [k1, p1] 7 times, k1.

Rows 32–41: Rep [Rows 30 and 31] 5 times.

Row 42: Rep Row 30, breaking off colors 5 and 6.

Rows 43–56: Rep Rows 29–42, using colors 7 and 8 instead of 5 and

6. At end of Row 56, break off colors 7 and 8 and center MC strand.

Rows 57–70: Rep Rows 15–28, using colors 9, 10, 11 and 12 instead of 1, 2, 3 and 4. At end of row 70, break off all strands except 1 MC.

Row 71: With MC [k1, p1] 5 times, k40, [k1, p1] 7 times, k1.

Rows 72–422: Maintaining established borders, work as right strip.

Work border as for right strip.

Finishing

With steam iron and pressing cloth, block strips to size, being careful not to touch iron to fabric. Allow strips to dry.

Using yarn needle and MC, sew strips tog, matching up beg of each block. Press seams if needed.

Optional edging

Using crochet hook and MC, work 1 rnd of sc around entire afghan, working 3 sc in corner, and being careful not to work too tightly. ❖

Skill Level

Intermediate***

Finished Size

Approximately 48½ x 61 inches

Materials

- Lion Brand Imagine 80 percent acrylic/20 percent mohair worsted weight mohair-look yarn, (22 yds/2.5 oz per skein): 6 skeins black #153 (MC)
- 10–40 different yarns (DK to heavy worsted weight) in various shades of deep rose and violet (CC1's) (see Pattern Notes)
- 10–40 different yarns (DK to heavy worsted weight) in various shades of blues and greenish blues (CC2's) (see Pattern Notes)
- Size 9 (5.5mm) straight and 36-inch circular needles or size needed to obtain gauge
- Tapestry needle

Gauge

17 sts and 30 rows = 4 inches/10cm in chart pat

To save time, take time to check gauge.

Pattern Notes

Each block of color uses approximately 11 yds of CC. Use this number to determine if you have enough of a particular yarn to complete a block. If you run out of yarn in middle of a block, you may simply finish that block in a closely matched color and type of yarn.

There are 165 blocks of color in the afghan. Use this number to determine how many different colors/yarns you would like to use. Sample afghan uses 32 yarns plus MC. Total amount of CC's is approximately 1,815 yds.

St gauge is more important than row gauge, as length may be adjusted by adding more blocks to each strip. To check gauge, cast on 18 sts with desired CC1 and work Rows 1–30 of chart. Piece should measure approximately 4¼ inches wide and 4 inches long, measuring above cast-on row.

Circular needle is used to pick up sts along side edges of panels for joining, and to pick up sts for borders. When using circular needle, do not join, but turn and work in rows or in 3-needle bind-off as indicated in pat.

First and last sts of each row of chart are selvage sts, and if you work them as directed in chart, you will have a neat edge on both sides of each strip. These edge sts make it much easier to pick up sts for joining strips, and keep horizontal MC garter ridges aligned throughout afghan.

Carry MC loosely up side of work throughout strip.

Each strip may be joined upon completion to strips already worked, or you may prefer to work all strips and then begin joining. There are a total of 11 strips.

Afghan

Strip 1

With straight needles and desired CC1 (deep rose), cast on 18 sts. Work [Rows 1–30 of chart] 14 times, changing CC after each rep and alternating deep rose and blue blocks throughout, then work [Rows 1–28] once more. (448 total rows worked)

Last block worked should be deep rose (a CC1). Bind off all sts. Strip should measure approximately 59 inches.

Strips 2, 4, 6, 8 and 10

Work as for Strip 1, beg and ending with a CC2 block.

Strips 3, 5, 7, 9 and 11

Work as for Strip 1.

Join Strip 1 and Strip 2

With MC and circular needle, RS of Strip 1 facing, beg at lower right corner of strip (at cast on edge), pick up and knit 1 st in edge of cast-on row, then 1 st in each edge st to upper right corner of strip, then 1 st in edge of bind off row. Do not break yarn. (226 sts)

(There is 1 edge st for every 2 rows of knitting, so if you pick up 1 st in each edge st plus 1 st at upper and lower edges, you will not need to count sts.)

Hold Strip 2 directly to left of last picked-up st of Strip 1. With RS facing, using same strand of MC and same needle, beg at bound off edge of Strip 2, pick up 1 st in edge of bound off row, 1 st in each edge st to lower end of Strip 2, then 1 st in edge of cast on row. (226 more sts)

You will now have both strips hanging from needle, and a total of 552 sts. Fold needle so both tips are tog, with RS of each strip facing outward. Using straight needle and MC, k first st on front and back needles tog, *k next st on both needles tog, bind off 1, rep from * until all sts are worked, fasten off.

Join remaining strips in same way, alternating colors, treating joined strips as Strip 1 and next strip to be joined as Strip 2, until all 11 strips have been joined.

Right Side Border

With MC and circular needle, RS facing, beg at lower right edge of Strip

Stained Glass Squares

Design by Laura Polley

Combine small amounts of many different yarns for a beautiful afghan that glows! Tips on page 73 make yarn selection easy.

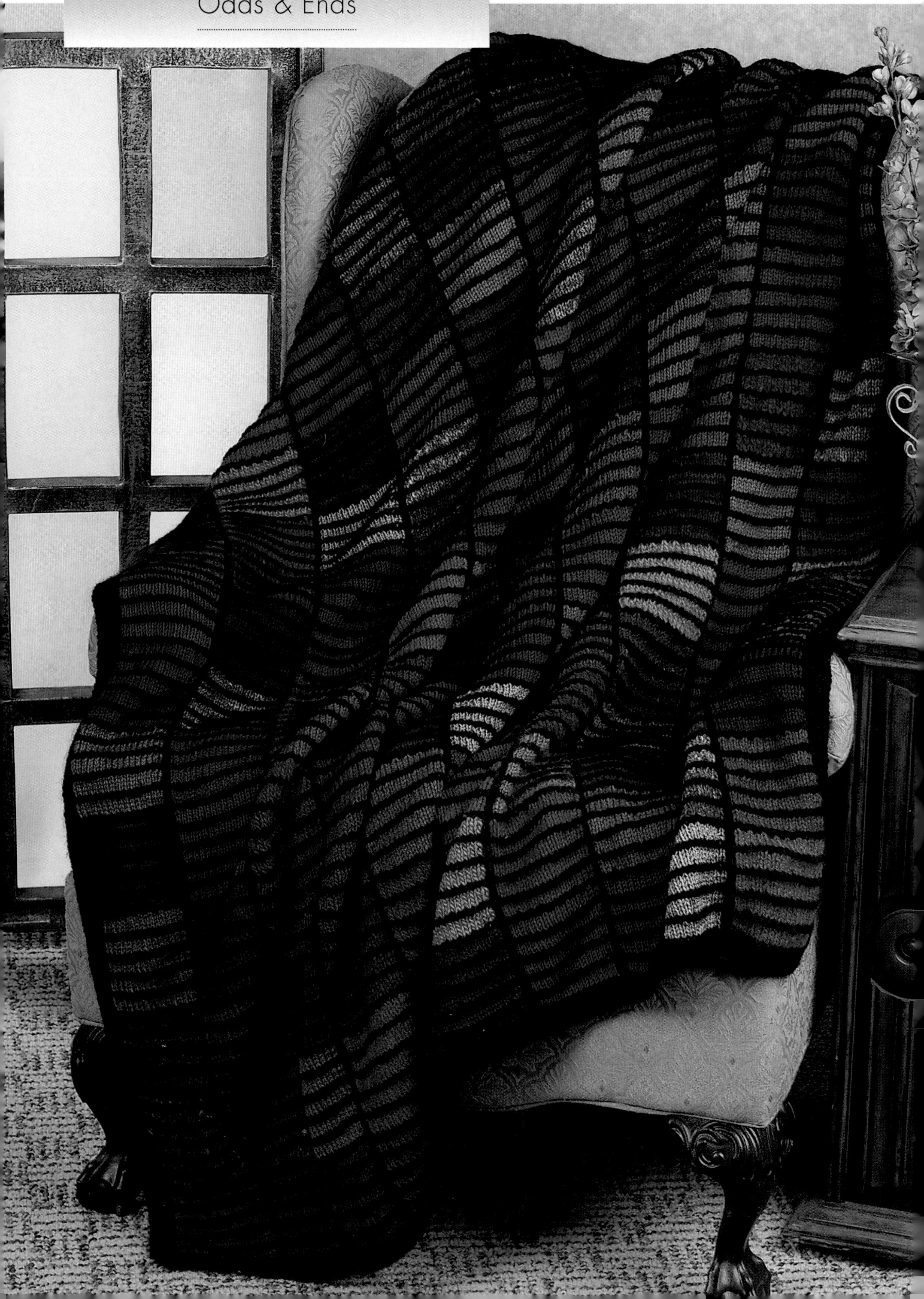

11, pick up and knit 1 st in edge of cast on row, 1 st in each edge st to upper right corner of strip, then 1 st in edge of bound off row. (226 sts)

Row 1 (WS): K into front and back of first st, k to last st, k into front and back of last st (228 sts)

Row 2 (RS): Knit.

Rep [Rows 1 and 2] twice more, then work Row 1 once more. (234 sts)

Bind off loosely purlwise on RS, leaving 10-inch tail for sewing corner.

Left Side Border

Pick up sts as for right border, beg at upper left (bound off) edge of Strip 1 and ending at lower left (cast on) edge of Strip 1.

Complete as for right border. (234 sts)

Upper Border

With MC and circular needle, RS facing, beg at upper right corner of Strip 11, pick up and k 17 sts in each color block across upper edge to left corner of Strip 1. (Do not pick up sts in MC joining/bound off rows) (187 sts)

Complete as for right border. (195 sts)

Lower Border

Pick up sts as for upper border,

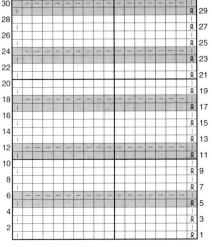

STITCH KEY

☐ K on RS, p on WS with CC
▧ K (RS) with MC
⊟ K (WS) with MC
⍀ K through back loop with CC
⍀ K through back loop with MC
⊡☐ Sl st with yarn held on WS

beg at lower left corner of Strip 1 and ending at lower right corner of Strip 11. (187 sts)

Complete as above.

Finishing

With tails of MC, sew corner seams.

Block piece by pinning flat without stretching, and steaming lightly above work. Do not rest iron on afghan. ❖

STAINED GLASS CHART

Tips for Working With Bits & Pieces

Afghan may be worked in any color scheme you desire. Choose odds and ends of many colors plus black or white for a vibrant afghan, or use odd balls of colors to match your home decor.

Squares are suggested, but if you have very small lengths of yarn, you can use them to make a crazy-stripe design, keeping MC ridges in place.

Feel free to combine yarns of

different weights, textures, and fibers. Any yarn between DK and heavy worsted weight can be used with this pattern, but try to balance weights by working a lighter weight square next to a heavier one and vice versa.

You can use fingering weight or sock weight yarns doubled to equal a strand of DK or worsted yarn. This is a great way to expand your possibilities.

Variegated yarns look great in this stained-glass pattern. Choose a yarn whose dominant color fits desired color scheme, even if there

are several other colors present.

For a larger or smaller afghan, simply adjust number of blocks in each strip, as well as number of strips. A smaller version in primary colors plus black would make a great kid's afghan.

For blocking and laundering, determine care requirements for most delicate yarn used, and treat entire afghan in this manner. If one square is dry-clean only, it's best to dry-clean the entire afghan! In most cases, a gentle-cycle or hand washing will be suitable. Lay flat to dry.

Yikes! Stripes!

Whether the stripes go across or up and down, they are colorful and full of life. Select an assortment of yarns and colors that look good together, and you're ready to start the projects in this section.

Fireside Warmer Afghan

Design by Carolyn Pfeifer

Create the tweed look of this striking afghan by using a slip-stitch pattern with alternating variegated and solid colors within a black framework.

Skill Level

Beginner*

Finished Size

Approximately 50 x 62 inches

Materials

- Red Heart Super Saver 100 percent acrylic worsted weight yarn from Coats & Clark (452 yds/8 oz per skein): 3 skeins black #312 (MC), 50 yds each of 14 variegated colors (A), 40 yds each of 16 solid colors (CC)
- Size 9 (5.5mm) 29-inch circular needle or size needed to obtain gauge
- Size H/8 (5mm) crochet hook (optional)
- Tapestry needle

Gauge

17 sts and 26 rows = 4 inches/10cm

To save time, take time to check gauge.

Pattern Notes

Sample was made with a different color for each stripe, alternating variegated and solid colors. Stripes are separated by 4 rows of MC.

Sl all sts purlwise unless otherwise instructed.

Afghan

With MC, cast on 211 sts.

Row 1 (RS): Sl 1 knitwise, *sl 1 wyif, k1, rep from * across.

Row 2: Sl 1, purl across.

Row 3: Sl 1 knitwise, *k1, sl 1 wyif, rep from * across, end k2.

Row 4: Sl 1, purl across.

Rows 1–4 form pat.

Rows 5 and 6: Drop MC but do not break off, attach first solid color (CC), rep Rows 1 and 2.

Rows 7 and 8: With MC, rep Rows 3 and 4.

Rows 9–14: Rep Rows 5–8, then rep Rows 5 and 6. Cut CC.

Rows 15–18: With MC only, work Rows 3 and 4, then Rows 1 and 2. Cut MC.

Rows 19–26: With first variegated color (A), work pat, beg with Row 3 and ending with Row 2. Cut A, attach MC.

Rows 27–30: With MC, rep Rows 15–18.

Drop MC but do not cut, attach next solid color (CC).

Rows 31–40: Beg with pat Row 3, work 2 rows CC, [2 rows MC, 2 rows CC] twice, ending with pat Row 4. Cut CC.

Rows 41–44: With MC, rep Rows 1–4. Cut MC.

Rows 45–52: Attach next variegated color (A), work [Rows 1–4] twice.

Rep [Rows 1–52] 6 times, then rep [Rows 1–44] once. This should give you 16 tweed stripes and 14 variegated stripes or approximately 62 inches.

Bind off all sts knitwise.

Finishing

Edge (optional)

With MC and crochet hook, work one rnd of sc around entire afghan.

Fringe

Cut a 3-inch-wide cardboard piece. Wrap MC yarn around it as many times as needed to have 1 strand in each st across top and bottom edges of afghan. Cut yarn on 1 edge of cardboard so that each piece is 6 inches. Fold each piece and loop through sts on top and bottom edges of afghan. Trim fringe evenly.

Steam block lightly with pressing cloth, being careful not to touch iron to fabric. ❖

Winterfest Afghan

Design by Barbara Venishnick

Knit a multicolored chevron afghan with great eye appeal. Three strands of DK weight or two strands of worsted weight yarns are held together throughout.

Skill Level

Easy**

Finished Size

Approximately 42 x 60 inches

Materials

- Wildflower DK 51 percent cotton/49 percent acrylic DK weight yarn from Plymouth Yarn Co. (136 yds/50g per ball): 21 balls natural #40 (A)
- Cotton Fleece 80 percent pima cotton/20 percent merino wool worsted weight yarn from Brown Sheep Co. (215 yds/100g per skein): 800g (8 skeins) of assorted colors (CC)
- Size 11 (8mm) 29-inch or longer circular needle or size needed to obtain gauge
- Size 17 needle (used to bind off trim)
- Tapestry needle

Gauge

13 sts and 14½ rows = 4 inches in pat with 3 strands of A or 2 strands of CC

To save time, take time to check gauge.

Pattern Notes

DK weight yarn (A) is used with 3 strands held tog throughout.

Worsted weight yarn (CC) is used with 2 strands held tog. The following colors were used in sample: barn red #CW201, goldenrod #CW340, lime light #CW840, candy apple #CW930, Navajo turquoise #CW480, obscure teal #CW465, raging purple #CW730, Malibu blue #CW570, cavern #CW005.

Pattern Stitch

Row 1 (WS): With A, k1 tbl, p to last st, sl 1 wyif.

Row 2: With A, k1 tbl, *p2tog, p6, yo, k1, yo, p6, p2tog, rep from * to last st, end sl 1 wyif.

Row 3: With A, k1 tbl, *k8, p1, k8, rep from * to last st, end sl 1 wyif.

Row 4: With A, k1 tbl, *p2tog, p6, yo, k1, yo, p6, p2tog, rep from * to last st, end sl 1 wyif.

Row 5: With CC, k1 tbl, p to last st, sl 1 wyif.

Row 6: With CC, k1 tbl, *k2tog, k6, yo, k1, yo, k6, ssk, rep from * to last st, end sl 1 wyif.

Rep Rows 1–6 for pat.

Afghan

With A (3 strands) and size 11 needle, cast on 138 sts. (8 reps of pat + 2 selvage sts)

Count cast on as Row 1 of pat. Work in pat beg with Row 2. Complete 30 reps of 6-row sequence, or desired length.

Work Rows 1–3 once more. Bind off purlwise on RS.

Side Trim

With A and size 11 needle, hold afghan with WS facing. Pick up and k 1 st in each selvage st, turn.

Note: *Pick up under both arms of knit st.*

[Knit 1 row, purl 1 row] twice. Using size 17 needle, bind off knitwise. Rep for other side. ❖

Imitation Rag Rug

Design by Kathleen Brklacich Sasser

Choose three colors of worsted weight yarn from your stash and knit this easy project. It'll add a warm, nostalgic touch to your home.

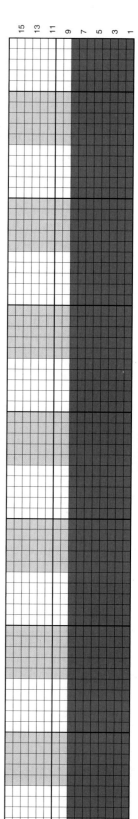

RUG CHART

Skill Level

Beginner

Finished Size

Approximately 24½ x 37½ inches

Materials

- Cascade 220 100 percent wool worsted weight yarn from Cascade Yarns (220 yds/100g per ball): 4 balls dark blue #7818 (A), 2 balls light blue #7815 (B)
- Encore 75 percent acrylic/25 percent wool worsted weight yarn from Plymouth Yarn Co. (200 yds/100g per ball): 2 balls ecru #256 (C)
- Size 11 (8mm) 24-inch circular needle or size needed to obtain gauge
- Tapestry needle
- Roll of nonskid backing material

Gauge

12 sts and 12 ridges = 4 inches/10cm in garter st

To save time, take time to check gauge.

Pattern Notes

Work entire rug in garter st pat (knit every row).

When changing colors, pick up new color under old to avoid holes. All color changes are made on RS rows.

Rug

Using 2 strands held tog throughout project, cast on 75 sts with A. Referring to chart, work [Rows 1–16] 13 times, then work 8 rows with A. Bind off loosely.

Lay nonskid material beneath rug to avoid slipping accidents! ❖

Skill Level

Intermediate***

Finished Measurements

3½ inches wide, 22-inch circumference

Materials

- X-press 60 percent merino wool/40 percent acrylic chunky weight yarn from Berroco Inc. (42 yds/39m per ball): 1 ball green #3611 (A)
- Baby 100 percent merino wool chunky weight yarn from Tahki/ Stacy Charles Inc. (60 yds/55m per ball): 1 ball white #1 (B)
- Size 10½ (6.5mm) needles or size needed to obtain gauge
- Tapestry needle

Gauge

5 sts and 6 rnds = 2 inches/5cm in St st

To save time, take time to check gauge.

Pattern Notes

1 skein of each yarn will make 2 ski bands.

Size may be changed by casting on more or less sts in 2 st increments to match the pat rep. For a narrower band (approximately 3 inches) omit 1 row of B on each side of band.

Ski Band

With A, cast on 55 sts using a long tail cast on. Turn work so the "purl bump" is toward outside (which will be RS of ski band) and yarn is attached on LH needle. Join by sl 1 st from RH needle to LH needle, then k first 2 sts tog. (54 sts)

With A, knit 1 row.

Rnds 1–3: With B, knit.

Rnd 4: *K1 A, k1 B, rep from * around.

Rnd 5: With A, knit.

Rnd 6: *K1 A, K1 B, rep from * around.

Rnds 7–9: With B, knit.

Rnd 10: With A, knit.

Bind off in purl, creating a garter ridge. ❖

Ski Band Stripes

Design by Virginia Vaughn

This is a quick, portable project that uses odd bits of yarn. You'll want to make many to give as gifts to your family and friends.

A Touch of Color Hat & Scarf

Designs by Virginia Vaughn

Combine different textures of yarn with simple garter stitch to create a stunning effect. The scarf is knit lenthwise, and the hat is knit on circular needles.

Skill Level

Easy**

Finished Measurements

Hat: Approximately 22-inch circumference

Scarf: 6 x 56 inches (excluding fringe)

Materials

- Lamb's Pride Bulky 85 percent wool/15 percent mohair chunky weight yarn from Brown Sheep Co. (125 yds/4 oz per skein): 2 skeins deep charcoal M06 (A)
- Alpaca Boucle from Plymouth Yarn Co. (115 yds/1.75 oz per skein): 1 skein #112 (B)
- Size 10½ (6.5mm) double-pointed and 16- and 24-inch circular needles or size needed to obtain gauge
- Tapestry needle

Gauge

12 sts and 16 rnds = 4 inches/10cm

in St st with Lamb's Pride Bulky

To save time, take time to check gauge.

Hat

With circular needle and A, cast on 65 sts. Join without twisting, pm at beg of rnd.

Rnds 1–5: Knit.

Rnd 6: With B, purl.

Rnd 7: With A, knit.

Rnds 8–15: Rep [Rnds 6 and 7] 4 times.

Cut B and knit every rnd with A until piece measures 6 inches.

Shape top

Rnd 1: [K11, k2tog] 5 times. (60 sts)

Rnd 2: [K10, k2tog] 5 times. (55 sts)

Rnd 3: [K9, k2tog] 5 times. (50 sts)

Continue to dec in this manner until 10 sts remain.

Last rnd: [K2tog] around. (5 sts)

Cut yarn, run through remaining sts and fasten off securely.

Scarf

Pattern Notes

Scarf is knit lengthwise, so adjust length by casting on fewer or more sts.

When changing yarn, leave a length of yarn for fringe as desired. Sample fringe is 5 inches.

Scarf

With A, cast on 168 sts.

Knit 4 rows with A.

Knit 2 rows with B.

Knit 6 rows with A.

[Knit 1 row B, knit 1 row A] 4 times.

Knit 1 row B.

Knit 5 rows A.

Knit 2 rows B.

Knit 4 rows A.

Bind off with A.

Add fringe or weave in ends. To add fringe, cut 12-inch lengths of yarn and add to ends of scarf, combining with previously cut ends. Trim evenly to desired length. ❖

Striped Tiptop Hats

Designs by Elizabeth Mattfield

Stripes and felting fun create these unique hats. Use two colors to match your favorite outfit or multiple colors for a hat that is ready for any occasion.

Skill Level

Easy**

Size

Woman's small (large) Instructions are given for smaller size, with larger size in parentheses. When only 1 number is given, it applies to both sizes.

Materials

- Lamb's Pride Bulky 85 percent wool/15 percent mohair bulky weight yarn from Brown Sheep Co. (125 yds/4 oz per skein): approximately 3 oz total per hat
- Size 13 (9mm) needles
- Tapestry needle

Gauge

In St st, before felting, very loose and airy, final gauge is determined by felting.

Pattern Notes

Basic hat instructions are given first; color instructions follow.

Finished size depends a lot on type and color of wool used and how tightly it felts. Easiest way to get correct head size is to dry, and complete felting process over something that is same size you want hat to be.

Hats may also be knitted circular, with 4 dpns and a short circular needle.

Hat

Beg at top, cast on 4 sts.

Row 1 (RS): Inc in each st. (8 sts)

Row 2: Purl.

Row 3: Knit, inc 8 sts evenly.

Row 4: Purl.

Rep Rows 3 and 4 until there are 72 (80) sts, placing incs so they are not directly above previous incs. Purl next RS row (turning ridge). Purl 1 row, dec 4 sts evenly.

Sides

Work 10 rows in St st, dec 4 sts evenly on last row. Work 3 rows garter st. Bind off all sts.

Finishing

Sew seam, then felt. Shape as desired and dry over padded pot or bowl that is desired size.

Blue & White Hat

White (MC) and blue (CC)

Cast on with MC and work to turning ridge. Change to CC, work 3 rows CC, then work pat referring to chart. Work last dec row on sides and garter band in CC.

Rep

HAT CHART

COLOR KEY
☐ MC
◇ CC

Shaded Stripes Hat

Red (A), purple (B), blue (C)

With A, cast on and work first 10 rows. Work [1 row B, 1 row A] twice, 2 rows B, 1 row C, 1 row B, 3 rows C (including turning row), [1 row B, 1 row C] twice, 2 rows B, 1 row A, 1 row B, 1 row A, complete hat with A. ❖

Tips for Felting

Different colors of the same yarn often do not felt equally. I believe it is because of differences in the way dyes bond to the wool.

I usually felt pieces by putting them in the washing machine, hot wash, with minimal water and some real soap. I leave the lid up, and don't let the machine go through the spin part of the cycle and dump all the hot water. I run several cycles that way until the texture looks about right. If the object is small enough, I pull it out of the hot water and dump it in a sink of cold water. Sometimes you can feel it felting in your hands when you do that. If the size or shape is critical, dry the felted object over a form or block, but if it is not critical, putting it in the dryer felts it even firmer.

Felted projects or experiments that go wrong get turned into gift or jewelry bags, cut to size, with braid or a fancy buttonhole stitch over the edges, and beads and trim added. Sewn buttonholes, button loops or hook and loop tape make good closures.

If you need to repair bits or seam pieces before felting, the darning has much more latitude than for normal wear, just make sure it is not very lumpy and is about the same thickness (same yarn) as the rest of the object.

If you sew a piece of yardage or flat object into a tube with light colorfast cotton yarn, it will usually felt more evenly than a flat piece.

Even though felted knitted material curls much less than unfelted stockinette, it can be useful to run a couple rows of garter stitch at the edge of any piece that really needs a firm, flat edge.

Rugged Felted Stripes

Design by Elizabeth Mattfield

Create a dense, warm fabric with subtle color changes by felting a loosely knit striped vest. It really is easy to stitch and to felt.

Skill Level

Intermediate***

Size

Adult's medium (large, extra-large) Instructions are given for smallest size, with larger sizes in parentheses. When only 1 number is given, it applies to all sizes.

Finished Measurements

Chest: Approximately 40 (45, 50) inches

Length: Approximately 23 inches

Materials

- Cascade 220 100 percent wool worsted weight yarn from Cascade Yarns (220 yds/100g per skein): 2 skeins each light blue #9325 (A), medium blue #9332 (B), dark blue #8339 (C)
- Size 10½ (6.5mm) circular needle or size needed to obtain gauge
- Stitch holders
- Tapestry needle

Gauge

12 sts = 4 inches/10cm in St st before felting

Gauge is not critical to this project (see notes).

Pattern Notes

Finished size depends a lot on the type of wool used and how tightly it will felt. Do not use superwash wool, as it is treated so it will not felt at all. Also different colors in the same yarn may react differently, so swatching and testing is important, especially if finished size is critical.

Fabric will be very loose before felting.

Color changes which create the shaded effect in the sample vest are given separately.

Color Sequence

Cast on and work first 21 rows with A. Beg with Row 21, work rows as follows: [1 A, 1 B] twice, 2 B, [3 A, 3 B] twice, 2 A, [3 B, 1 A] twice, work in B.

Several rows after joining all pieces, rep color sequence, using B in place of A and C in place of B.

Back

Beg at shoulder with A, cast on 22 (25, 28) sts.

Row 1 (RS): Knit.

Row 2: P7, turn. (Short row to lengthen neck edge)

Row 3: K across, cast on 2 sts at end of row (neck edge).

Row 4: P18, turn.

Row 5: K across, cast on 2 (2, 3) sts at end of row.

Row 6 and remaining WS rows: Purl.

Row 7: Knit, cast on 2 (3, 3) sts at end of row.

Row 9: Knit, cast on 3 (3, 3) sts at end of row. (29, 33, 37 sts)

Leave sts on holder or spare needle.

Work 2nd shoulder, reversing shaping and working short rows as RS rows.

Row 10 (WS): Beg with 2nd shoulder, p across, cast on 9 (10, 11) sts for back neck, p across other shoulder. (67, 76, 85 sts)

Rows 11–70: Work even in St st, beg color sequence on Row 21.

Shape underarms

At beg of row, cast on [2 sts] 2 (2, 0)

Actual size of stitches before felting.

times, [3 sts] 4 (2, 4) times, and [4 sts] 0 (2, 2) times. (83, 94, 105 sts)

Leave all sts on holder or spare needle.

Front

With A, cast on 22 (25, 28) sts.

Beg with a k row, work 24 rows in St st.

Beg with next RS row, inc 1 st at end of row (neck edge) [every 4th row] 8 (7, 6) times, then [every other row] until there are 35 (40,

45) sts on needle. Continue to work in St st until 70 rows are completed.

Shape underarm

At beg of WS rows, cast on [2 sts] 1 (1, 0) time, [3 sts] 2 (1, 2) times, and 4 sts 0 (1, 1) time. (43, 49, 55 sts)

Leave sts on holder or spare needle.

Work 2nd front, reversing shaping.

Body

Making sure all RS are facing same

way, work across a front, cast on 12 (14, 15) underarm sts, work across back, cast on 12 (14, 15) underarm sts, work across other front. (193, 220, 245 sts)

Work 80 rows in St st.

Next row: Dec 6 sts evenly across.

Work 18 more rows in St st. Bind off all sts.

Finishing

Graft shoulder sts, then felt. ❖

Mohair Stripes Scarf & Pigtail Hat

Designs by Edie Eckman

This project, which uses garter stitch and stripes, is a perfect way to introduce the beginning knitter to the joy of working with mohair!

Skill Level

Beginner*

Finished Measurements

Scarf: 7 x 60 inches (without fringe)

Hat: 22–23 inch circumference

Materials
- Mohair Classic 78 percent mohair/13 percent wool/9 percent nylon bulky weight yarn from Berroco, (93 yds/1.5 oz per ball): 2 balls pink #1488 (MC), 1 ball each orange #1487 (A), purple #1110 (B), yellow #8222 (C), blue #1486 (D), lime #1485 (E)
- Size 10½ (7mm) needles or size needed to obtain gauge
- Tapestry needle

Gauge

10¼ sts and 18 rows = 4 inches/10cm in striped garter st

To save time, take time to check gauge.

Pattern Note

When working scarf, carry MC up side on contrasting color rows. Do not carry contrasting colors along side.

Continued on page 119

Summer Stripes Crop Tops

Designs by Patsy Leatherbury

Colorful stripes are popular with the younger set today. Your little one will stay cool and look cool in these easy-to-knit crop tops.

Skill Level

Easy**

Size

Child's 2 (4, 6, 8) Instructions are given for smallest size, with larger sizes in parentheses. When only 1 number is given, it applies to all sizes.

Finished Measurement

Chest: 22 (25, 28, 31) inches

Summer Stripe Crop Top Variation A

Materials

- Sirdar Silky Look DK 93 percent acrylic/7 percent nylon DK weight yarn distributed by Knitting Fever (148 yds/50g per ball): 1 ball each green #287 (A), light peach #928 (B), dark peach #917 (C)
- Size 3 (3.25mm) straight and 16-inch circular needles
- Size 5 (3.75mm) needles or size needed to obtain gauge
- Stitch holders
- Tapestry needle

Gauge

20 sts and 26 rows = 4 inches/10cm in St st with larger needles

To save time, take time to check gauge.

Stripe Pattern

Work 6 rows A, 6 rows B, 8 rows C, 6 rows B, remainder of rows in A.

Back

With smaller needles and A, cast on 55 (63, 71, 79) sts.

Working in k1, p1 rib, work 2 rows of A, 2 rows of B, 2 rows of C, 2 rows of B, 2 rows of A. Change to larger needles and work in stripe pat in St st for 14 (16, 18, 20) rows.

Shape armholes

Maintaining St st and stripe pat throughout, bind off at beg of row [4 sts] 0 (2, 2, 2) times, [3 sts] twice, [2 sts] 4 (2, 4, 4) times, dec [1 st at each edge] 2 (2, 1, 2) times. (37, 41, 47, 53 sts)

Work 8 (8, 10, 10) more rows.

Shape neck

K13 (15, 17, 19), sl remaining sts to holder or a piece of thread. Turn and work back to arm edge. Bind off at neck edge on alternate rows [0 (3, 4, 4) sts] once, [2 sts] 2 (1, 1, 1) time, [1 st] 1 (1, 1, 2) time. Work on remaining 8 (9, 10, 11) sts for 14 (16, 18, 20) more rows. Bind off.

Sl sts from holder back to needle and attach yarn at neck edge. Bind off 11 (11, 13, 15) sts, leaving 13 (15, 17, 19) sts on needle. Work as for first side of neck, reversing shaping.

Front

Work as for back until armhole decrease is completed. Continuing in St st and stripe pat, work 4 (4, 6, 6) more rows. Shape neck as for back until 8 (9, 10, 11) sts remain. Work 18 (20, 22, 24) more rows. Bind off.

Finishing

Sew shoulders tog. Beg at right shoulder, with smaller circular needle and A, RS facing, pick up and k 51 (57, 63, 71) sts around back of neck, 55 (61, 67, 75) sts around front of neck. (106, 118, 130, 146 sts)

Working in k1, p1 rib, work 2 rows A, 2 rows C, 1 row B. Bind off rib.

With smaller needles and A, pick up and k 63 (71, 79, 89) sts around armhole. Working in k1, p1 rib, work 2 rows A, 2 rows C, 1 row B. Bind off rib. Rep for other armhole.

Sew side seams.

Summer Stripe Crop Top Variation B

Materials

- Sirdar Silky Look DK 93 percent acrylic/7 percent nylon DK weight yarn distributed by Knitting Fever (148 yds/50g per ball): 1 ball each violet (A), light blue (B), aqua (C), light green (D)
- Size 3 (3.25mm) straight and 16-inch circular needles
- Size 5 (3.75mm) needles or size needed to obtain gauge
- Stitch holders
- Tapestry needle

Gauge

20 sts and 26 rows = 4 inches/10cm in St st with larger needles

To save time, take time to check gauge.

Stripe Pattern

16 rows A, 16 rows B, 16 rows C, remainder of rows in D.

Back

With smaller needles and A, cast on 55 (63, 71, 79) sts.

Working in k1, p1 rib, work 2 rows of A, 1 row of B, 1 row of C, 2 rows of D, 1 row of C, 1 row of B, 2 rows of A. Change to larger needles and work in stripe pat in St st for 28 (32, 38, 44) rows.

Shape armholes

Maintaining St st and stripe pat throughout, bind off at beg of row [4 sts] 0 (2, 2, 2) times, [3 sts] twice, [2 sts] 4 (2, 4, 4) times, dec [1 st at each edge] 2 (2, 1, 2) times. (37, 41, 47, 53 sts)

Work 8 (8, 10, 10) more rows.

Shape neck

K13 (15, 17, 19), sl remaining sts to holder or a piece of thread. Turn and work back to arm edge. Bind off at neck edge on alternate rows [0 (3, 4, 4) sts] once, [2 sts] 2 (1, 1, 1) time, [1 st] 1 (1, 1, 2) time. Work on remaining 8 (9, 10, 11) sts for 14 (16, 18, 20) more rows. Bind off.

Sl sts from holder back to needle and attach yarn at neck edge. Bind off 11 (11, 13, 15) sts, leaving 13 (15, 17, 19) sts on needle. Work as for first side of neck, reversing shaping.

Front

Work as for back until armhole decrease is completed. Continuing in St st and stripe pat, work 4 (4, 6, 6) more rows. Shape neck as for back until 8 (9, 10, 11) sts remain. Work 18 (20, 22, 24) more rows. Bind off.

Finishing

Sew shoulders tog. Beg at right shoulder, with smaller circular needle and A, RS facing, pick up and k 51 (57, 63, 71) sts around back of neck, 55 (61, 67, 75) sts around front of neck. (106, 118, 130, 146 sts)

Working in k1, p1 rib, work 2 rows D, 1 row C, 1 row B, 1 row A. Bind off rib.

With smaller needles and A, pick up and k 63 (71, 79, 89) sts around armhole. Working in k1, p1 rib, work 2 rows D, 1 row C, 1 row B, 1 row A. Bind off rib. Rep for other armhole.

Sew side seams. ❖

Popsicle Stripes

Design by Svetlana Avrakh

Knit this colorful classic with a two-row shaker rib stitch, drop shoulders and a buttoned neckline. Let your child choose his or her favorite colors for the stripes.

Skill Level

Easy**

Size

Child's 2 (4, 6, 8, 10) Instructions are given for smallest size, with larger sizes in parentheses. When only 1 number is given, it applies to all sizes.

Finished Measurements

Chest: 27 (29, 31, 33, 35) inches

Materials

- Patons Look at Me! 60 percent acrylic/40 percent nylon sport weight yarn from Spinrite Yarns (152 yds/50g per ball): 2 (3, 3, 3, 4) balls white #6351 (MC), 2 (2, 2, 3, 3, 4) balls each lilac #6358 (A), green apple #6362 (B)
- Size 4 (3.5mm) needles
- Size 5 (3.75mm) needles or size needed to obtain gauge
- Stitch holders
- 2 (¼-inch) buttons

Gauge

24 sts and 48 rows = 4 inches/10cm in shaker rib pat

To save time, take time to check gauge.

Special Abbreviation

K1B (knit 1 below): Knit into next st 1 row below, sl both sts off needle.

Pattern Stitch

Shaker Rib Pat

Row 1 (RS): Sl 1, knit across.

Row 2: Sl 1, *p1, k1B, rep from * to last 2 sts, end p1, k1.

Rep Rows 1 and 2 for shaker rib pat.

Back

With smaller needles and A, cast on 81 (87, 93, 99, 105) sts.

Row 1 (RS): K1, *p1, k1, rep from * across. Break A.

Row 2: With MC, p1, *k1, p1, rep from * across.

With MC, [rep Rows 1 and 2] 6 (6, 8, 8, 9) times more.

Change to larger needles and work in stripe pat as follows:

Rows 1–8: Work pat Rows 1 and 2 with A.

Rows 9–12: Work pat Rows 1 and 2 with B.

Rows 13–20: Work pat Rows 1 and 2 with A.

Rows 21–28: Work pat Rows 1 and 2 with MC.

Rows 29–36: Work pat Rows 1 and 2 with B.

Rows 37–40: Work pat Rows 1 and 2 with A.

Rows 41–48: Work pat Rows 1 and 2 with B.

Rows 49–56: Work pat Rows 1 and 2 with MC.

Continue in stripe pat until piece measures 14¼ (16¼, 17½, 19½, 21¼) inches from beg, ending with a WS row.

Shape shoulders

Bind off 24 (25, 27, 30, 31) sts at beg of next 2 rows. Sl remaining 33 (37, 39, 39, 43) sts to a holder.

Front

Work as for back until piece measures 10 (11½, 12, 13¼, 14¼) inches from beg, ending with a WS row.

Left yoke

Next row: Maintaining established pat throughout, work across 35 (38, 40, 43, 46) sts. Turn and leave remaining sts on a holder or spare needle.

Continue to work in pat until placket opening measures 2¾ (3, 3, 3½, 4) inches, ending with a WS row.

Shape neck

Next row: Work in pat across 29 (31, 32, 35, 37) sts to neck edge. Turn and leave remaining 6 (7, 8, 8, 9) sts on a st holder.

Dec 1 st at neck edge [every row] 4 times, then [every other row] until 24 (25, 27, 30, 31) sts remain.

Work even until piece measures

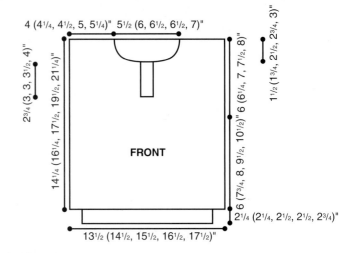

4 (4¼, 4½, 5, 5¼)"   5½ (6, 6½, 6½, 7)"

2¾ (3, 3, 3½, 4)"

14¼ (16¼, 17½, 19½, 21¼)"

1½ (1¾, 2½, 2¾, 3)"

6 (6¼, 7, 7½, 8)"

6 (7¾, 8, 9½, 10½)"

FRONT

2¼ (2¼, 2½, 2½, 2¾)"

13½ (14½, 15½, 16½, 17½)"

same as back, ending with a WS row. Bind off all sts.

Right Yoke

With RS facing, join yarn to remaining sts. Bind off 11 (11, 13, 13, 13) sts, work in pat to end of row.

Maintaining established pat throughout, continue to work until placket opening measures 2¾ (3, 3, 3½, 4) inches, ending with a RS row.

Shape neck

Next row: Work across 29 (31, 32, 35, 37) sts to neck edge. Turn and leave remaining 6 (7, 8, 8, 9) sts on a st holder.

Dec 1 st at neck edge [every row] 4 times, then [every other row] until 24 (25, 27, 30, 31) sts remain.

Work even until piece measures same as back, ending with a WS row. Bind off all sts.

Sleeves

With smaller needles and MC, cast on 47 (49, 51, 53, 57) sts.

With MC, work in k1, p1 ribbing for 12 (12, 16, 16, 18) rows as for back, ending with a WS row.

Change to larger needles and work in stripe pat, at the same time, beg on 5th row inc 1 st at each end [every 6th row] 12 (13, 17, 19, 20) times. (71, 75, 85, 91, 97 sts)

Continue to work even until sleeve

measures 8½ (9½, 11, 12½, 14) inches from beg, ending with a WS row. Bind off all sts.

Finishing

Buttonhole band

With MC and smaller needles, RS facing, pick up and k 22 (24, 24, 28, 32) sts along left placket opening.

Row 1 (WS): P1, *k1, p1, rep from * across.

Row 2: Sl 1, *p1, k1, rep from * across.

Rows 3–7: Rep Rows 1 and 2, ending with Row 1.

Row 8 (RS): Rib 7 sts, yo, k2tog, rib 6 (8, 8, 12, 16) sts, yo, k2tog, rib 5 sts.

Continue to work in ribbing for 6 more rows.

With A, work 1 row in ribbing. Bind off in ribbing.

Button band

With MC and smaller needles, RS facing, pick up and k 22 (24, 24, 28, 32) sts along right placket opening. Work as given for buttonhole band omitting buttonholes.

Neck band

Sew shoulder seams. With MC and smaller needles, RS facing, beg at center of top

edge of button band, pick up and k 6 sts, k6 (7, 7, 7, 9) from right front st holder, pick up and k 21 (23, 25, 27, 29) sts along right front neck edge, k33 (37, 39, 39, 43) from back neck holder, pick up and k 21 (23, 25, 27, 29) sts along left front neck edge, k6 (7, 7, 7, 9) from left front st holder, pick up and k 6 sts to center of top edge of buttonhole band. (99, 109, 115, 119, 131 sts)

Work in k1, p1 ribbing until collar measures 3 inches from pick up row.

With A, work 1 row in ribbing. Bind off in ribbing.

Place markers on front and back side edges 6 (6½, 7, 7½, 8) inches down from shoulder seams. Sew in sleeves between markers. Sew side and sleeve seams. Sew on buttons to correspond to buttonholes. ❖

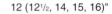
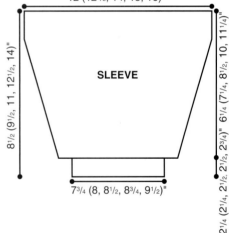

12 (12½, 14, 15, 16)"

SLEEVE

8½ (9½, 11, 12½, 14)"

2¼ (2¼, 2½, 2½, 2¾)" 6¼ (7¼, 8½, 10, 11¼)"

7¾ (8, 8½, 8¾, 9½)"

Skill Level

Intermediate***

Size

Child's 18 months (2, 4, 6)
Instructions are given for smallest size, with larger sizes in parentheses. When only 1 number is given, it applies to all sizes.

Finished Measurements

Chest (buttoned): 25 (28½, 31, 33½) inches

Length: 13 (14, 16, 18) inches

Materials

- Bernat Berella "4" 100 percent acrylic worsted weight yarn from Spinrite Yarns (220 yds/ 3 oz per skein): 2 (2, 2, 3) skeins country print variegated #9112 (MC)
- Worsted weight acrylic yarn: 85 (105, 130, 160) yds each light blue (A), lavender (B), pink (C), 175 (200, 240, 280) yds mint green (D)
- Size 7 (4.5mm) straight, 16- and 29-inch circular needles
- Size 9 (5.5mm) straight, double-pointed, 16- and 29-inch circular needles or size needed to obtain gauge
- Tapestry needle
- 4 (4, 5, 7) ¾-inch buttons

Gauge

20 sts and 22 rows = 4 inches/10cm in St st and chart pat with larger needles

To save time, take time to check gauge.

Pattern Notes

Yarn amounts given for each size will make both sweater and hat.

Body of sweater is worked in 1 piece to armholes, then divided for fronts and backs. Sleeves are worked flat.

COLOR KEY
- ■ Variegated (MC)
- ■ Light blue (A)
- ■ Lavender (B)
- ■ Pink (C)
- ■ Mint green (D)

Circular needle is used to accommodate large number of sts, do not join, but turn and work in rows throughout body of sweater.

Pat is worked in St st from chart. When working from chart, strand color not in use loosely across WS of work. For best results, always pick up CC from under MC, and always pick up MC over CC. Carry yarns to edge of work for a neater side edge.

Body of sweater is worked over full reps of chart pat (a multiple of 6 sts).

After dividing for armholes, and when working sleeves, chart will not come out even. For help in keeping pat correct, note that each 3-st group of color shifts 1 st to left or right on each row, until 4 rows have been worked, then shifts 1 st in opposite direction for 4 rows.

Pattern Stitch

K2, P2 Rib (multiple of 4 sts + 2)

Row 1 (RS): K2, *p2, k2, rep from * across.

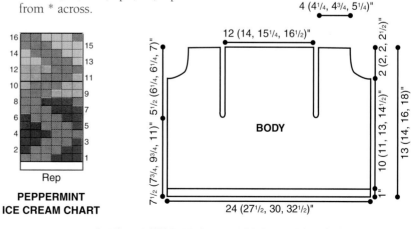

Rep
**PEPPERMINT
ICE CREAM CHART**

Row 2: P2, *k2, p2, rep from * across.

Rep Rows 1 and 2 for pat. To work in rnds for hat, rep Row 1 every rnd.

Sweater

Body

With smaller circular needle and D, cast on 118 (138, 150, 162) sts.

Work 6 rows in k2, p2 rib, inc 2 (0, 0, 0) sts evenly across last row. (120, 138, 150, 162 sts)

Change to larger circular needle and work Row 1 of chart pat across all sts. Continue to work in chart pat until piece measures 7½ (7¾, 9¾, 11) inches from beg, end with a WS row.

Divide for fronts and back

Next row (RS): Work in pat across first 30 (34, 37, 40) sts and place on a holder for right front, work in pat across next 60 (70, 76, 82) sts and place on a holder for back,

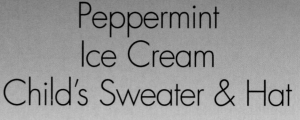

4 (4¼, 4¾, 5¼)"

12 (14, 15¼, 16½)"

5½ (6¼, 6¼, 7)"

7½ (7¾, 9¾, 11)"

2 (2, 2, 2½)"

10 (11, 13, 14½)"

13 (14, 16, 18)"

BODY

1"

24 (27½, 30, 32½)"

work in pat across remaining 30 (34, 37, 40) sts.

Left Front

Work even in established pat on 30 (34, 37, 40) sts, until left front measures 11 (12, 14, 15½) inches from beg, ending with a RS row.

Shape neck

Next row (WS): Bind off 5 (7, 8, 8) sts at beg of row, work in pat to end. (25, 27, 29, 32 sts)

Work 1 row even in pat.

Bind off 3 sts at beg of next row, work in pat to end. (22, 24, 26, 29 sts)

Continue in pat, dec 1 st at neck edge [every other row] 2 (2, 2, 3) times. (20, 22, 24, 26 sts)

Work even in pat until piece measures 13 (14, 16, 18) inches from beg, ending with a WS row.

Bind off all sts, using solid color from last row worked.

Right Front

With larger needles, rejoin yarn to WS of 30 (34, 37, 40) sts on holder for right front. Maintaining established pat, work as for left front, reversing shaping by beg neck shaping on a RS row. Bind off all sts, using solid color from last row worked.

Back

With larger needles, rejoin yarn to WS of 60 (70, 76, 82) sts on remaining holder. Maintaining established pat, work even on all sts until back measures 13 (14, 16, 18) inches from beg, ending with a WS row.

Next row: Bind off first 20 (22, 24, 26) sts, work in pat across next 20 (26, 28, 30) sts and place on holder for back neck, bind off remaining 20 (22, 24, 26) sts.

Sleeves

With smaller needles and D, cast on 38 (38, 38, 42) sts. Work 6 rows of k2, p2 rib, inc 4 (4, 4, 6) sts evenly across last row. (42, 42, 42, 48 sts)

Work in pat from chart, maintaining

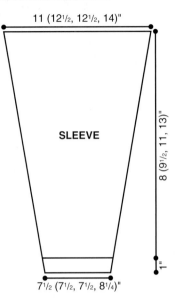

11 (12½, 12½, 14)"

SLEEVE

8 (9½, 11, 13)"

1"

7½ (7½, 7½, 8¼)"

established pat as new sts are added, *at the same time,* inc 1 st at each end [every 4th row (last row of every stripe)] 6 (11, 11, 11) times. (54, 64, 64, 70 sts)

Work even, maintaining pat, until sleeve measures 9 (10½, 12, 14) inches from beg, ending with a WS row. Bind off all sts using solid color from last row worked.

Finishing

Sew shoulder seams.

Neck band

With smaller needles and D, RS facing, beg at right front neck edge, pick up and k 21 (22, 23, 26) sts along shaped neck edge to shoulder, k across 20 (26, 28, 30) sts from back neck holder, pick up and k 21 (22, 23, 26) sts along shaped neck edge of left front. (62, 70, 74, 82 sts)

Beg with Row 2, work 5 rows in k2, p2 rib. Bind off all sts in rib.

Button band

With smaller needles and D, RS facing, beg at upper edge of left front neck band, pick up and k 58 (62, 70, 78) sts evenly along front of sweater to lower edge.

Beg with Row 2, work 7 rows in k2, p2 rib. Bind off all sts loosely in rib.

Buttonhole band

With smaller needles and D, RS facing, beg at lower edge of right front, pick up and k 58 (62, 70, 78) sts evenly along front of sweater to upper edge of neck band.

Beg with Row 2, work 3 rows in k2, p2 rib.

Buttonhole row (RS):

18-month size: K2, p2, k2, [p2tog, yo, k2, p2, k2, p2, k2, p2, k2] 3 times, p2tog, yo, k2.

Size 2: K2, p2, k2, p2, k2, [p2tog, yo, k2, p2, k2, p2, k2, p2, k2] 3 times, p2tog, yo, k2.

Size 4: K2, [p2tog, yo, k2, p2, k2, p2, k2, p2, k2] 4 times, p2tog, yo, k2.

Size 6: K2, [p2tog, yo, k2, p2, k2, p2, k2] 6 times, p2tog, yo, k2.

All sizes: Beg with Row 2, work 3 more rows in k2, p2 rib. Bind off all sts loosely in rib.

Sew sleeves into armhole openings, easing to fit. Sew sleeve seams. Sew on buttons.

Hat

Size

Child's 18 months–2 years (3–6 years) Instructions are given for smaller size, with larger size in parentheses. When only 1 number is given, it applies to both sizes.

Finished Measurement

Circumference: Approximately 18 (20½) inches

Instructions

With smaller 16-inch circular needle and D, cast on 88 (96) sts.

Pm and join without twisting.

Brim

Work 3 (4) inches in k2, p2 rib, working Row 1 for all rnds, inc 2 (6) sts evenly on last rib rnd. (90, 102 sts)

Main section

Change to larger 16-inch circular

needle. Work in pat from chart for 16 (20) rnds. Change to D.

Shape crown

Note: Switch to dpns as needed.

Dec Rnd 1: With D, *[k2tog, k43 (15)], rep from * 1 (6) times. (88, 96 sts)

Work 2 rnds k2, p2 rib as before.

Dec Rnd 2: *[K2, p2, k2, p2tog], rep from * 11 (12) times. (77, 84 sts)

Work 1 rnd even in rib, working p1 over dec sts of last rnd.

Work in St st from this point.

Dec Rnd 3: *[K5, k2tog], rep from * 11 (12) times. (66, 72 sts)

Knit 1 rnd.

Dec Rnd 4: *[K4, k2tog], rep from * 11 (12) times. (55, 60 sts)

Knit 1 rnd.

Dec Rnd 5: *[K3, k2tog], rep from * 11 (12) times. (44, 48 sts)

Knit 1 rnd.

Dec Rnd 6: *[K2, k2tog], rep from * 11 (12) times. (33, 36 sts)

Dec Rnd 7: *[K1, k2tog], rep from * 11 (12) times. (22, 24 sts)

Dec Rnd 8: K1 (0), *[k2tog], rep from * 10 (12) times, k1 (0). (12 sts)

Cut D, leaving a 10-inch tail. If omitting braid, weave tail through 12 remaining sts twice, then draw tight to close gap at top of crown. Finish hat as described below.

I-Cord Braid (optional)

Rearrange sts if necessary so that there are 4 sts on each of 3 dpns. Join MC to any group of 4 sts, leaving remaining sts on other

dpns. K4, do not turn, *sl sts to other end of needle, pull yarn across back, k4, rep from * until I-cord when firmly tugged and stretched, measures approximately 8 (9) inches from first MC row. Bind off sts until 1 loop remains. Cut MC, leaving an 8-inch tail, and draw tail through loop.

Attach MC to next group of 4 sts and rep for 2nd and 3rd I-cords.

From RS, using attached 10-inch tail of D, thread through 12 sts of last D rnd at base of I-cords. Thread through these 12 sts again.

Draw up tightly, closing the gap at top of crown. Bring strand through to WS of hat to weave in later.

Braid 3 I-cord strands tog tightly, pulling cords downward as you go to keep them stretched. Braid to very end of cords, then continue to braid 3 yarn tails tog for a further 2 inches. Holding all 3 tails tog, tie 1 knot at end of braid, and another at base of I-cord portion of braid. Trim ends to about 1½ inches.

Finishing

Fold half of hat brim under to WS and st in place loosely. ❖

Skill Level

Beginner*

Finished Size

Approximately 14 x 70 inches
(blocked)

Materials

- Unger Boodles 60 percent
  acrylic/20 percent wool/20 percent nylon worsted weight yarn
  from JCA Inc. (82 yds/50g per
  skein): 1 skein beige (A)
- Katia Folk 50 percent wool/36
  percent silk/14 percent cotton
  worsted weight yarn from KFI
  Inc. (93 yds/50g per skein): 1
  skein natural (B)
- On Line Taiga 100 percent wool
  worsted weight yarn from Euro
  Yarns (82 yds/50g per skein): 2
  skeins beige variegated (C)
- Reynolds Eternity 51 percent
  wool/49 percent microfiber
  worsted weight yarn from JCA
  Inc. (88 yds/50g per skein): 1
  skein white (D)
- Toison et Soie 90 percent wool/10
  percent silk worsted weight yarn
  from K1C2 (110 yds/50g per
  skein): 1 skein fawn (E)
- Size 10½ (6.5mm) needles or
  size needed to obtain gauge
- Size G/6 (4mm) crochet hook

Gauge

12 sts = 4 inches/10cm in St st

Gauge is not critical to this project.

Scarf

With A cast on 41 sts. Knit 55 rows.

Change to B.

Moss Diamonds Pat

Row 1: K2, *[k3, p1] twice, k1,
p1, rep from * to last 9 sts, end
k3, p1, k5.

Row 2: K2, *[p3, k1] twice, p1,
k1, rep from *·to last 9 sts, end
p3, k1, p3, k2.

Row 3: K4, p1, k1, p1, *[k3, p1]

Continued on page 119

Textured Blocks Scarf

Design by Sue Childress

*Every beginning knitter works up a
sampler of different stitches. Why not
put it to good use as a beautiful scarf!*

Color Splash Cardigan for the Family

Design by Kennita Tully

Sized for the whole family, these cardigans can be worn by all. Pick your color combo and change colors at will.

Skill Level

Intermediate***

Size

Child's extra-small (small, medium, large, extra-large) [adult's extra-small (small, medium, large, extra-large, 2X-large)] Instructions are given for smallest size, with larger sizes in parentheses, adult size is shown in brackets. When only 1 number is given, it applies to all sizes.

Finished Measurements

Chest: 28¼ (30¼, 32, 35, 36½) [39 (42¾, 45½, 48¼, 52½, 56)] inches

Length: 16 (17, 18, 19, 20) [21 (22, 23½, 25, 27, 29)] inches

Materials

• Prairie Silk 72 percent wool/18 percent mohair/10 percent silk worsted weight yarn from Brown Sheep Co. (88 yds/50g per skein): 7 (8, 9, 10, 11) [12 (13, 13, 14, 14, 15)] skeins buck #PS450 (MC)
• Handpaint Originals 70 percent mohair/30 percent wool worsted weight yarn from Brown Sheep Co. (88 yds/50g per skein): 1 skein or less each of forest floor #HP70, tropical water #HP60, strawberry patch #HP40, chestnut #HP35, plum purple #HP45, ink blue #HP55, seaglass #HP15 (CC's)
• Size 8 (5mm) needles or size needed to obtain gauge
• 4 (4, 4, 4, 5) [5 (6, 6, 7, 7, 8)] (¾-inch) buttons
• Tapestry needle

Gauge

18 sts and 28 rows = 4 inches/10 cm in pat

To save time, take time to check gauge.

Pattern Notes

Due to large pat rep, not all sizes beg with the same multiple of sts. Because of this, Rows 3–5 vary to fit the size needed. Follow the version given for desired size.

Sleeve incs are made using M1. Work inc sts into pat, keeping edge sts in St st throughout.

Special Abbreviation

M1 (make 1): Inc by making a backward loop over right needle.

Pattern Stitches

Version A (multiple of 9 sts + 6)

Row 1 (RS): With MC, knit.

Row 2: With MC, purl.

Row 3: With CC, k1, sl 1 wyif, k1, *sl 2 wyib, k1, [sl 1 wyif, k1] 3 times, rep from *, end sl 2 wyib, k1.

Row 4: With CC, p1, *sl 2 wyif, p7, rep from *, end sl 2 wyif, p3.

Row 5: With MC, k2, sl 1 wyif, *k2, sl 1 wyif, [k1, sl 1 wyif] 3 times, rep from *, end k3.

Row 6: With MC, purl.

Row 7: Rep Row 1.

Row 8: Rep Row 2.

Rows 9 and 13: Rep Row 3.

Rows 10 and 14: Rep Row 4.

Rows 11 and 15: Rep Row 5.

Rows 12 and 16: Rep Row 6.

Rep Rows 1–16 for pat.

Version B (multiple of 9 sts + 4)

Row 3: With CC, k2, *sl 2 wyib, k1, [sl 1 wyif, k1] 3 times, rep from *, end k2.

Row 4: With CC, p2, *p7, sl 2 wyif, rep from *, end p2.

Row 5: With MC, k1, sl 1 wyif, *k2, sl 1 wyif, [k1, sl 1 wyif] 3 times, rep from *, end k2.

Version C (multiple of 9 sts + 7)

Row 3: With CC, *k1, [sl 1 wyif, k1] 3 times, sl 2 wyib, rep from *, end k1, [sl 1 wyif, k1] 3 times.

Row 4: With CC, p7, *sl 2 wyif, p7, rep from *.

Row 5: With MC, k2, sl 1 wyif, [k1, sl 1 wyif] twice, k2, *sl 1 wyif, [k1, sl 1 wyif] 3 times, k2, rep from *, end [sl 1 wyif, k1] twice, sl 1 wyif, k2.

Version D (multiple of 9 sts)

Row 3: With CC, k2, [sl 1 wyif, k1] 3 times, *sl 2 wyib, k1, [sl 1 wyif, k1] 3 times, rep from *, end k1.

Row 4: With CC, p8, *sl 2 wyif, p7, rep from *, end sl 2 wyif, p8.

Row 5: With MC, k1, *sl 1 wyif, [k1, sl 1 wyif] 3 times, k2, rep from *, end last rep k1 instead of k2.

Version E (multiple of 9 sts + 1)

Row 3: With CC, k1, [sl 1 wyif, k1] twice, *sl 2 wyib, k1, [sl 1 wyif, k1] 3 times, rep from *, end sl 2 wyib, k1, sl 1 wyif, k1.

Row 4: With CC, p3, *sl 2 wyif, p7, rep from *, end sl 2 wyif, p5.

Row 5: With MC, k2, sl 1 wyif, k1, sl 1 wyif, k2, *sl 1 wyif, [k1, sl 1 wyif] 3 times, k2, rep from *, end sl 1 wyif, k2.

Back

With MC, cast on 64 (69, 73, 79, 82) [87 (96, 103, 109, 118, 126)] sts.

Row 1 (RS): K3 (4, 3, 3, 3) [4 (4, 3, 3, 3, 4)], *p1, k2, rep from *, end p1, k3 (4, 3, 3, 3) [4 (4, 3, 3, 3, 4)].

Row 2: K the knit sts and p the purl sts.

Continue in ribbing for 1 inch for children's sizes and 1 (1¼, 1¼, 1¼, 1½, 1½) inches for adult sizes.

Next row (RS): Beg with Row 1 follow pat version E (A, E, C, E) [A (A, B, E, E, D)].

Continue to work even until piece measures 10 (10½, 11, 11½, 12) [12½ (13, 14, 15, 16½, 18)] inches.

Mark armhole for children's sizes, on adult sizes, bind off each side for armhole 4 (7, 9, 10, 12,14) sts. [79, 82, 85, 89, 94, 98 sts]

Continue to work in pat until piece measures 16 (17, 18, 19, 20) [21 (22, 23½, 25, 27, 29)] inches.

Shape shoulders

At beg of next RS row, bind off 7 (8, 8, 9, 9) [8 (8, 9, 9, 9, 10)] sts, k across 16 (17, 18, 20, 20) [17 (18, 18, 19, 20, 20)] sts, join new ball of yarn and bind off center 18 (19, 21, 21, 24) [29 (30, 31, 33, 36, 38)] sts, k across remaining sts.

Next row: Working both sides at once with separate balls of yarn, bind off 7 (8, 8, 9, 9) [8 (8, 9, 9, 9, 10)] sts at shoulder edge, complete row.

Continue working shoulder shaping as follows: bind off 7 (8, 8, 9, 9) [8 (8, 8, 9, 9, 9)] sts 2 (1, 2, 2, 2) [1 (2, 2, 1, 2, 2)] times, then 0 (7, 0, 0, 0) [7 (0, 0, 8, 0, 0)] sts once, and *at the same time,* dec 1 st at each neck edge [every other row] twice for all sizes.

Left Front

With MC, cast on 31 (33, 34, 37, 40) [42 (46, 49, 52, 58, 60)] sts.

Row 1 (RS): K3 (4, 3, 3, 3) [4 (4, 3, 3, 3, 4)], *p1, k2, rep from *, end p1, k3 (4, 3, 3, 3) [4 (4, 3, 3, 3, 4)].

Row 2: K the knit sts and p the purl sts.

Continue until ribbing measures same as for back.

Next row: Beg with Row 1, work pat version B (A, C, E, B) [A (E, B, C, B, A)].

Work as for back until piece measures approximately 15 (16, 17, 18, 19) [19½ (20½, 22, 23½, 25, 27)] inches.

Beg neck shaping: At neck edge, bind off {4 (4, 4, 4, 6) [5 (5, 5, 5, 6, 6)] sts} once, then {2 (2, 2, 2, 2) [3 (3)] sts} 1(1, 1, 1, 1) [2 (2, 2, 2, 2, 2)] times, then 0 (0, 0, 0, 0) [0 (0, 0, 0, 2, 0)] sts} 0 (0, 0, 0, 0) [0 (0, 0, 0, 1, 0)] times, then dec 1 st [every other row] 4 (4, 4, 4, 5) [4 (4, 4, 5, 5, 6)] times. *At the same time,* work shoulder shaping to correspond to back.

Right Front

Work as for left front, reversing shapings.

Child's Sleeves

With MC, cast on 31 (31, 34, 37, 37) sts.

Next row (RS): K3 [3], *p1, k2, rep from *, end p1, k3 [3].

Row 2: K the knit sts and p the purl sts.

Continue in ribbing for 2 inches, ending with a WS row.

Next row (RS): Beg with Row 1, work pat version B (B, C, E, E). *At the same time,* beg on 3rd row for all sizes, inc 1 st each side [every 4th row] 10 (12, 11, 13, 17) times, then [every 6th row] 2 (2, 4, 3, 1) times, working new sts into pat, and keeping 2 sts at each edge in St st. (55, 59, 64, 69, 73 sts)

Ending with MC, k 1 row, p1 row, bind off all sts.

Adult Sleeves

With MC, cast on 40 (43, 49, 52, 52, 55) sts.

Next row (RS): K3, *p1, k2, rep from *, end p1, k3.

Row 2: K the knit sts and p the purl sts.

Continue in ribbing for 2½ (2½, 2½, 2½, 3, 3) inches, ending with a WS row.

Next row (RS): Beg with Row 1, work pat version B (C, B, C, C, E). *At the same time,* beg on 3rd row <all sizes>, inc 1 st each side [every 6th (6th, 6th, 6th, 4th, 4th) row] 19 (19, 16, 14, 8, 10) times, then [every 8th (8th, 8th, 8th, 6th, 6th) row] 0 (0, 2, 5, 13, 12) times. (78, 81, 85, 90, 94, 99 sts)

Work even for 1 (1½, 2, 2½, 2½, 2¾) inches. Ending with MC, k 1 row, p 1 row, bind off all sts.

Finishing

Block all pieces to measurements. Sew shoulder seams, sew in sleeves and join sleeve and side seams.

Right band

With MC, RS facing, pick up and k 61 (64, 67, 70, 73) [79 (82, 88, 94, 100, 109)] sts along right front.

Row 1 (WS): P3, *k1, p2, rep from *, end k1, p3.

Row 2: K3, *p1, k2, rep from *, end p1, k3.

Rep Rows 1 and 2 until band measures ¾ (¾, ¾, ¾, 1) [1 (1, 1, 1, 1, 1¼)] inches, bind off all sts in pat.

Left band

Work as for right band, placing 4 (4, 4, 4, 5) [5 (6, 6, 7, 7, 8)] buttonholes evenly spaced along band. For man's cardigan, work buttonholes in right band.

Neck band

With MC, RS facing, pick up and k 15 (15, 15, 17, 21) [21 (21, 21, 21, 23, 23)] sts across right front neck, 25 (26, 28, 28, 31) [33 (34, 34, 36, 39, 41)] sts across back and 15 (15, 15, 17, 21) [21 (21, 21, 21, 23, 23)] sts across left front. Work in pat as for bands, bind off in pat when piece measures same as for center bands.

Sew on buttons to correspond to buttonholes. ❖

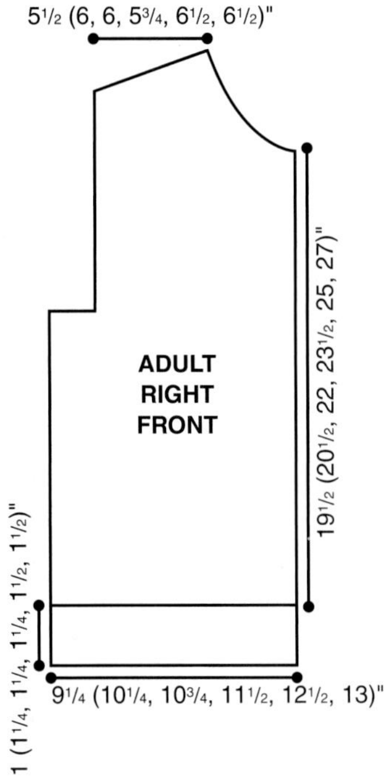
5 1/2 (6, 6, 5 3/4, 6 1/2, 6 1/2)"
ADULT
RIGHT
FRONT
19 1/2 (20 1/2, 22, 23 1/2, 25, 27)"
1 (1 1/4, 1 1/4, 1 1/4, 1 1/2, 1 1/2)"
9 1/4 (10 1/4, 10 3/4, 11 1/2, 12 1/2, 13)"

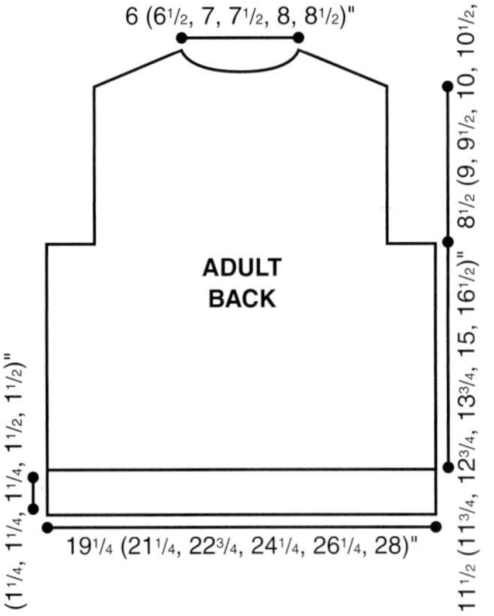
6 (6 1/2, 7, 7 1/2, 8, 8 1/2)"
ADULT
BACK
8 1/2 (9, 9 1/2, 10, 10 1/2, 11)"
11 1/2 (11 3/4, 12 3/4, 13 3/4, 15, 16 1/2)"
1 (1 1/4, 1 1/4, 1 1/4, 1 1/2, 1 1/2)"
19 1/4 (21 1/4, 22 3/4, 24 1/4, 26 1/4, 28)"

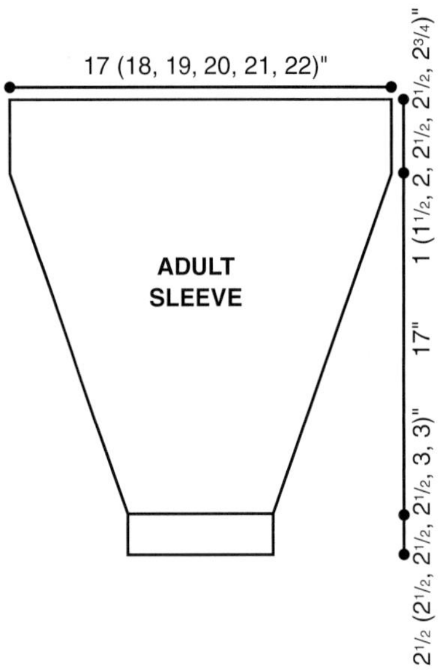
17 (18, 19, 20, 21, 22)"
ADULT
SLEEVE
1 (1 1/2, 2, 2 1/2, 2 1/2, 2 3/4)"
17"
2 1/2 (2 1/2, 2 1/2, 2 1/2, 3, 3)"

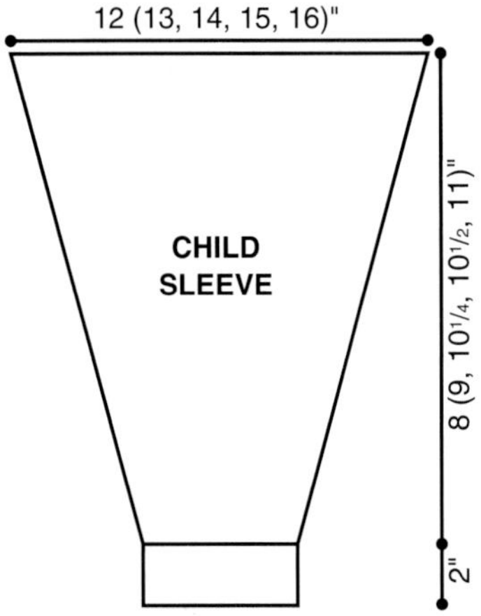
12 (13, 14, 15, 16)"
CHILD
SLEEVE
8 (9, 10 1/4, 10 1/2, 11)"
2"

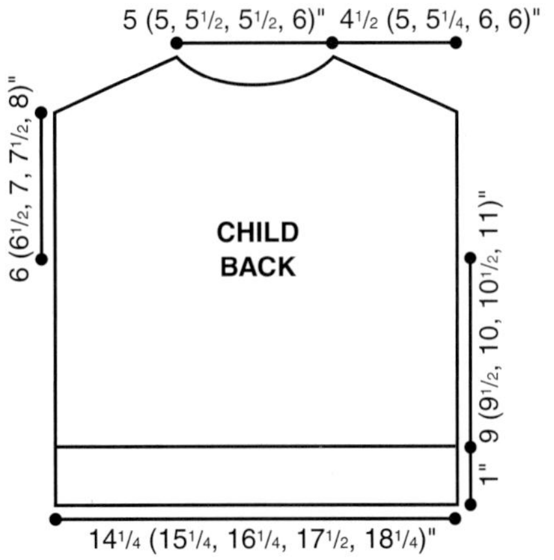
5 (5, 5 1/2, 5 1/2, 6)"
4 1/2 (5, 5 1/4, 6, 6)"
6 (6 1/2, 7, 7 1/2, 8)"
CHILD
BACK
9 (9 1/2, 10, 10 1/2, 11)"
1"
14 1/4 (15 1/4, 16 1/4, 17 1/2, 18 1/4)"

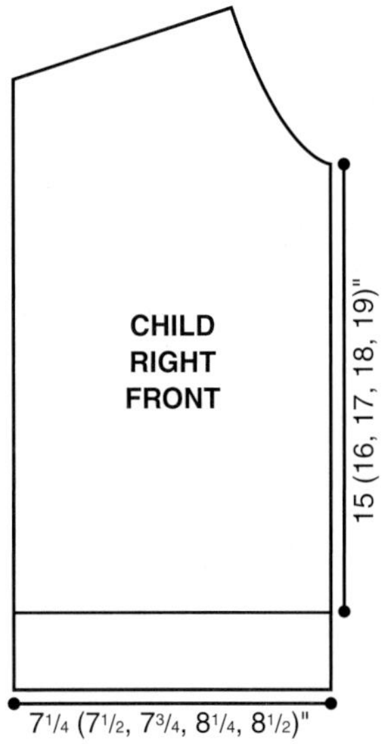
CHILD
RIGHT
FRONT
15 (16, 17, 18, 19)"
7 1/4 (7 1/2, 7 3/4, 8 1/4, 8 1/2)"

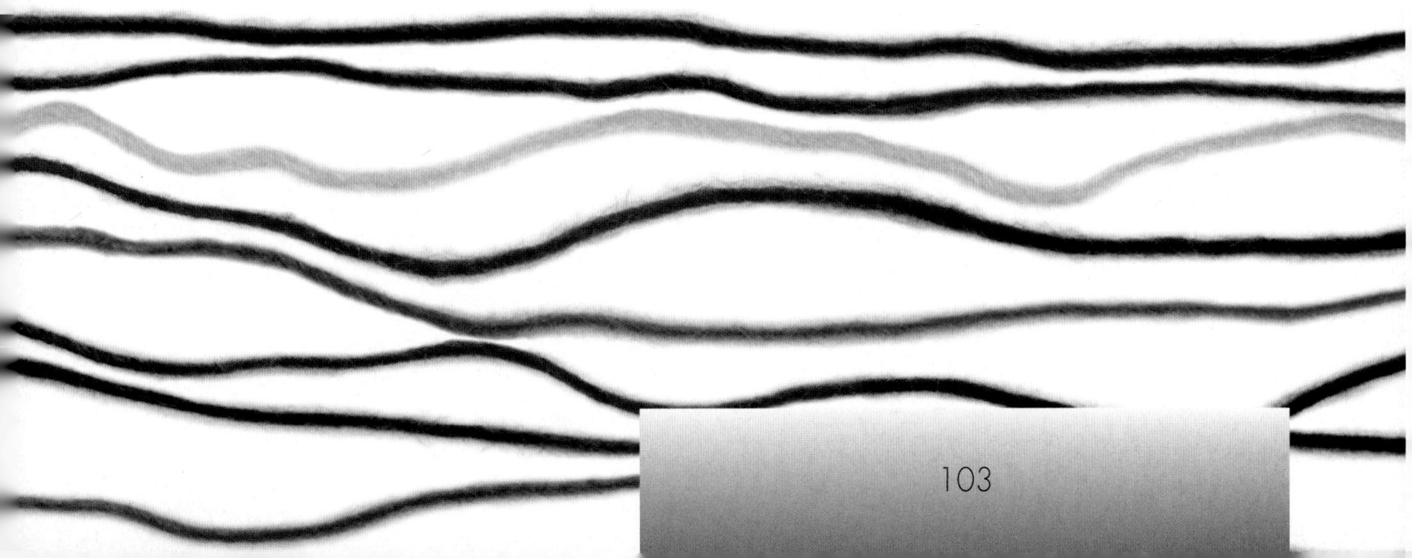

Sideways Knit Striped Cardigan

Design by Kennita Tully

Select yarns of similar weight and pleasing color combinations from your stash and knit up this easy garter-stitch cardigan, changing color every other row. Weaving in your ends as you go will make for very little finishing in the end!

Skill Level

Intermediate***

Size

Woman's small (medium, large) Instructions are given for smallest size, with larger sizes in parentheses. When only 1 number is given, it applies to all sizes.

Finished Measurements

Chest: 38 (42, 46) inches

Length: 23½ inches

Materials

- Assortment of worsted weight yarns (95–135 yds/50g per skein): Approximately 14 (15, 16) skeins
- Size 7 (4.5mm) straight and circular needles or size needed to obtain gauge
- 4 buttons
- Stitch markers
- Tapestry needle

Gauge

16 sts and 32 rows = 4 inches/10cm in garter st.

To save time, take time to check gauge.

Pattern Notes

Sample sweater was completed with the following yarns from Classic Elite Inc.: Atmosphere 100 percent cotton (used double strand), Avignon 15 percent tussah silk/85 percent pima cotton, Believe 77 percent cotton/23 percent rayon, Fame 75 percent rayon/25 percent silk, Vision 45 percent cotton/45 percent viscose/10 percent linen, Mistral 85 percent pima cotton/15 percent superfine alpaca, Mini-Mohair 74 percent mohair/13 percent wool/13 percent nylon.

Color changes are at will. For best random effect, change colors every 2 rows.

Bind off rows should be done with a smooth yarn.

Special Abbreviation

W/t (wrap and turn): With yarn in back, sl next st, bring yarn to front, replace st on LH needle, turn work.

Body

Beg at left front edge, cast on 94 sts. Knit 1 row.

Changing colors every 2 rows, short row as follows to form V-neck: RS row, k52, w/t, knit back.

Next RS row: K55, w/t, knit back.

Next RS row: K58 sts, w/t, knit back.

Continue in this manner, working [3 sts more each RS row] 3 times, then [4 sts more] 6 times for a total of 24 rows. Piece should measure 3 inches.

Knit even until piece measures 7½ (8½, 9½) inches, ending with a RS row.

Shape armhole

On WS, bind off 32 (36, 40) sts.

Continue to work even over 62 (58, 54) sts for 4 inches. At end of next RS row, cast on 32 (36, 40) sts, work 4½ (5½, 6½) inches, pm, knit 6 inches more, pm, knit 4½ (5½, 6½) inches more, ending with a RS row.

Shape armhole

Bind off 32 (36, 40) sts at beg of next WS row. Work even for 4 inches, cast on 32 (36, 40) as before and work even for 4½ (5½, 6½) inches.

Beg short rowing on next RS row as follows: K90, w/t, knit back.

Close-up of buttonhole rows.

Next RS row: K86, w/t, knit back.

Next RS row: K82, w/t, knit back.

On each remaining RS row, knit [4 sts less] 3 times, then [3 sts less] 6 times to correspond to left front shaping. When 52 sts remain, knit across all sts on next RS row and bind off on WS.

Sleeves

Beg at cuff, cast on 32 (36, 40) sts. Knit, inc 1 st at each side on 7th (7th, 5th) row, then [every 8 (8, 6) rows] 8 (18, 7) times, then [every 10 (0, 8) rows] 8 (0, 13) times. (66, 74, 82 sts)

Work even for 2 more inches or to desired length. Bind off all sts.

Finishing

Wash, dry and press all pieces to measurements. Sew shoulder seams and set in sleeves. Sew sleeve seams. Sew on buttons.

Front band

Mark buttonhole spacing for 4 buttons along right center front. With RS facing, pick up and k 94 sts along right front, skipping 1 st at each buttonhole and using a knit cast on of 3 sts in each place, 24 sts across back neck and 94 sts along left center front. Bind off all sts on next row. Rep this edging along bottom edge, picking up 1 st for each garter ridge. ❖

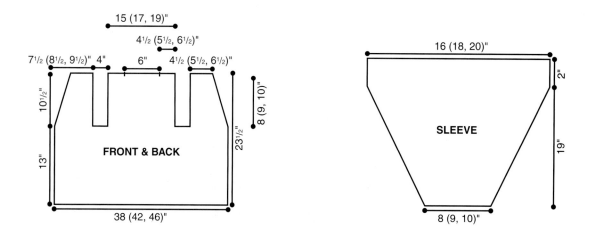

Skill Level

Advanced ****

Size

Woman's small (medium, large)
Instructions are given for smallest size, with larger sizes in parentheses. When only 1 number is given, it applies to all sizes.

Finished Measurements

Chest: 36½ (40, 45) inches

Side to underarm: 14 (15, 16) inches

Sleeve length: 17½ (18, 18½) inches

Armhole depth: 7½ (8, 8½) inches

Materials

- Nature Spun 100 percent wool sport weight yarn from Brown Sheep Co. (184 yds/50g skein): 5 (6, 7) skeins ash #720 (MC), 1 skein each stone #701(A), beet red, #235 (B), red fox #N46 (C), orange crush #861 (D), orange you glad #N54 (E), impasse yellow #305 (F), lullaby #307 (G)
- Size 5 (3.75mm) straight and 16-inch circular needles or size needed to obtain gauge
- Stitch markers
- Stitch holders
- Tapestry needle

Gauge

28 sts and 30 rows = 4 inches/10cm in color pat

24 sts and 30 rows = 4 inches/10cm in St st

To save time, take time to check gauge.

Color Sequence

Pattern is a 10-row rep with color changing every 5 rows. Background is worked in MC throughout, while leaves follow sequence *A, B, C, D, E, F, G, rep from *. Because there are 7 colors (3½ reps of chart), each time a given color appears in sequence, it will be on other side of pat panel.

Back

Border

With MC, cast on 115 (125, 139)

sts. Beg with a WS row, knit 1 row, then knit 2 rows each of A, MC, B, MC, A, MC.

Inc row: With MC, knit across, inc 12 (14, 16) sts evenly. (127, 139, 155 sts)

Break yarn, sl sts to other needle to beg Row 1 of chart as a RS row. Work back and forth in St st following chart until Rows 1–10 have been worked 9 (10, 10) times, then rep [Rows 1–5] 1 (0, 1) time.

Shape armhole

Maintaining pat throughout, bind off 13 (14, 16) sts at beg of next 2 rows. (101, 111, 123 sts)

Continue to work in pat, dec [every RS row] 11 (12, 14) times as follows: K1, ssk, work to last 3 sts, k2tog, k1. (79, 87, 95 sts remain)

Work even until Rows 1–10 of chart have been worked a total of 5 (5, 6) times above underarm, bind off, rep [Rows 1–5] 1 (0, 1) time.

Shape shoulders

At beg of row, bind off [7 (8, 10) sts] 4 (6, 2) times, [6 (0, 9) sts] 2 (0, 4) times. Break yarn, put remaining 39 sts on holder for back of neck.

Front

Work to match back until Rows 1–10 of chart have been worked a total of 3 (3, 4) times above underarm, rep [Rows 1–5] 0 (1, 0) time.

Beg working back and forth on first 26 (30, 34) sts, leaving rest of sts on needle unworked.

Shape neck

Dec 1 st at neck edge on RS rows to match underarm decs 6 times. (20, 24, 28 sts)

When armhole is same depth as back, at armhole edge, bind off [7 (8, 10) sts] 2 (3, 1) times, [6 (0, 9) sts] 1 (0, 2) times.

Put 27 sts on holder for neck front. Work 2nd shoulder as mirror image of first, attaching yarn at neck edge.

Sleeves

With MC, cast on 41 (47, 53) sts. Make cuff to match body border, but inc 8 (12, 16) sts evenly on last MC k row. (49, 59, 69 sts)

Work back and forth in MC from this point, inc 1 st at each end of RS row [every 4th row] 19 (20, 21) times. (87, 99, 111 sts)

Work even until sleeve measures 17½ (18, 18½) inches. Bind off 13 (14, 16) sts at beg of next 2 rows. (61, 71, 79 sts)

Shape sleeve cap

Dec row (RS): K1, ssk, k to last 3 sts, k2tog, k1.

Rep dec row 15 (17, 19) more times. (29, 35, 39 sts remain)

At beg of row, bind off [2 sts] 8 (6, 6) times, [3 sts] 0 (2, 2) times. Bind off remaining 13 (17, 21) sts.

Finishing

Sew shoulder seams. Sew sleeves to armholes. Sew sleeve and side seams, beg at bottom of sleeve.

Neck band

Using circular needle and MC, RS facing, sl 39 back neck sts from holder to needle. Sl first 20 sts, pm for beg of rnd, k19, pick up and k 15 (20, 25) sts along side neck, pm, k 27 front neck sts from holder, pm, pick up and k 15 (20, 25)

107

sts along side neck, k20 sts to center back. (96, 106, 116 sts)

Purl 1 rnd. Change to A and work

border to match bottom and cuffs by working [knit 1 rnd, purl 1 rnd]. On knit rnds, [dec 1 st on side neck edges at marker] 6 times,

k to 2 sts before marker, k2tog, k across front to marker, ssk, k rest of rnd. On last set of 2 MC rnds, bind off purlwise on 2nd rnd. ❖

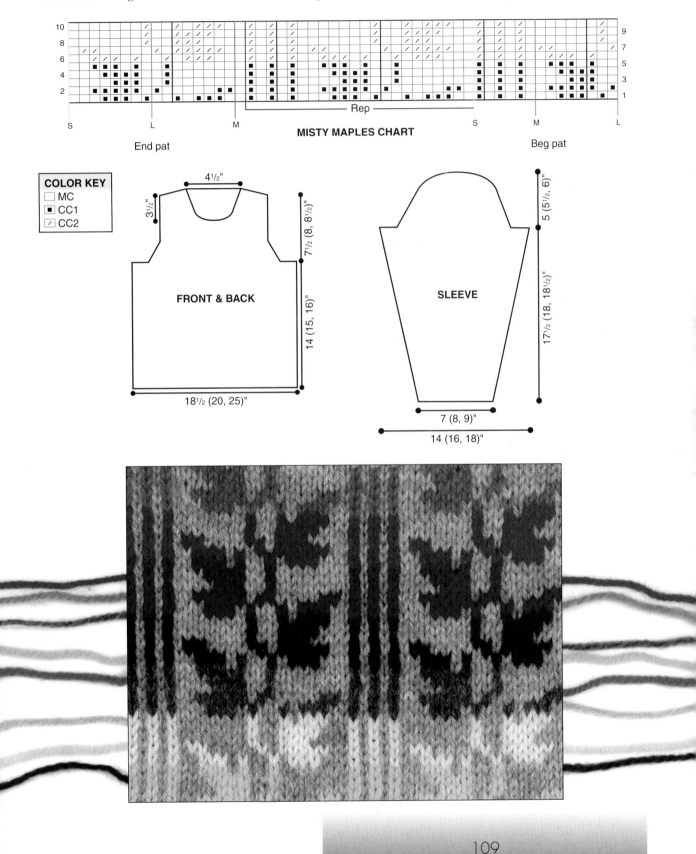

MISTY MAPLES CHART

End pat

Beg pat

COLOR KEY
☐ MC
■ CC1
⬕ CC2

FRONT & BACK

4½"

3½"

7½ (8, 8½)"

14 (15, 16)"

18½ (20, 25)"

SLEEVE

5 (5½, 6)"

17½ (18, 18½)"

7 (8, 9)"

14 (16, 18)"

Kaleidoscope Triangles Jacket

Design by Barbara Venishnick

An ever-changing vivid array of color can flow from your needles one triangle after another as you create a unique work of art!

Skill Level

Intermediate***

Size

Woman's medium/large

Finished Measurements

Chest: 52 inches

Length: 28 inches

Materials

- A variety of worsted weight tweed and space dyed yarns: Approximately 2660 yds total
- Size 7 (4.5mm) double-pointed and 30-inch circular needles or size needed to obtain gauge
- Tapestry needle

Gauge

17 sts = 4 inches/10cm in garter st

Each equilateral triangle measures 5 inches on each side (blocked)

Pattern Note

Sample project uses 13 different shades. All yarns should be worsted weight, that is, yarns that yield from 4½–5 sts per inch.

Special Abbreviation

Cdd (central double decrease): Sl next 2 sts as if to k2tog, k1, p2sso.

Triangles

Cast on 63 sts and divide evenly on 3 dpn. (21 sts on each needle)

Bring needles into a triangle, hold first cast on st in left hand and last cast on st in right hand.

Join without twisting and work in rnds.

Rnd 1: [Sl 1 from right to left needle, with 4th dpn, cdd, k18] 3 times. (19 sts on each needle)

Rnd 2: [K1, p18] twice, k1, p17, sl last st to LH needle.

Rnd 3: [Cdd, k16] 3 times. (17 sts)

Rnd 4: [K1, p16] twice, k1, p15, sl last st to LH needle.

Rnd 5: [Cdd, k14] 3 times. (15 sts)

Rnd 6: [K1, p14] twice, k1, p13, sl last st to LH needle.

Rnd 7: [Cdd, k12] 3 times. (13 sts)

Rnd 8: [K1, p12] twice, k1, p11, sl last st to LH needle.

Rnd 9: [Cdd, k10] twice, cdd, k9, sl last st to LH needle. (11 sts)

Rnd 10: [Cdd, p8] twice, cdd, p7, sl last st to LH needle. (9 sts)

Rnd 11: [Cdd, k6] twice, cdd, k5, sl last st to LH needle. (7 sts)

Rnd 12: [Cdd, p4] twice, cdd, p3, sl last st to LH needle. (5 sts)

Rnd 13: [Cdd, k2] twice, cdd, k1, sl last st to LH needle. (3 sts)

Rnd 14: [Cdd] 3 times. (1 st)

Cut yarn leaving a 2-inch tail. Using a tapestry needle, draw yarn through last 3 sts and pull through to back side.

Note: When working in stripes of many colors it is best to weave in ends as you knit to avoid a large task at end.

Half Triangle A

Cast on 33 sts and work back and forth on 2 dpn.

Row 1: Ssk, k18, cdd, k10. (30 sts total)

Row 2: K10, p1, k18, p1.

Row 3: Ssk, k16, cdd, k9. (27 sts)

Close-up of Triangle.

Yikes! Stripes

Close-up of Half Triangle.

Row 4: K9, p1, k16, p1.

Row 5: Ssk, k14, cdd, k8. (24 sts)

Row 6: K8, p1, k14, p1.

Row 7: Ssk, k12, cdd, k7. (21 sts)

Row 8: K7, p1, k12, p1.

Row 9: Ssk, k10, cdd, k6. (18 sts)

Row 10: K5, p3tog, k8, p2tog. (15 sts)

Row 11: Ssk, k6, cdd, k4. (12 sts)

Row 12: K3, p3tog, k4, p2tog. (9 sts)

Row 13: Ssk, k2, cdd, k2. (6 sts)

Row 14: K1, p3tog, p2tog. (3 sts)

Cut yarn and draw through last 3 sts.

Half Triangle B

Cast on 33 sts and work back and forth on 2 dpn.

Row 1: K10, cdd, k18, k2tog. (30 sts total)

Row 2: P1, k18, p1, k10.

Row 3: K9, cdd, k16, k2tog. (27 sts)

Row 4: P1, k16, p1, k9.

Row 5: K8, cdd, k14, k2tog. (24 sts)

Row 6: P1, k14, p1, k8.

Row 7: K7, cdd, k12, k2tog. (21 sts)

Row 8: P1, k12, p1, k7.

Row 9: K6, cdd, k10, k2tog. (18 sts)

Row 10: P2tog, k8, p3tog, k5. (15 sts)

Row 11: K4, cdd, k6, k2tog. (12 sts)

Row 12: P2tog, k4, p3tog, k3. (9 sts)

Row 13: K2, cdd, k2, k2tog. (6 sts)

Row 14: P2tog, p3tog, p1. (3 sts)

Cut yarn and draw through last 3 sts.

Jacket

Make 146 triangles, 10 A half triangles and 10 B half triangles.

Finishing

Join A and B half triangles by sewing each pair together along shortest cast on edge, making 10 pairs of joined half triangles.

Referring to Fig. 1, sew all triangles tog and place half triangle pairs along center front edges and at bottom of sleeves. See notes about color placement.

Front band

Hold jacket with RS facing. Beg at bottom of right side, with circular needle, pick up and k 108 sts along right side edge, 24 sts across back neck edge, and 108 sts down left side edge. (240 sts)

Knit 1 row on WS. Continue in St st for 1½ inches. Work 1 knit row on WS for a turning ridge, then continue in St st as established for an additional 1½ inches. Bind off all sts loosely.

Fold band along turning ridge and sew to inside.

Sleeve cuff

Pick up and k 60 sts along bottom edge of sleeve and work back and forth. Knit 1 row on WS, knit 1 row on RS, bind off knitwise on WS.

Fold jacket in half along top of shoulder. Sew underarm seams. Sew triangles tog along side seams.

Notes on Color Placement

While any combination is possible (think of old crazy quilts), a little organization can be a good thing. I chose not to sew triangles together until I could lay them all out and make sure that the colors were evenly distributed. This is especially important if you are using just small scraps and may have a color in just a few triangles.

The triangles were made with several different stripe variations.

Stripe I

I used this stripe for half of triangles. It is begun with black, or a color that is very close to black. I ran out of one yarn so I used a close cousin and I think that, if anything, it adds to the richness of the design. The result is the appearance of triangles floating on a black background.

Rnds 1–4: Black or near black.

Rnds 5–6: Multicolored.

Rnds 7–10: Solid color.

Rnds 11–14: Multicolored.

Stripe II

Rnds 1–2: Solid color.

Rnds 3–4: Multicolored.

Rnds 5–6: Different solid color.

Rnds 7–8: Same multicolored.

Rnds 9–10: 3rd solid color.

Rnds 11–12: Same multicolored.

Rnds 13–14: 4th solid color.

Stripe III

As stripe II but using only 1 solid color and 1 multicolored.

Stripe IV

Rnds 1–2: Solid color.

Rnds 3–6: 2nd solid color.

Rnds 7–8: Multicolored.

Rnds 9–12: 2nd multicolored again.

Rnds 13–14: 3rd multicolored.

Stripe V

Rnds 1–2: Solid color.

Rnds 3–4: 2nd solid color.

Rnds 5–8: First solid color again.

Rnds 9–10: Multicolored.

Rnds 11–14: 3rd solid color.

The Half Triangles were all worked the same way. I alternated 2 rows of black with 2 rows of a multicolored. ❖

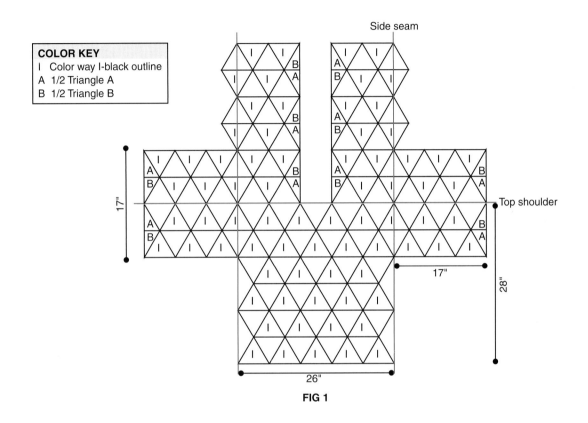

COLOR KEY
I   Color way I-black outline
A   1/2 Triangle A
B   1/2 Triangle B

Side seam

Top shoulder

17"

17"

28"

26"

FIG 1

Fiesta Grande Shawl

Design by Patsy Leatherbury

Inspired by the brilliant colors of a southwestern fiesta, this shawl is a great way to use small amounts of several colors!

Skill Level

Easy**

Finished Size

Approximately 34 x 84 inches (excluding fringe)

Materials

- Katia Siesta 50 percent viscose/50 percent acrylic sport weight yarn from KFI Inc. (126 yds/50g per ball): 4 balls black #820 (MC), 3 balls each aqua #815, lime #816, pink #814, 2 balls each purple #818, turquoise #817, yellow #811, orange #812, red #813
- Size 3 (3.25mm) 29-inch circular needle or size needed to obtain gauge

Gauge

Approximately 20 sts = 4 inches/ 10cm in garter st

Gauge is not critical to this project.

Pattern Notes

This project is a good way to use small amounts of different colors of the same yarn, or to combine many different yarns of the same weight.

The garter st stripe pattern is reversible, and the size can easily be adjusted by casting on more or less sts.

Shawl

Cut 2 (374-inch) pieces of MC, knot pieces tog 6 inches from 1 end and cast on 400 sts, using long tail cast on. At end, knot both pieces again, leaving 6-inch tails.

*Tie next strand to previous strand, knit across, cut yarn, leaving a 6-inch tail. Rep from * for 225 rows, changing colors as desired, cutting yarn at end of every row, and being sure to knot yarns securely each time.

Bind off all sts, leaving 6-inch ends and knotting as before. Trim fringe even.

Sample project was worked in the following color sequence:

Rows 1–3: Black (MC).

Rows 4–6: Red.

Rows 7–9: Pink.

Rows 10 and 11: Orange.

Rows 12 and 13: Black.

Rows 14–17: Purple.

Rows 18–20: Turquoise.

Rows 21 and 22: Yellow.

Rows 23–25: Aqua.

Rows 26–29: Black.

Rows 30–33: Red.

Rows 34–37: Yellow.

Rows 38–41: Turquoise.

Rows 42 and 43: Black.

Rows 44 and 45: Lime.

Rows 46 and 47: Black.

Rows 48–55: [Rep Rows 44–47] twice.

Rows 56–60: Pink.

Rows 61–64: Purple.

Rows 65–69: Aqua.

Rows 70 and 71: Black.

Rows 72–74: Red.

Rows 75–77: Pink.

Rows 78–80: Orange.

Rows 81–83: Yellow.

Rows 84–86: Lime.

Rows 87–89: Aqua.

Rows 90–92: Turquoise.

Rows 93–95: Purple.

Rows 96 and 97: Black.

Rows 98–100: Pink.

Rows 101 and 102: Lime.

Rows 103 and 104: Pink.

Rows 105–108: Rep Rows 101–104.

Rows 109 and 110: Lime.

Rows 111–113: Pink.

Row 114–116: Black.

Rows 117–119: Purple.

Row 120: Turquoise.

Rows 121 and 122: Purple.

Rows 123 and 124: Turquoise.

Row 125: Purple.

Rows 126–128: Turquoise.

Row 129: Aqua.

Rows 130 and 131: Turquoise.

Rows 132 and 133: Aqua.

Row 134: Turquoise.

Rows 135–137: Aqua.

Row 138: Lime.

Rows 139 and 140: Aqua.

Rows 141 and 142: Lime.

Row 143: Aqua.

Rows 144–146: Lime.

Row 147: Yellow.

Rows 148 and 149: Lime.

Rows 150 and 151: Yellow.

Row 152: Lime.

Rows 153–155: Yellow.

Row 156: Orange.

Rows 157 and 158: Yellow.

Rows 159 and 160: Orange.

Row 161: Yellow.

Rows 162–164: Orange.

Row 165: Pink.

Rows 166 and 167: Orange.

Rows 168 and 169: Pink.

Row 170: Orange.

Rows 171–173: Pink.

Row 174: Red.

Rows 175 and 176: Pink.

Rows 177 and 178: Red.

Row 179: Pink.

Rows 180–182: Red.

Rows 183 and 184: Black.

Rows 185 and 186: Aqua.

Rows 187 and 188: Black.

Rows 189 and 190: Aqua.

Rows 191 and 192: Black.

Rows 193 and 194: Aqua.

Rows 195 and 196: Black.

Rows 197–199: Pink.

Rows 200–202: Yellow.

Rows 203–205: Orange.

Rows 206–208: Red.

Rows 209 and 210: Black.

Rows 211–213: Lime.

Rows 214–216: Aqua.

Rows 217–219: Turquoise.

Rows 220–222: Purple.

Rows 223–225: Black.

Bind off with black. ❖

Nautical Vest

Design by Ann E. Smith

Pockets nested within the color work serve to enhance this exciting design. You'll enjoy wearing this striking vest for an evening out or for an afternoon with friends.

Skill Level

Easy**

Size

Woman's small (medium, large, extra-large) Instructions are given for smallest size, with larger sizes in parentheses. When only 1 number is given, it applies to all sizes.

Finished Measurements

Chest (buttoned): 38¾ (42¼, 46, 50¼) inches

Length: 25 (25½, 26, 26½) inches

Materials

- Lion Brand Wool-Ease 80 percent acrylic/20 percent wool worsted weight yarn (197 yds/3 oz per skein): 2 (2, 3, 3) skeins blue feather #107 (MC), 1 skein of hunter green #132 (A), 2 (2, 3, 3) skeins tartan twist #185 (B), 1 skein green heather #130 (C)
- Size 6 (4mm) circular needle
- Size 8 (5mm) 29-inch circular needle or size needed to obtain gauge
- Tapestry needle
- 5 (⅝-inch) buttons

Gauge

18 sts and 24 rows = 4 inches/10cm in pat with larger needles

To save time, take time to check gauge.

Special Abbreviations

Sl 1p: With yarn on WS, sl st purlwise.

Sl 3p: With yarn on WS, sl 3 sts purlwise.

Pattern Stitches

Ribbing (multiple of 5 sts + 3)

Row 1 (RS): With A, * k1, sl 1p, k1, p2, rep from * across, end k1, sl 1p, k1.

Row 2: With A, *p3, k2, rep from * across, end p3.

Rows 3 and 4: With B, rep Rows 1 and 2.

Rows 5 and 6: With C, rep Rows 1 and 2.

Rows 7–12: Rep Rows 1–6.

Rows 13–16: Rep Rows 1–4.

Pattern A (any number of sts)

Row 1: With circular needle and C, knit across, push sts to right end of needle without turning.

Row 2: With A, knit across, turn.

Row 3: With C, purl across, push sts to right end of needle without turning.

Row 4: With A, purl across, turn.

Rep Rows 1–4 for Pat A.

Pattern B (multiple of 4 sts + 1)

Row 1: With A, knit.

Row 2: With A, purl.

Row 3: With B, k1, *sl 3p, k1, rep from * across.

Row 4: With B, p2, *sl 1p, p3, rep from * across, end sl 1p, p2.

Row 5: With B, knit.

Row 6: With B, purl.

Rows 7–10: With B, rep Rows 3–6.

Rows 11–14: With MC, rep Rows 3–6.

Rows 15–18: With A, rep Rows 3–6.

Rows 19–22: With C, rep Rows 3–6.

Rows 23–26: With B, rep Rows 3–6.

Rows 27 and 28: With MC, rep Rows 3 and 4.

Pattern Note

Vest is worked in 1 piece to underarm, then divided for front and back yokes.

Pocket Linings

Make 2

With larger needle and C, cast on 23 sts. Beg with a purl row, work in St st to approximately 5 inches from beg, ending with a RS row. Place sts on a holder.

Lower Body

Beg at lower edge with smaller needle and A, cast on 168 (188, 203, 223) sts. Work ribbing Rows 1–16. Change to larger needle and Pat A, adjusting st count to 169 (185, 201, 221) on first row. Continue in pat to approximately 7½ inches from beg, ending with a WS row.

Pockets

Maintaining established pat, work across first 9 (11, 13, 15) sts, *place next 23 sts on a holder for pocket, with WS facing, k with current color across 23 pocket lining sts*. Continue in pat to last 32 (34, 36, 38) sts, rep from * to * for pocket, then work to end.

Continue to work pat A, ending with Row 4. Cut C, leaving a tail to weave in later. Beg Pat B. Work even through completion of Row 28. With MC, work in St st until piece measures approximately 16 inches from beg, ending with a WS row.

Right Front

Work in pat across first 32 (35, 38, 45) sts, turn, leaving remaining sts for later. Dec 1 st at armhole edge [every other row] 6 times, continue in pat on 26 (29, 32, 39) sts until piece measures approximately 18 inches from beg, ending with a WS row.

Shape neck

Dec 1 st at neck edge [every other row] 1 (3, 4, 12) times, then dec 1 st at neck edge [every 4th row] 9 (8, 8, 5) times. Continue pat on remaining 16 (18, 20, 22) sts to approximately 25 (25½, 26, 26½) inches from beg, ending with a WS row. Bind off all sts.

Back

With RS facing, join MC in next st, bind off 18 (20, 22, 20) sts, continue pat across 69 (75, 81, 91) sts for back. Dec 1 st at each armhole edge [every other row] 6 times. (57, 63, 69, 79 sts)

Work even to approximately 24½ (25, 25½, 26) inches from beg, ending with a WS row.

Right shoulder

K 16 (18, 20, 22) sts, turn. Purl 1 row. Bind off all sts knitwise. With RS facing, join MC in st next to right shoulder, bind off 25 (27, 29, 35) sts, k to end. P1 row. Bind off remaining sts.

Left Front

With RS facing, join MC in next st, bind off 18 (20, 22, 20) sts, continue in pat across row. Work as for right front, reversing armhole and neck shaping.

Finishing

Join shoulder seams.

Pockets

Make 2

With RS facing, sl sts from holder to smaller needle. Join A and knit 2 rows. Bind off all sts knitwise. Join edges of garter st trim to body of vest. Sew pocket linings to WS of fabric.

Arm bands

With smaller needle and MC, RS facing, beg at center of underarm, pick up and k 90 (96, 100, 104) sts evenly around armhole. Pm at beg of rnd.

Rnds 1–5: *K1, p1, rep from * around.

Bind off all sts in ribbing.

Right front band

With smaller needle and B, RS facing, pick up and k 92 sts evenly spaced from lower edge to first V-neck dec.

Row 1 (WS): *P1, k1, rep from * across, end p2.

Row 2: K2, *p1, k1, rep from * across.

Row 3: Rep Row 1.

Row 4: Work established pat across first 6 sts, * yo, k2tog, rib 18 sts, rep from * for 5 buttonholes, ending rib to end.

Rows 5 and 7: Rep Row 1.

Row 6: Rep Row 2.

Bind off all sts in pat.

Left front band

With smaller needle and B, RS facing, pick up and k 92 sts evenly from first V-neck dec to lower edge.

Row 1 (WS): P2, *k1, p1, rep from * across.

Row 2: *K1, p1, rep from * across end k2.

Rows 3–6: Rep Rows 1 and 2.

Row 7: Rep Row 1.

Bind off all sts in pat.

Neck band

With smaller needle and B, RS facing and beg directly above right front band, pick up and k 27 (29, 31, 33) sts evenly to shoulder, 25 (27, 29, 35) sts across back neck, and 27 (29, 31, 33) sts evenly to just above left front band. (79, 85, 91, 101 sts)

Row 1 (WS): P1, *k1, p1, rep from * across.

Row 2: K1, *p1, k1, rep from * across.

Rows 3–6: Rep Rows 1 and 2.

Row 7: Rep Row 1.

Bind off all sts in pat.

Sew band edges tog. Sew buttons opposite buttonholes. ❖

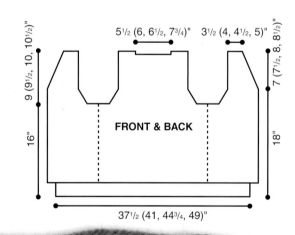

9 (9½, 10, 10½)"

5½ (6, 6½, 7¾)"   3½ (4, 4½, 5)"

7 (7½, 8, 8½)"

16"

FRONT & BACK

18"

37½ (41, 44¾, 49)"

Mohair Stripes Scarf & Pigtail Hat

Continued from page 88

Stripe Pattern

Rows 1 and 2: With A, knit

Rows 3 and 4: With MC, knit.

Rows 5 and 6: With B, knit.

Rows 7 and 8: With MC, knit.

Rows 9 and 10: With C, knit.

Rows 11 and 12: With MC, knit.

Rows 13 and 14: With D, knit.

Row 15 and 16: With MC, knit.

Row 17 and 18: With E, knit.

Rows 19–24: With MC, knit.

Rep Rows 1–24 for stripe pat.

Scarf

With MC, cast on 18 sts. Knit 5 rows. Work 11 reps of stripe pat. With MC, bind off loosely.

Fringe

Cut 20 (16-inch) lengths of MC and 10 (16-inch) lengths of each CC. Using 1 strand of each CC and 2 of MC, attach four-strand fringe along each end of scarf.

Hat

With MC, cast on 58 sts. Knit 7 rows. Work 1 rep of stripe pat. With MC, knit 8 rows.

Eyelet row: K1, *yo, k2tog, rep from * to last st, k1.

Knit 7 rows. Bind off all sts.

Sew side seam.

Tie

Cut 3 (32-inch) strands of each CC, and 6 of MC. Holding all strands tog, tie an overhand knot approximately 2 inches from 1 end. Divide strands into 3 groups, evenly distributing colors. Braid, leaving approximately 3½ inches free. Tie overhand knot at end of braid. Trim ends. Weave through eyelets, gather and tie. ❖

Textured Blocks Scarf

Continued from page 99

twice, k1, p1, rep from * to last 4 sts, end k4.

Row 4: K2, p2, k1, p1, k1, *[p3, k1] twice, p1, k1, rep from * to last 4 sts, p2, k2.

Row 5: K2, [p1, k1] 3 times, *[k2, p1] twice, [k1, p1] twice, rep from * to last 3 sts, end k3.

Row 6: K2, [p1, k1] 3 times, *[p2, k1] twice, [p1, k1] twice, rep from * to last 3 sts, end p1, k2.

Row 7: K4, p1, k1, p1, *[k3, p1] twice, k1, p1, rep from * to last 4 sts, end k4.

Row 8: K2, p2, k1, p1, k1, *[p3, k1] twice, p1, k1, rep from * to last 4 sts, end p2, k2.

Row 9: K2, *[k3, p1] twice, k1, p1, rep from * to last 9 sts, k3, p1, k5.

Row 10: K2, *[p3, k1] twice, p1, k1, rep from * to last 9 sts, end p3, k1, p3, k2.

Row 11: K5, p1, *k2, [p1, k1] twice, p1, k2, p1, rep from * to last 5 sts, end k5.

Row 12: K2, p3, k1, *p2, [k1, p1] twice, k1, p2, k1, rep from * to last 5 sts, end p3, k2.

Rows 13–60: [Rep Rows 1–12] 4 times.

Change to C. Work 55 rows of St st, ending with a RS row.

Change to D. Purl 1 row.

Mosaic St

Row 1: K2, p3, *k1, p3, k1, p1, k1, p3, rep from * to last 6 sts, end k1, p3, k2.

Row 2: K5, *p1, k3, p1, k1, p1, k3, rep from * to last 6 sts, end p1, k5.

Rows 3 and 4: Rep Rows 1 and 2.

Row 5: K2, p2, *k1, p1, [k1, p3] twice, rep from * to last 7 sts, end k1, p1, k1, p2, k2.

Row 6: K4, *p1, k1, [p1, k3] twice, rep from * to last 7 sts, end p1, k1, p1, k4.

Rows 7 and 8: Rep Rows 5 and 6.

Rows 9–56: [Rep Rows 1–8] 6 times.

Change to E. Knit every row until section measures 12 inches. Bind off all sts.

Edging (optional)

With crochet hook and C, join yarn at any corner and work 1 rnd of sc around entire scarf, being careful not to pull too tight. Sl st to first sc.

For best appearance, wet block scarf. ❖

Little Bitties

Select bits of yarn from your stash and sit down for a quiet evening of knitting. Before long you'll have the satisfied feeling that comes when you complete a creative little project.

Mini-Mitts & Hat Garland

Design by Diane Zangl

Miniature mittens and hats make delightful tree ornaments or package trims. When strung together, these tiny Christmas treasures form a garland for trimming the mantel, staircase or Christmas tree.

Skill Level

Intermediate***

Finished Size

Hat: approximately 2 inches high x 1¼ inch wide (without tassel)

Mitt: approximately 2 inches wide x 2¾ inches tall

Garland: 72 inches long, or desired length

Materials

- Brown Sheep Nature Spun Sport 100 percent wool sport weight yarn (184 yds/50g per skein): 10–15 yds for each hat or mitt, your choice of colors. Colors used in this project were natural #730, meadow green #N56, and scarlet #N48
- Size 2 (2.75mm) double-pointed needles
- Size F/5 (3.75mm) crochet hook
- Small stitch holder

Gauge

5 sts and 8½ rows = 1 inch in St st

Gauge is not critical for this project.

Hat

Cast on 20 sts, divide onto 3 dpn.

Join without twisting, pm between first and last st.

Work in k1, p1 ribbing for 5 rnds, inc 2 sts on last rnd. (22 sts)

Work in St st for 10 rnds, adding a CC stripe on 2nd rnd if desired.

Shape top

Next rnd: [K2tog] around. (11 sts)

Knit 1 rnd. Cut yarn and draw end through remaining sts twice.

Tassel

Wind CC yarn around tip of

Work in k1, p1 ribbing for 6 rnds, inc 2 sts on last rnd. (18 sts)

Beg thumb gusset

Rnd 1: K2, pm, inc 2 sts in next st, pm, k to end of rnd.

Rnds 2, 4 and 6: Knit.

Rnd 3: K2, inc in next st, k1, inc in next st, k to end of rnd.

Rnd 5: K2, inc in next st, k3, inc in next st, k to end of rnd.

Rnd 7: K2, removing markers, sl next 7 sts to holder for thumb, cast on 2 sts, k to end of rnd.

Hand

On next rnd, k2tog over 2 cast on sts. (18 sts)

Work even for a total of 14 rnds above cuff ribbing.

Shape top

Rnd 1: *K1, k2tog, rep from * around. (12 sts)

Rnd 2: Knit.

Rnd 3: [K2tog] around. (6 sts)

Cut yarn and draw through remaining sts.

Thumb

Sl sts from holder to 2 needles, having 4 sts on first needle and 3 sts on 2nd. Join yarn. Pick up and k 3 sts above 2 cast on sts. (10 sts)

Next rnd: Knit, dec 2 sts evenly. (8 sts)

Knit 2 rnds.

Dec rnd: [K2tog] around. (4 sts)

Cut yarn and draw through remaining sts.

Finishing

With crochet hook, join yarn to cuff edge of 1 mitt, ch 12, sl st in cuff edge of 2nd mitt. Fasten off.

With CC, referring to Fig. 1, embroider snowflake pat on back of each mitt, using 3 long sts.

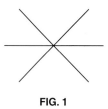

FIG. 1

Garland

Note: You will need 1 hat or set of mini-mitts for every 6 inches of desired garland length.

Working with 2 dpn only, cast on 4 sts. [K4, sl sts back to LH needle] twice.

***Join hat:** K1, [pick up 1 st behind tassel and k2tog (I-cord st and hat st)] twice, k1.

or

Mitts: K2, place joining ch of mitts between LH and RH needles, k2.

[K4, sl sts back to LH needle] until I-cord measures 6 inches from last hat or mitt.*

Rep from * to * until garland is 72 inches long, or desired length, ending with hat or mitts. K4tog. Fasten off last st. Cut yarn and run end back into I-cord. ❖

forefinger 8–10 times. Tie 1 end of loops with separate strand of yarn. Cut opposite end.

Tie tassel to top of hat, trim evenly.

If using as a package trim or individual ornament, attach yarn under tassel. Crochet a ch approximately 2 inches long, join to first ch, fasten off.

Mitten

Make 2 alike

Cast on 16 sts, divide onto 3 dpn. Join without twisting, pm between first and last st.

Easy Santa Ornament & Lapel Pin

Designs by Kathie Ballard

These easy Santas not only make good ornaments, but you can also knit the head and beard for cute lapel pins or package toppers!

Skill Level

Beginner*

Finished Size

Santa head and beard lapel pin: 3¾ inches high

Santa ornament with toy bag: 6½ inches high

Materials

- Sport weight yarn: small amounts pink, peach, red
- Worsted weight yarn: small amounts white, tan, black
- Size 4 (3.5mm) needles or size needed to obtain gauge
- Tapestry needle
- 2 (1-inch) pompom
- Small amount fiberfill
- 12 inches (⅛-inch-wide) green satin ribbon
- 2 (10mm) green jingle bells
- Small safety pin or pin back for lapel pin
- Small teddy bear, toy or package for bag

Gauge

6 sts and 8 rows = 1 inch/2.5cm in St st with sport weight yarn

5 sts and 8 rows = 1 inch/2.5cm in St st with worsted weight yarn

Gauge is not critical for this project.

Pattern Note

When changing colors, leave a 15-inch end for sewing seams when finishing.

Santa Ornament

Body

Beg at bottom with white, cast on 18 sts.

Rows 1–5: Knit.

Rows 6–9: Change to red, work in St st for 4 rows, beg with a knit row.

Row 10: K2tog, k to last 2 sts, k2tog. (16 sts)

Rows 11–13: Work in St st.

Rows 14–17: Rep Rows 10–13. (14 sts)

Row 18: Rep Row 10. (12 sts)

Row 19: Purl.

Head and Hat

Rows 20–25: Change to pink, work in St st, beg with a knit row.

Rows 26–30: Change to white, knit.

Rows 31–36: Change to red, work in St st, beg with a knit row.

Row 37: K2tog, k to last 2 sts, k2tog. (10 sts)

Row 38: Purl.

Rows 39–44: Rep Rows 37 and 38. (4 sts remain)

Bind off remaining sts, leaving a 15-inch end to sew seam.

Beard

Using white and leaving a 15-inch end, cast on 16 sts.

Rows 1–4: Knit.

Row 5: K2tog, k to last 2 sts, k2tog. (14 sts)

Row 6: Knit.

Rows 7–15: Rep Rows 5 and 6, ending with Row 5. (4 sts remain)

Bind off remaining sts, fasten off end.

Arms and Hands

Using red and leaving a 12-inch end, cast on 6 sts.

Rows 1–8: Beg with a knit row, work in St st.

Rows 9–12: Change to white, knit.

Rows 13–16: Change to black, work in St st, beg with a knit row.

Rows 17–20: Change to white, knit.

Rows 21–27: Change to red, work in St st, beg with a knit row.

Bind off all sts, leaving a 12-inch end.

Feet

With black, cast on 8 sts.

Rows 1–4: Knit.

Rows 5 and 7: Purl.

Row 6: Knit.

Bind off all sts, leaving a 15-inch end.

Toy Bag

With tan, cast on 18 sts.

Work in St st for 20 rows.

Bind off all sts, leaving a 24-inch end for seaming.

Finishing

Beg at hat, sew back seam, changing colors to match each section. Stuff head and body with fiberfill as you go.

Making sure seam is centered at back,

sew bottom (cast on) white edges tog.

Sew side edges of feet, fold with seam at 1 side, then sew bottom edge (garter st) tog. Sew to bottom of body.

Sew red ends of arm piece in center back of body, ½ inch below top of red suit.

Referring to photo, center point of beard in front, sew ends in back of head, st top edge to face. Using small straight sts, embroider mouth with red and eyes with black. Bend top of hat down to side, and glue hat end to side of hat; glue pompom to end of hat.

Sew bottom and side of toy bag. Beg at center front (opposite seam), make a couple of sts near top edge of toy bag with two 12-inch pieces of red yarn held tog; thread one end through loop made by arms and hands. Stuff bag with fiberfill and glue tiny toys or packages to top of fiberfill. Pull yarn to tighten slightly and tie ends in a bow.

Toy Bag Ornament

Work toy bag as for Santa ornament.

Finishing

Sew bottom and side of toy bag. Beg

at center front (opposite seam), thread green ribbon around top edge of bag ending back at center front; at center back (seam) pull out a 2-inch loop of ribbon and tie a knot close to edge of bag to prevent ribbon from slipping back into bag—this will act as hanger. Stuff bag with fiberfill and glue tiny toys or packages to top of fiberfill. Pull ribbon to tighten slightly and tie ends in a bow. Tie one bell to each end of ribbon.

Santa Hat-and-Beard Lapel Pin

Head and Hat

Row 1: With peach, cast on 12 sts. Rep Rows 20–44 of Santa ornament head and hat.

Beard

Work beard of Santa as directed for ornament.

Finishing

Beg at hat, sew back seam, changing colors to match each section. Stuff head and hat with fiberfill before closing seam at bottom of head. Referring to photo, center point of beard in front, sew ends in back of head, st top edge to face. Using small straight sts, embroider mouth with red and eyes with black. Bend top of hat down to side, and glue hat end to side of hat; glue pompom to end of hat. Glue or sew pin back to back of head. ❖

Mini Christmas Stocking Set

Designs by Edie Eckman

Knit up a set of wee socks for your Christmas decorating or use them to embellish gifts. Each sock just uses bits of yarn.

Skill Level

Intermediate***

Finished Size

Approximately 5 inches long

Materials

- Worsted weight wool yarn: small amounts dark green (A), red (B) and off-white (C)
- Size 8 (5mm) double-pointed needles or size needed to obtain gauge
- Stitch marker
- Tapestry needle
- Size G/6 (4mm) crochet hook

Gauge

20 sts and 28 rows = 4 inches/ 10cm in St st

Gauge is not critical in this project, and will probably vary among socks.

Sock #1 (4-rnd stripes)

With A, cast on 20 sts, leaving a 10-inch tail. Divide sts evenly on 3 needles and join without twisting.

Rnds 1–4: *K1, p1, rep from *. Cut A.

Rnds 5–8: With C, knit. Cut C.

Rnds 9–12: With B, knit. Cut B.

Heel

Sl last 5 sts of previous rnd to free needle, sl next 5 sts onto same needle, sl remaining 10 sts to holder for instep. Turn and work in rows on heel sts only.

Row 1 (WS): With A, p10.

Rows 2, 4, 6, 8 and 10: Sl 1 purlwise, k across.

Rows 3, 5, 7 and 9: Sl 1 purlwise, p across.

Turn heel

Row 1 (WS): P5, p2tog, p1, turn.

Row 2: Sl 1 knitwise, k1, ssk, k1, turn.

Row 3: Sl 1 purlwise, p2, p2tog, p1, turn.

Row 4: Sl 1 knitwise, k3, ssk, k1. (6 sts) Cut A.

Gusset and Foot

Sl last 3 sts worked onto free needle. Mark center of heel bottom as beg of rnd. With C and free needle, knit 3 sts from heel bottom, pick up and k 5 sts along right edge of heel flap; on 2nd needle, k 10 instep sts from holder; on 3rd needle, pick up and k 5 sts along right edge of heel, k 3 remaining heel sts onto same needle. (26 sts)

Rnds 1 and 3: With C, on first needle, k to last 3 sts, k2tog, k1; on 2nd needle, k across; on 3rd needle, k1, ssk, k to end.

Rnd 2: With C, knit.

Rnd 4: With B, knit.

Rnds 5: With B, rep Rnd 1. (20 sts)

Rnds 6 and 7: With B, knit. Cut B.

Rnds 8–11: With C, knit. Cut C.

Toe

Rnd 1: With A, knit.

Rnd 2: On first needle, k to last 3 sts, k2tog, k1; on 2nd needle, k1, ssk, knit to last 3 sts, k2tog, k1; on 3rd needle, k1, ssk, knit to end.

Rnds 3 and 4: Rep Rnds 1 and 2.

Rnd 5: On first needle, k2tog, k1; on 2nd needle, k1, ssk, k2tog, k1; on 3rd needle, k1, ssk. (8 sts)

K sts from first needle onto 3rd needle.

Finishing

With tapestry needle, graft toe sts tog. Using 10-inch tail left from cast on, crochet an 8-st ch. Fasten off and turn to form loop. Sew in end.

Sock #2 (2-rnd stripes)

Work as for Sock #1 through Rnd 4.

Rnds 5 and 6: With C, knit.

Rnds 7 and 8: With B, knit.

Rnds 9 and 10: With C, knit.

Rnds 11 and 12: With B, knit.

Work heel as for Sock #1.

With C, pick up sts for gusset as for Sock #1. Shape gusset and foot as for Sock #1 and at the same time, continue established 2-rnd stripe pat.

Cut B and C. Work toe shaping and finishing as for Sock #1.

Sock #3 (1-rnd stripes)

Work as for Sock #1 through Rnd 4.

Rnd 5: With C, knit.

Rnd 6: With B, knit.

Rnds 7–12: Rep Rnds 5 and 6.

Continuing in 1-rnd stripes, complete as for Sock #1.

Sock #4 (checks)

Work as for Sock #1 through Rnd 4.

Rnds 5–12: Work Rows 1–4 of Checks Chart twice.

Work heel flap and shaping as for Sock #1.

Gusset and Foot

Sl last 3 sts worked onto free needle. Mark center of heel bottom as beg of rnd. With C and free needle, k1 from heel bottom. With B, k2 from heel bottom. Along right edge of heel flap, pick up and k 2 C, 2 B, 2 C; on 2nd needle, k instep sts from holder in established pat; on 3rd needle, pick up and k 2 C, 2 B, 2 C sts along edge of heel, k 2 B, 1 C heel sts onto same needle. (26 sts)

Make adjustments as needed

on following rows to maintain established pat.

Rnd 1: On first needle, k to last 3 sts, k2tog, k1; on 2nd needle, k across; on 3rd needle, k1, ssk, k to end. (24 sts)

Rnd 2: Rep Rnd 1. (22 sts)

Rnd 3: Work even.

Rnd 4: Rep Rnd 1. (20 sts)

Rnds 6–9: Work even.

Work toe and finishing as for Sock #1.

Sock #5 (spiral)

Work as for Sock #1 through Rnd 4.

Rnds 5–12: Work Rows 1–4 of Spiral Chart twice.

Work heel flap and shaping as for Sock #1.

Gusset and Foot

Sl last 3 sts worked onto free needle. Mark center of heel bottom as beg of rnd. With B and free needle, k 3 sts from heel bottom, along right edge of heel flap, pick up and k 5 sts; on 2nd needle, join C and k instep sts from holder in established pat; on 3rd needle, with B, pick up and k 5 sts, carrying C and catching it loosely behind work approximately every 3 sts, k 3 heel sts onto same needle. (26 sts)

Work gusset and foot shaping as for Sock #1, maintaining spiral pat across instep and catching C loosely behind work along solid part of foot.

Work toe and finishing as for Sock #1. ❖

Rep
CHECKS CHART

COLOR KEY
■ Red (B)
□ Off-white (C)

Rep
SPIRAL CHART

Little Lamb Ornament

Design by Diane Elliott

Knit up a flock of darling little garter-stitch ornaments to give as gifts or to decorate your packages for Christmas.

Skill Level

Beginner*

Finished Size

3 inches high

Materials

- Sport weight acrylic/wool blend yarn: approximately 25 yds white or cream, 5 yds black
- Size 3 (3.25mm) needles or size needed to obtain gauge
- Tapestry needle
- Small amount of fiberfill
- 8 inches (¼-inch) ribbon
- Small crochet hook

Gauge

6 sts = 1 inch/2.5 cm in garter st

Gauge is not critical to this project, but should be firm enough that filling won't poke through.

Pattern Note

Lamb may be worked with scrap yarns of any weight, using appropriate needle size to make a fairly firm fabric.

Body

With white, cast on 12 sts.

Row 1: Knit across, inc 1 in each st. (24 sts)

Rows 2–21: Knit.

Row 22: [K2tog] across. (12 sts)

Cut yarn, leaving a 12-inch end.

Thread yarn in tapestry needle and run through sts, pull tight. Sew body seam, stuff firmly with fiberfill. Run yarn through cast-on sts, pull tight and fasten off securely.

Head

With white, cast on 10 sts.

Row 1: Knit across, inc 1 in each st. (20 sts)

Rows 2–10: Knit.

Row 11: [K2tog] across. (10 sts)

Row 12: Knit. Cut white, leaving a 6-inch end.

Row 13: Attach black, knit.

Row 14: Purl.

Row 15: [K2tog, k3] twice. (8 sts)

Row 16: Purl.

Row 17: [K2tog] across. (4 sts)

Cut yarn, leaving a 6-inch end.

Thread yarn in tapestry needle and run through sts, pull tight. Sew seam, matching colors, stuff firmly with fiberfill. Run yarn through cast-on sts, pull tight and fasten off securely.

Ears

Make 2

With white, cast on 3 sts.

Row 1 (RS): Knit, inc in first and last sts. (5 sts)

Rows 2–6: Work in St st.

Cut yarn, leaving a 6-inch end.

Thread yarn in tapestry needle and run through sts, pull tight. Referring to photo, sew ears to sides of head.

Tail

With white, cast on 3 sts. Work 6 rows of garter st. Cut yarn, leaving a 6-inch end.

Thread yarn in tapestry needle and run through sts, pull tight. Sew to back of body, about 3 rows above center.

Legs

Make 4

With black, cast on 8 sts.

Knit 1 row. Cut black, attach white and work 9 rows of garter st. Bind off all sts. Cut yarn, leaving a 6-inch end.

Sew leg seam, matching colors. Stuff each leg firmly with fiberfill, sew in place to bottom of body.

Finishing

Sew head to body. Using black, embroider eyes between muzzle and ears.

With small crochet hook, attach white to top of head, work hanging loop, fasten off. Tie ribbon bow around neck. ❖

Easter Basket & Eggs

Designs by Edie Eckman

Six multicolored eggs sit amongst loops of green grass in a hand-knit basket. Here comes the Easter bunny hopping down the trail.

Skill Level

Advanced****

Finished Size

Basket: approximately 7 x 3 inches

Eggs: approximately 2 inches long

Materials

- Cotton Fleece 80 percent pima cotton/20 percent merino wool worsted weight yarn from Brown Sheep Co. (215 yds/100g per skein): 1 skein each putty #CW105 (A), lime light #CW840 (B)
- Cotton Fine 80 percent pima cotton/20 percent merino wool fingering weight yarn from Brown Sheep Co. (222 yds/50g per skein): small amounts cherry moon #CF810 (C), sunburst #CF830 (D), cotton ball #CF100 (E), raging purple #CF730 (F), Malibu blue #CF570 (G)
- Size 7 (4.5mm) double-pointed and 16-inch circular needles or size needed to obtain gauge
- Size 0 (2mm) double-pointed needles
- Tapestry needle
- Fiberfill stuffing

Gauge

22 sts and 32 rows = 4 inches/10cm in St st with larger yarn and needles

Gauge is not critical in this project.

Pattern Note

All pieces are worked in the round on double pointed needles. When there are enough sts on

basket and grass, change to circular needles.

Special Abbreviations

M1: Inc by k1 in top of st below next st on LH needle.

K1f&b: Inc by k1 in front and back of same st.

Yb: Yarn back.

Yf: Yarn forward.

Pattern Stitch

Basketweave (multiple of 8 sts)

Rnds 1–4: *P5, k3, rep from * around.

Rnds 5–8: P1, *k3, p5, rep from * to last 7 sts, end k3, p4.

Rep Rnds 1–8 for pat.

Easter Basket

With larger dpn and A, cast on 8 sts. Join without twisting.

Rnd 1: Knit.

Rnd 2: [K1f&b] around. (16 sts)

Rnds 3–5: Knit.

Rnd 6: Rep Rnd 2. (32 sts)

Rnds 7–9: Knit.

Rnd 10: *K1, k1f&b, rep from * around. (48 sts)

Rnds 11–13: Knit.

Rnd 14: *K2, k1f&b, rep from * around. (64 sts)

Rnds 15–17: Knit.

Rnd 18: *K3, k1f&b, rep from * around. (80 sts)

Rnds 19–21: Knit.

Rnd 22: *K4, k1f&b, rep from * around. (96 sts)

Rnds 23–25: Knit.

Rnd 26: *K5, k1f&b, rep from * around. (112 sts)

Rnd 27: Knit.

Rnd 28: Purl.

Work [Rnds 1–8 of basketweave pat] twice, then [Rnds 1–4] once more. Work 3 garter-stitch ridges (p 1 rnd, k 1 rnd). Bind off all sts.

Grass

With larger dpns and B, cast on 8 sts. Join without twisting.

Rnd 1: Knit.

Rnd 2: [K1f&b] around. (16 sts)

Rnd 3 (loop rnd): *K1, leaving st on needle, yf between needles, wrap yarn around thumb, yb between needles, k same st and slide off needle, yo, pass 2 sts on RH needle over yo, sl loop off thumb (loop made), rep from * around.

Note: Vary loop sizes as you work by holding thumb closer to or further from work.

Rnds 4 and 5: Knit.

Rnd 6: [K1f&b] around.

Rnds 7–9: Rep Rnds 3–5.

Rnd 10: *K1, k1f&b, rep from * around. (48 sts)

Rnds 11–13: Rep Rnds 3–5.

Rnd 14: *K2, k1f&b, rep from * around. (64 sts)

Rnd 15: Rep Rnd 3.

Rnd 16: [K1 tbl] around.

Rnd 17: Knit.

Rnd 18: *K3, k1f&b, rep from * around. (80 sts)

Rnd 19: Rep Rnd 3.

Rnd 20: [K1 tbl] around.

Finishing

Sew grass piece ½ inch below top edge around inside edge of basket, leaving a 4-inch opening. Lightly stuff basket with fiberfill. Sew opening closed.

Eggs

Note: *Refer to Charts A–F for pat and colors.*

With smaller needles and MC, cast on

8 sts. Divide onto 3 dpn and join without twisting.

Rnd 1: Knit.

Rnd 2: *M1, k1, rep from * around. (16 sts)

Rnds 3 and 4: Knit.

Rnd 5: *K1, M1, k1, rep from * around. (24 sts)

Rnds 6 and 7: Knit.

Rnd 8: Rep Rnd 5. (36 sts)

Rnds 9–22: Knit, working pat from chart.

Rnd 23: Knit with MC.

Rnd 24: *K2, k2tog, rep from * around. (27 sts)

Rnds 25 and 26: Knit. Using tail left from cast-on, close cast-on edge. Turn egg inside out, weave in ends.

Rnd 27: *K1, k2tog, rep from * around. (18 sts)

Rnds 28–30: Knit. Stuff egg with fiberfill before continuing.

Rnd 31: [K2tog] around. (9 sts)

Rnd 32: Knit.

Rnd 33: [K2tog] 4 times, k1.

Cut yarn and pull through remaining sts.

Secure end by passing needle through stuffing. ❖

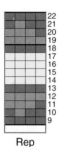

Rep
CHART A
Knit top & bottom in cherry moon (C).

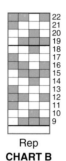

Rep
CHART B
Knit top & bottom in malibu blue (G).

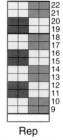

Rep
CHART C
Knit top & bottom in sunburst (D).

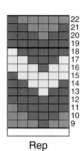

Rep
CHART D
Knit top & bottom in raging purple (F).

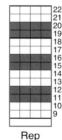

Rep
CHART E
Knit top & bottom in raging purple (F).

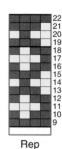

Rep
CHART F
Knit top & bottom in cherry moon (C).

COLOR KEY
■ Cherry moon (C)
▫ Sunburst (D)
□ Cotton ball (E)
▨ Raging purple (F)
▩ Malibu blue (G)

Glitzy Earrings

Designs by Edie Eckman

Here's a novel way to accessorize your favorite sweater. You'll want to stitch all three styles of knitted earrings, attaching them to earring findings.

Skill Level

Beginner*

Finished Size

Approximately 1–1¼ inches

Materials

- Metallica 85 percent rayon/15 percent metallic worsted weight yarn from Berroco Inc. (85 yds/25g per skein): a few yards each gold #1001, black/gold #1003
- 2 size 6 (4.5mm) double-pointed needles

- Post-type earring findings
- Clear-drying craft glue

Gauge

Gauge is not important in this project.

Teardrop Earring

Make 2

Cast on 4 sts. *Do not turn. Sl sts to other end of same needle. [K1, p1] twice, rep from * 6 times. Do not turn. Sl sts to other end of needle. K4tog. Cut yarn, leaving a 4-inch tail.

Bring tail through last st and pull tight. Weave tail through earring fabric.

Knot

Make 2

Cast on 3 sts. *Do not turn. Sl sts to other end of needle, k3, rep from * until cord is 2¼ inches long. Do not turn. K3tog. Cut yarn, leaving a 4-inch tail. Bring tail through last st and pull tight. Weave tail through earring fabric. Tie into overhand knot.

Curlicue

Make 2

Cast on 20 sts. [K2tog] twice. Insert needle through first st on RH needle and pull over 2nd st (1 st bound off). *K2tog, bind off 1 st; rep from * until all sts are bound off. Cut yarn, leaving a 4-inch tail. Bring tail through last st and pull tight. Weave tail through earring fabric. Twist into curl shape.

Finishing

Trim ends and dab with glue. Glue earrings to findings. ❖

Fashion Doll Cheerleader Outfit

Designs by Thelma Jean Young

Use your favorite team colors and short row shaping to bring out the cheers for your little doll. Any little girl would love this outfit for her doll.

Skill Level
Easy**

Size
Fits 11½-inch fashion doll

Materials
- Patons Kroy 3-ply 85 percent wool/ 15 percent nylon fingering/sock weight yarn: 40 yds each yellow and green or desired colors, 5 yds black (optional for shoes).
- Size 0 (2mm) 4 double-pointed needles for shoes and socks
- Size 1 (2.25mm) needles
- Size 2 (2.75mm) to cast on or bind off sts
- 2 (7mm) white faceted beads
- 2 elastic hair bands
- Tapestry needle
- Size 5 (1.7mm) steel crochet hook
- Hook and eye sets
- 2 small snaps
- Sewing and embroidery needles
- 5 yards green embroidery floss

Pattern Notes
Review all abbreviations, diagrams and instructions before beginning.

Knit each item and note finishing procedures.

These items take very little yarn. To save time, wrap each 40-yd color onto pieces of cardboard.

Special Abbreviations
Cns: Change needles to size given.

Pp1: Pick up and p 1 st.

Up-1: K1 in top of st in row below. (1 new st)

Uku (up-1, k1, up-1): Work up-1 as above, then knit next st on needle, work another up-1. (2 new sts)

Wrap and turn: Wyib, sl next st purlwise, bring yarn to front between needles, sl st purlwise back to LH needle, turn work.

Pp-1(2): With crochet hook, pick up 1 (2) sts from edge and place loop on needle.

Rt: Right

Lt: Left

Bodice

Refer to Fig. 1 throughout.

Beg just above waist, with yellow and size 1 needles, cast on 40 sts.

Rows 1–3: Cns 0, k2, *k1, p1, rep from * across, end k2.

Row 4: Cns 1, k2, purl across, end k2.

Row 5: K5, uku, k10, uku, k6, uku, k10, uku, end k5. (48 sts)

Rows 6, 8, 10 and 12: K2, purl across, end k2.

Rows 7 and 11: Knit.

Row 9: K19, uku, k8, uku, k19. (52 sts)

Divide for front and back

Row 13: K11, k2tog (Lt back); front, ssk, k22, k2tog, turn. (24 sts, * to * on Fig. 1). Leave last 13 sts for Rt back.

Rows 14 and 16: Working on front sts only, k2, p20, k2.

Row 15: Knit.

Row 17: K9, bind off next 8 sts (front neck), k7. (8 sts on each side of neck)

Right Front

Row 18 (WS): (At turn) K2, p6.

Row 19: Ssk, k6. (7 sts)

Row 20: K2, p5.

Row 21: Ssk, k5. (6 sts)

Rows 22, 24 and 26: K2, p4.

Rows 23 and 25: Knit.

Row 27: Bind off all sts knitwise, cut yarn, leaving a 5-inch tail to join shoulders (E to E).

Left Front

Row 18 (WS): Attach new strand of yarn, leaving a 5-inch tail to close neck sts, p6, k2. (8 sts)

Row 19: K6, k2tog. (7 sts)

Row 20: P5, k2.

Row 21: K5, k2tog. (6 sts)

Rows 22, 24 and 26: P4, k2.

Rows 23 and 25: Knit.

Row 27: Bind off all sts knitwise, cut yarn, leaving a 5-inch tail to join shoulders (D to D).

Left Back

Row 14 (WS): Attach new strand of yarn, leaving a 5-inch tail to close neck sts, k2, p8, k2.

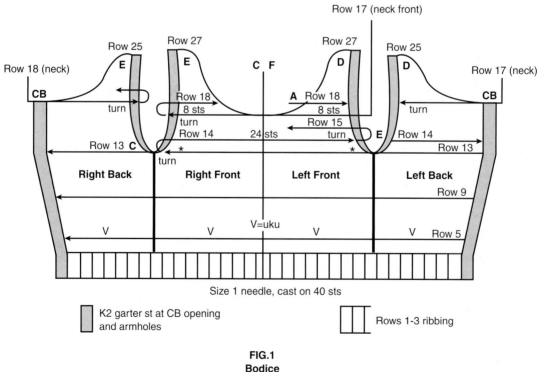

FIG.1
Bodice

Row 15: Knit.

Row 16: K2, p8, k2.

Row 17: Bind off 4 sts (back neck), k7. (8 sts)

Row 18: K2, p6.

Row 19: Ssk, k6. (7 sts)

Row 20: K2, p5.

Row 21: Ssk, k5. (6 sts)

Rows 22 and 24: K2, p4.

Row 23: Knit.

Row 25: Bind off all sts knitwise, cut yarn.

Right Back

Row 13 (RS): Attach new strand of yarn, leaving a 5-inch tail to close neck sts, ssk, (armhole) k11. (12 sts)

Rows 14 and 16: K2, p8, k2.

Rows 15 and 17: Knit.

Row 18: Bind off 4 sts purlwise (back neck), p5, k2. (8 sts)

Row 19: K6, k2tog. (7 sts)

Row 20: P5, k2.

Row 21: K5, k2tog. (6 sts)

Rows 22 and 24: P4, k2.

Row 23: Knit.

Row 25: Bind off all sts knitwise. Cut yarn.

Finishing

Referring to Fig. 1, join shoulder seams D to D and E to E. Sew on snaps. Work stem st around neck with green embroidery thread and make 3 small French knots for buttons. Decorate front with a bow or team's initials.

Panty

Refer to Fig. 2 throughout.

Beg at top with green and size 2 needles, cast on 36 sts.

Row 1: Knit.

Row 2: Cns 1, purl.

Row 3: [K4, up-1, k10, up-1, k4] twice. (40 sts)

Row 4: [P13, turn, k6, turn, p13] twice. (for hips)

Divide for front and back

Row 5: K30, turn, leave last 10 sts on needle for Lt back.

Row 6: P20 (front), leave last 10 sts on needle for Rt back.

Row 7: Working on front sts only, k1, ssk, k14, k2tog, k1. (18 sts)

Rows 8 and 10: Purl.

Row 9: K1, ssk, k12, k2tog, k1. (16 sts)

Row 11: [K1, ssk] twice, k4, [k2tog, k1] twice. (12 sts)

Row 12: P3, turn, k3, turn, p2, p2tog, p8, turn, k3, turn, p3. This makes hip sts slightly higher. (11 sts)

Row 13: K2, ssk, k3, k2tog, k2. (9 sts)

Row 14: Purl.

Row 15: Bind off all sts (crotch), cut yarn.

Back

Join center backs (CB) by placing all sts on 1 needle (see Fig. 4b of sock).

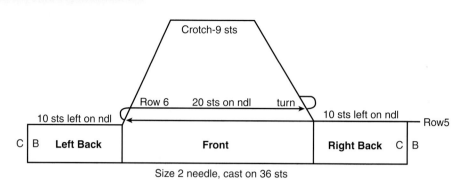

Crotch-9 sts

Row 6   20 sts on ndl   turn

10 sts left on ndl   10 sts left on ndl — Row5

C | B **Left Back**   **Front**   **Right Back** C | B

Row5

Size 2 needle, cast on 36 sts

FIG. 2
RS facing

With RS facing, k2, ssk, k13, k2tog, k1. (18 sts)

Complete as for front from Row 8. Join crotch sts with blind st. Sew hook and eye at back opening.

Full Skirt

Refer to Fig. 3 throughout.

Skirt is knitted from side to side, with rows being vertical from waist. Following 5 rows will make 1 panel. Change yarn color for each panel. Work 30 panels total.

With yellow or green yarn and size 2 needle, cast on 15 sts.

Row 1: Cns 1, (at waist) k14, k1 tbl.

Row 2: (At hem) k1 tbl, k11, wrap and turn, k12.

Row 3: (At hem) k5, wrap and turn, k5.

Row 4: (At hem) k9, wrap and turn, k9.

Row 5: K15.

Change color and rep Rows 1–5. On Row 5 of 30th panel, cns 2, bind off all sts knitwise.

Finishing

With crochet hook, ch 35 for tie, then continue with sc around waist for band, being careful not to pull too tightly. At end of band, ch 35 to make 2nd tie, cut yarn leaving a 5-inch tail. At end of each tie, attach a bead by pulling ch through bead and with tail make a large French knot (wrap needle 5 times) then secure with 2 or 3 sts. Join skirt edges with blind st from hem up to band. Note that reverse side of skirt is equally interesting, hence ties.

Slim Skirt

Work as above, omitting Row 4.

Finishing

Finish as above, or with hook and eye at waist instead of ties.

Place skirt on doll over panty just under cast on sts. As an option, while skirt and panty are on doll, st skirt to panty, making 1 unit.

Shoes and Socks

Refer to Figs. 4 and 5.

Beg at top with size 2 needle and green, cast on 13 sts.

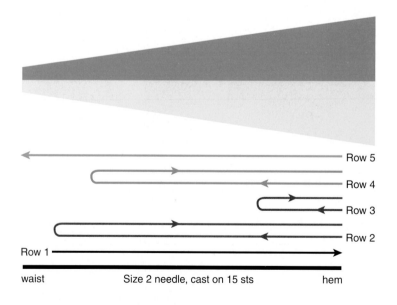

Row 5

Row 4

Row 3

Row 2

Row 1

waist   Size 2 needle, cast on 15 sts   hem

FIG.3

Socks

Row 1: *K1, p1, rep from * across, end k1. Cut yarn short.

Row 2: Cns 0, attach yellow, leaving a 5-inch tail to join center backs, purl across.

Rows 3–7: *K1, p1, rep from * across, end k1.

Row 8: P5, p2tog, p6. (12 sts)

Row 9: Divide for front (arch) and back (heel), k9, turn.

Row 10: At turn, p6 (see Fig. 4a). (arch sts)

Row 11: K6.

Row 12: P2tog, p2, p2tog tbl. (4 sts)

Row 13: Bind off sts knitwise, cut yarn. Place 6 yellow heel sts onto 1 needle, center backs facing (see Fig. 4b).

With tail, seam center backs. Double st to reinforce.

Shoes

See Fig. 4b. With RS of 6 heel sts facing, attach green.

Rows 1 and 3 (RS): With green, k6.

Row 2: Purl.

Row 4: P2tog, p2, p2tog tbl. (4 sts)

Row 5: K4, with crochet hook pp-1 on green edge and pp-1 on yellow edge. (6 sts)

Row 6: P2tog, p4, with crochet hook, pick up on RS as in Row 5. (7 sts)

Row 7: K2tog tbl, k5, pp-1 on arch edge. (7 sts)

Row 8: P2tog, p2 (CB of heel), with 3rd needle, p3, pp-1 on arch edge. (7 sts)

Row 9: K2tog, k2, (CB of heel), k3, pp-4 (arch sts). (10 sts)

With 4th needle, k first 3 sts again (CB of heel), work in rnds from this point.

Rnd 10: Knit.

Rnd 11: [K2, k2tog] twice, end k2. (8 sts)

Rnd 12: Knit, cut yarn, leaving an 8-inch tail.

Finishing

Thread tail in needle, run through sts to gather for toe. Place shoe/sock on doll, close any holes and work stem st across arch for strap. See Fig. 5.

Shakers

For each shaker, cut 10 (3-inch) lengths of yarn (5 of each color), tie at center. Work 2 or 3 buttonhole sts on each side of center tie, wrap around doll's hand and tie. With tapestry needle, split each yarn then trim neatly.

Hair

Tie ponytails with elastic hair bands. Make 1-inch pompoms, trim and tie around hair bands on ponytails. ❖

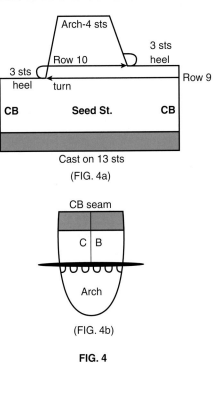

FIG. 4

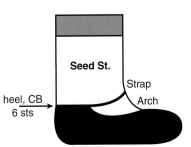

FIG. 5
Shoe & Sock
Knit as one unit

Summer Dream Suit

Designs by Thelma Jean Young

An embroidered hat and purse enhance an already exciting three-piece suit that is perfect for summer knitting, using small amounts of fingering weight yarn.

Skill Level

Intermediate

Size

Fits 11½-inch fashion doll

Materials

- Fingering weight yarn: 50g flamingo (MC), 25g white (CC)
- Size 0 (2mm) 4 double-pointed needles for bodice, skirt top
- Size 1 (2.25mm) 4 double-pointed needles for skirt
- Size 2 (2.75mm) 2 double-pointed needles for working rib
- Size 3 (3mm) needles to cast on
- Stitch markers
- Size 1 (2mm) crochet hook
- Size 4 (1.75mm) crochet hook
- Hook and eye sets (skirt back opening)
- Small snaps (bodice and jacket openings)
- 6 (⅛-inch) white faceted beads (for buttons)
- Embroidery floss and needle: yellow, green, pink, blue
- Sewing and tapestry needles
- T-pins for blocking

Gauge

32 sts and 40 rows = 4 inches/10cm in St st with MC and size 1 needles

37 sts and 50 rows = 4 inches/10cm in St st with white and size 0 needles

Pattern Notes

Review all abbreviations, diagrams and instructions before beginning.

Outfit is completed in this order; knit bodice, skirt, jacket, hat and purse. Embroider flowers on hat, bodice and purse. Sew on beads (buttons) and snaps.

To knit skirt front ribbing, jacket right front and one sleeve make a 2nd ball using 20 yards of MC.

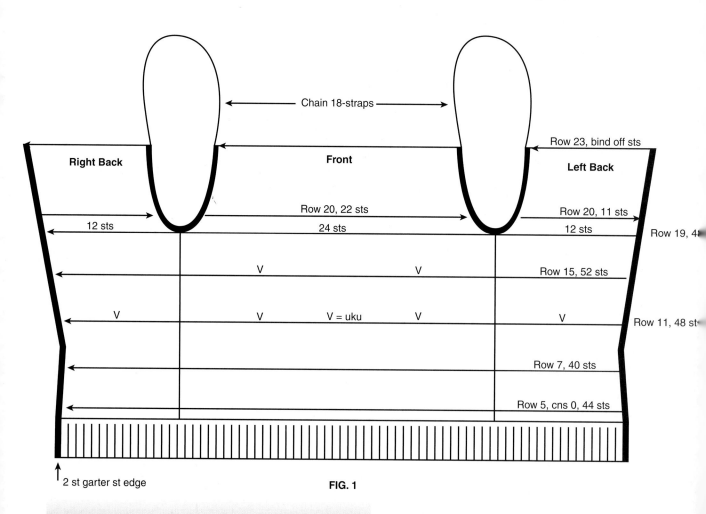

Right Back
Front
Left Back

Chain 18-straps

Row 23, bind off sts
Row 20, 22 sts
Row 20, 11 sts
12 sts
24 sts
12 sts
Row 19, 4?
V
V
Row 15, 52 sts
V
V
V = uku
V
V
Row 11, 48 st?
Row 7, 40 sts
Row 5, cns 0, 44 sts

2 st garter st edge

FIG. 1

Special Abbreviations

Up-1: K1 in top of st in row below. (1 new st)

Uku (up-1, k1, up-1): Work up-1 as above, then knit next st on needle, work another up-l. (2 new sts)

Cns: Change needles to size given.

RF: Right Front

LF: Left Front

RB: Right Back

LB: Left Back

N1, 2 or 3: Needle 1, 2 or 3

(~): Work extra garter st edge rows at each end of marked rows to prevent pulling as follows: k3 (bodice) or k4 (jacket fronts), sl next st purlwise, turn work, take yarn to back as if to k, sl same st, then k3 (4). Continue to work pat as written, but pick up wrapped yarn and knit it tog with 4th (5th) st. Continue in pat to end of row then rep extra row, purling wrap tog with 4th (5th) st of row.

Spaghetti Strap Bodice

Knitted in 1 piece. Refer to Fig. 1.

Note (~) to knit extra rows at garter st edges, at beg and end of Rows 5, 9 and 15.

Band

With white and size 2 needle, cast on 47 sts.

Rows 1 and 3: Cns 1, k3 *k1 tbl, p1, rep from * across, end k1 tbl, k3.

Rows 2 and 4: K3, *p1 tbl, k1, rep from * across, end p1 tbl, k3.

Beg St st, cns 0.

Row 5: (~) k6, k2tog, [k15, k2 tog] twice, k5. (~)(44 sts)

Rows 6–18 (WS rows): K3, p across, end k3.

Row 7: K10, k2tog, k2tog tbl, k16, k2tog, k2tog tbl, k10. (40 sts)

Row 9: (~) Knit across. (~)

Row 11: K6, [uku, k9, uku, k6] twice. (48 sts)

Row 13: Knit.

Row 15: (~) k19, uku, k8, uku, k19. (~) (52 sts)

Row 17: Knit.

Shape armholes

Row 19: (LB) k11, k2tog (12 sts); (front) k2tog tbl, k22, k2tog (24 sts); (RB) k2tog tbl, k11. (12 sts)

Work on RB sts only.

Row 20 (WS): K3, p7, p2tog tbl, turn. (11 sts)

Row 21: K2tog tbl, k9. (10 sts)

Row 22: K3, p7.

Row 23: K2tog tbl, bind off to last 2 sts, k2tog. Fasten off.

Front

Row 20 (WS): P2tog, p20, p2tog tbl. (22 sts)

Row 21: K2tog tbl, k18, k2tog. (20 sts)

Row 22: P2tog, p16, p2tog tbl. (18 sts)

Row 23: Work as for RB.

Left Back

Row 20 (WS): P2tog, p7, k3. (11 sts)

Row 21: K9, k2tog. (10 sts)

Row 22: P7, k3.

Row 23: Work as for RB.

Finishing

Sew 2–3 snaps at back opening so RB overlaps LB. With white and size 1 hook, ch 18 sts for each strap. Attach inside of bodice with 2–3 sts at each end.

Skirt

Refer to Fig 2. 2½-inch ribbing at bottom of skirt is worked in 2 sections on same needle. (1 front, 1 back)

With MC large ball and size 3 needle, cast on 35 sts for back; with 2nd ball, cast on 35 sts for front. Work each row across both sections.

Row 1: Cns 2, k1, p1, *k1 tbl, p1, rep from * across, end k1.

Row 2: P1, *k1, p1 tbl, rep from * across, end k1, p1.

Rows 3–19: Rep Rows 1 and 2, ending with Row 1.

Row 20: Cns 1, p3, *p2tog, p1, rep from * across, end p2. (25 sts each side)

Cut 2nd ball, leave main ball attached.

Join to work in rnds.

Row 21: N1, k13 (center back of

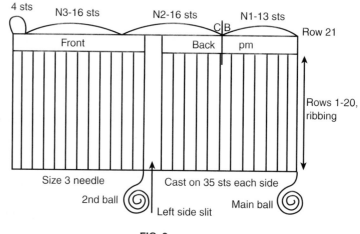

FIG. 2

skirt, beg of rnds) pm; N2, k11, k2tog, k4 (16 sts); N3, k16, sl remaining 4 sts to N1. With empty needle, k3, k2tog, k12. (16 sts)

You are again at CB. (48 sts)

Rnds 22–34: Knit even.

Rnd 35: [K9, k2tog, k2, k2tog, k9] twice. (44 sts)

Rnds 36–48: Knit even.

Rnd 49: [K8, k2tog, k2, k2tog, k8] twice. (40 sts)

Rnds 50–59: Knit even.

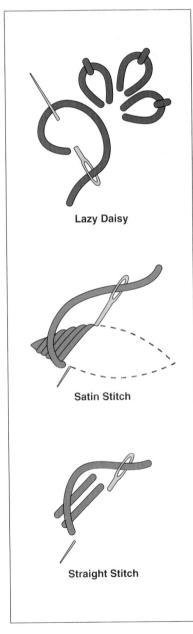

Lazy Daisy

Satin Stitch

Straight Stitch

Shape hips

Work in rows from this point.

Row 60: Purl.

Row 61: Cns 0, [k7, k2tog, k2, k2tog, k7] twice. (36 sts)

Row 62: Purl.

Row 63: K6, k2tog, k2, k2tog, k1, turn; sl 1, p5, turn; sl 1, k16, k2tog, k2, k2tog, k1, turn; sl 1, p5, turn; sl 1, k10. (32 sts)

Bind off all sts knitwise.

Finishing

Reinforce top of each slit with a double st. Sew hook and eyes at back opening.

Referring to Fig. 2a, block skirt, pinning slits closed.

Jacket

Back

With MC and size 3 needles, cast on 25 sts.

Rows 1 and 3: Cns 2, k1, *k1 tbl, p1, rep from * across, end k1 tbl, k1.

Rows 2 and 4: P1, *p1 tbl, k1, rep from * across, end p1 tbl, p1.

Rows 5–20: Cns 1, work even in St st.

Shape armholes

Row 21: Bind off 2 sts knitwise, k across. (23 sts)

Row 22: Bind off 2 sts purlwise, p across, end p2tog tbl. (20 sts)

Row 23: K2tog tbl, k across, end k2tog. (18 sts)

Row 24: P2tog, p across. (17 sts)

Rows 25–30: Work even in St st.

Shape neck

Row 31: Cns 0, k7, attach 2nd ball of yarn, bind off next 5 sts, k5. (6 sts each side)

Row 32 (Left shoulder-WS): P6, turn, k6, place sts on holder.

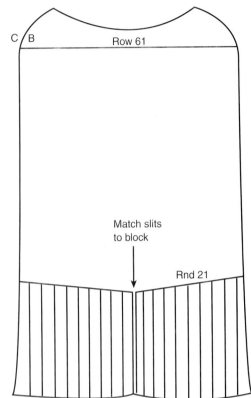

C B   Row 61

Match slits to block

Rnd 21

FIG. 2A

(Right shoulder-WS) Work as for left. Set aside.

Front

Referring to Fig. 3, work right and left fronts on same needle with center fronts facing and using 2 balls of yarn.

Note (~) to knit extra rows at garter st edges, at beg and end of Rows 5, 11, and 17.

Band

With MC (2 balls) and size 3 needles, cast on 16 sts for each side.

Rows 1 and 3 (RS): LF, k1, *k1 tbl, p1, rep from * across, end k1 tbl, k4; RF, (attach 2nd ball), k4 *k1 tbl, p1, rep from * across, end k1 tbl, k1.

Rows 2 and 4: RF, p1, *p1 tbl, k1, rep from * across, end p1 tbl, k4; LF, k4, *p1 tbl, k1, rep from * across, end p1 tbl, p1.

Row 5: Cns 1, LF, k across (~); RF, (~) k across.

Rows 6, 8 and 10 (WS): RF, p12, k4; LF, k4, p12.

Rows 7 and 9: Knit.

Row 11: LF, k8, uku, k7 (~); RF, (~) k7, uku, k8. (18 sts on each side)

Rows 12, 14 and 16: P14, k4, k4, p14.

Rows 13 and 15: Knit.

Row 17: LF, k10, uku, k7, (~); RF, (~) k7, uku, k10. (20 sts each side)

Neck

Row 18: RF, p16, k4. (20 sts)

LF, bind off 4 sts purlwise, p15. (16 sts)

Row 19: K14, k2tog. (15 sts)

Bind off 4 sts, k15. (16 sts)

Shape armholes

Row 20: Bind off 2 sts purlwise, p11, p2tog tbl. (13 sts)

P2tog, p11, p2tog tbl. (13 sts)

Row 21: Bind off 3 sts knitwise, k7, k2tog. (9 sts)

K2tog tbl, k9, k2tog. (11 sts)

Row 22: P2tog, p7, p2tog tbl. (9 sts)

P2tog, p5, p2tog tbl. (7 sts)

Row 23: K2tog tbl, k5. (6 sts)

K2tog, k4, k2tog tbl. (6 sts)

Rows 24–34: Work even in St st.

Row 35: Knit.

Place RF and RB sts on 2 needles. Bind off right shoulder sts as follows: Hold needles containing shoulder sts parallel, RS tog; with 3rd needle, k first st of front and back needles tog, *k next st on both needles tog, bind off 1, rep from * until all sts are worked, fasten off. Rep for left shoulder. Block pieces.

Sleeves

With 2 balls of MC and size 3 needles, cast on 13 sts for each sleeve. Work each row across both sleeves.

Rows 1 and 3 (RS): Cns 2, k1, *k1 tbl, p1, rep from * across, end k1 tbl, k1.

Rows 2 and 4: P1, *p1 tbl, k1, rep from * across, end p1 tbl, p1.

Rows 5–10: Cns 1, work even in St st.

Row 11: K3, up-1, k7, up-1, k3. (15 sts)

Rows 12–24: Work even in St st.

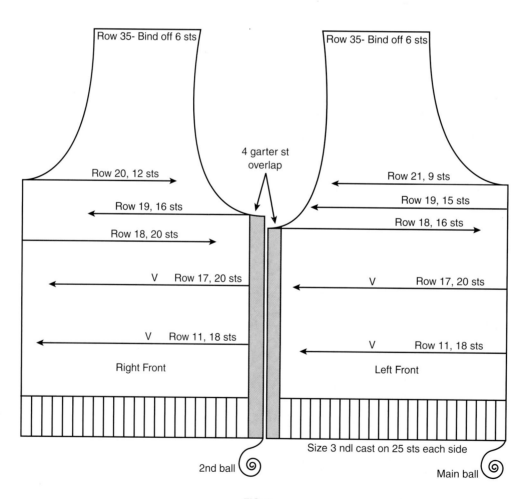

FIG. 3

Row 25: K3, up-1, k9, up-1, k3. (17 sts)

Rows 26–29: Work even in St st.

Row 30: Bind off 2 sts purlwise, k14. (15 sts)

Row 31: Bind off 2 sts knitwise, p12. (13 sts)

Row 32 and 34: Purl.

Row 33: K2tog tbl, k9, k2tog. (11 sts)

Row 35: K2tog tbl, k7, k2tog. (9 sts)

Row 36: Purl.

Bind off all sts knitwise. Block sleeves.

Finishing

Set in sleeves, then sew sleeve and underarm seams. Sew on snaps then beads as shown.

Tip: To join these small pieces, split yarn into 2 strands, and crochet tog with size 4 hook working in sl st.

Note: When putting jacket on doll, cover hands with small pieces of thin plastic to allow hands to slide easily into sleeves.

Sun Hat

With white and size 2 needle, cast on 8 sts, turn. Cns 1, purl across.

Crown

Row 1: Inc in each st across. (16 sts)

Row 2: Purl.

Join and work in rnds from this point.

Rnd 3: Beg with 8 sts on each needle *inc in first st, k1, rep from * around. (24 sts)

Rnds 4 and 6: Knit.

Rnd 5: *Inc in first st, k2, rep from * around. (32 sts)

Rnd 7: K4, up-1, *k8, up-1, rep from * around, end k4. (36 sts)

Rnd 8: Purl. (last rnd of crown)

Rnds 9–18: Cns 0, knit even.

Brim

Rnd 19: K1, up-1, *k3, up-1, rep from * around, end k2. (48 sts)

Rnds 20, 22 and 23: Knit.

Rnd 21: K3, up-1, *k6, up-1, rep from * around, end k3. (56 sts)

Rnd 24: K2, up-1, *k4, up-1, rep from * around, end k2. (70 sts)

Rnds 25, 26 and 28: Knit.

Rnd 27: K2, up-1, *k5, up-1, rep from * around, end k3. (84 sts)

Rnd 29: *K1, p1, rep from * around.

Rnd 30: *P1, k1, rep from * around.

Cns 3, turn work with WS facing, bind off all sts knitwise.

Finishing

Split embroidery threads into 2 or 3 strands and embroider flowers, buds and leaves, referring to photos and embroidery st guides on page 141. To prevent threads showing on underside of brim, skim sts into top surface of knitting.

To firm brim edge, turn hat so WS of brim is facing, with 12-inch piece of white sewing thread, work hidden sts along 1 side of bound off sts around. Then very gently pull threads just a little to tighten brim. Secure with 2 or 3 sts.

Purse

Make 2

With white and size 1 needle, cast on 8 sts, turn. Cns 0, purl across.

Work Rows and Rnds 1–6 of sun hat crown instructions. (32 sts)

Rnd 7: *Inc in first st, k3, rep from * around. (40 sts)

Cns 2, bind off all sts knitwise.

Finishing

Embroider flowers on RS of each knitted circle, keeping clear of bound-off edges.

With WS facing, hold circles in place with 2 or 3 thread tacks of CC and mark a 1-inch opening. Beg at 1 end of opening, and with size 4 hook, crochet tog 1 loop of each bound off st on front and back of circles; *work loop of next st on both sides tog, bind off 1, rep from *until you reach opposite end of opening. Secure with 2 or 3 sts. Remove thread tacks.

Strap

Beg at 1 end of opening with size 1 hook, ch 45. Secure at opposite end of opening with 2 or 3 sts.

Tip: So purse will hang better, place a coin inside. ❖

Checkerboard Doll Pullover

Design by Edie Eckman

Practice a slip-stitch check pattern and use up some of your stash to create a little sweater for a favorite doll or bear.

Skill Level

Intermediate**

Size

Fits 18-inch doll

Finished Measurements

Chest: 14 inches

Length: 5½ inches

Materials

- Worsted weight yarn: Approximately 85 yds dark green (A), 45 yds white (B), 45 yds red (C)
- Size 8 (5mm) needles or size needed to obtain gauge
- Tapestry needle

Gauge

20 sts and 36 rows = 4 inches/10cm in sl st check pat

To save time, take time to check gauge.

Pattern Notes

This may look like a Fair Isle pat, but it's really a sl st pat that uses only 1 color on each row. Colors not in use may be carried loosely up side.

Sl all sts purlwise with yarn of WS of fabric.

Pattern Stitch

Slip Stitch Check (multiple of 4 sts + 2)

Sl sts purlwise.

Row 1 (RS): With B, k1, sl 1, *k2, sl 2, rep from *, end k2, sl 1, k1.

Row 2: With B, p1, sl 1, *p2, sl 2, rep from *, end p2, sl 1, p1.

Row 3: With A, knit.

Row 4: With C, p2, *sl 2, p2, rep from * across.

Rows 5: With C, k2, *sl 2, k2, rep from * across.

Row 6: With A, purl.

Rep Rows 1–6 for pat.

Back

With A, cast on 34 sts. Work in k1, p1 rib for 3 rows.

Change to pat and work even until piece measures 4¾ inches from beg, ending with a WS row.

Shape neck

Maintaining pat, work 11 sts, join new ball of yarn and bind off next 12 sts, work to end. Working both sides at once with separate balls of yarn, bind off 1 st at each neck edge once. (10 sts each side)

Work even until back measures 5½ inches from beg. Bind off with A.

Front

Work as for back until front measures 4 inches from beg, ending with a WS row.

Shape neck

Maintaining pat, work 14 sts, join new ball of yarn and bind off next 6 sts, work to end. Working both sides at once with separate balls of yarn, work 1 row even, then [bind off 2 sts at each neck edge] twice. (10 sts remain on each side)

Work even until front measures 5½ inches from beg. Bind off with A.

Sleeves

With A, cast on 30 sts. Work in k1, p1 rib for 3 rows.

Beg pat, inc 1 st each side [every 6th row] twice, working new sts into pat. (34 sts)

Work even until sleeve measures 4½ inches from beg, ending with Row 2 or 5 of pat. Bind off with A.

Finishing

Sew left shoulder seam. With A, pick up and k 44 sts around neck. Work 3 rows in k1, p1 rib. Bind off all sts. Sew right shoulder and neck seams. Sew sleeve to sides of body. Sew underarm and sleeve seams. ❖

A Norwegian Couple: Knute & Ragnhild

Designs by Rita G. Knudson

These two dolls were knitted with Rita's husband's Norwegian roots in mind. Their names come from the Knudson family tree. She stayed faithful to Norwegian knitting techniques when she designed their miniature clothing.

Skill Level

Advanced****

Finished Sizes

Approximately 13 inches tall

Materials

- Sock yarn or fingering weight yarn (50g per skein): 2 skeins black, 1 skein each cream, maroon, tan, flesh color
- Small amount bouclé yarn in cream (Knute)
- 2 sets size 1 (2.5mm) double-pointed knitting needles or size needed to obtain gauge
- Stitch holders
- Tapestry needle
- Doll hair (Ragnhild)
- Fiberfill
- Blue, pink and brown embroidery floss
- 9 silver flat type beads
- 9 silver seed beads
- 5 black doll buttons
- 1 cream colored doll button
- Approximately 12 inches (¼-inch-wide) elastic
- Beading needle
- Sewing needle and thread

Gauge

30 sts and 40 rows = 4 inches/10cm in St st

To save time, take time to check gauge.

Special Abbreviation

Cdd (central double decrease): Sl next 2 sts as if to k2tog, k1, p2sso.

Dolls

Legs

Cast on 20 sts using waste yarn, which will be removed and discarded later. Divide sts onto 3 needles. Join without twisting, k 2 rnds. Change to black (shoe color), k 12 rnds, change to maroon for stockings, for Ragnhild, k 26 rnds; for Knute, k 3 rnds. Work in k1, p1 ribbing, 3 rnds for Ragnhild; 15 rnds for Knute, bind off in rib.

Using flesh-color yarn, working in tops of sts in rnd before beg of ribbing, pick up and k 20 sts from inside of stocking. Knit 22 rnds for Ragnhild; 45 rnds for Knute. Leave leg on needles and rep for 2nd leg.

Once both legs are completed, remove waste yarn at bottom of leg, thread a tapestry needle with black, draw through loops and pull tight. Secure yarn end inside of leg.

Turn legs inside out and work in ends. Turn legs right side out.

Body

Note: This is very awkward at first, but after a few rnds, it becomes much easier. There is a lot of stress and strain in these first few rnds. You may have to readjust your needles frequently and use 4 or 5 dpn at once.

Beg with first leg with first dpn, attach flesh-color yarn, k1, inc 1, k7, inc 1, k2 (10 unworked sts remaining on needles in back); cast on 2 sts (crotch); on 2nd leg, k2, inc 1, k7, inc 1, k1 (10 unworked sts remaining on needles in back. (see Fig. 1, 26 sts on first needle)

Use 2nd dpn, k1, inc 1, k7, inc 1, k2; when you come to 2-st crotch, k 2 cast on sts; with 3rd dpn, k2, inc 1, k7, inc 1, k1. (50 sts)

On Rnd 2, at 2-st crotch area, k2. As you work around to back and come to 2 crotch sts again, pick up and k 2 sts from purl backs of sts created in first rnd. (52 sts)

K 30 rnds for both Ragnhild and Knute.

Divide for arms

Note: Bodies are now worked back and forth in rows.

K 26 front sts for 10 rows, place on holder. K 26 back sts for 10 rows, place on holder. Stuff legs and body with fiberfill to underarm.

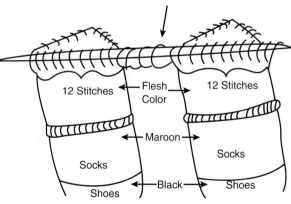

FIG. 1

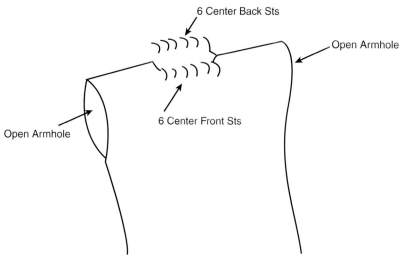

6 Center Back Sts

Open Armhole

Open Armhole

6 Center Front Sts

FIG. 2

Grafting shoulders

Take first 10 sts for front and first 10 sts from back and graft them tog. Rep for last 10 sts of front and back. Center 6 neck sts will remain in front and back (see Fig. 2).

Neck

Divide 12 neck sts evenly on dpn, join, k 2 rnds.

Rnd 3: Inc 12 sts evenly around. (24 sts)

Rnd 4: Knit.

Rnd 5: Inc 12 sts evenly. (36 sts)

Head

K 14 rnds.

Divide for front and back

Working on 18 front sts, bind off on each side [1 st] once, then [3 sts] once. (10 sts remain)

For Ragnhild, work same shaping on back 18 sts.

For Knute, using cream-colored bouclé yarn, k18 from back, pick up and k 4 sts along bound off sts, k10 front sts, then pick up and k4 sts along bound off sts. (36 sts)

Join, k 4 rnds, then [k2tog] around. (18 sts)

K 1 rnd, cut yarn, leaving a 6-inch

end. Using tapestry needle, run yarn through remaining sts, pull tight and secure loose end inside of head. Use armhole openings to access head to insert stuffing.

Finish Ragnhild's head by grafting 10 front and 10 back sts tog, seam bound off sts at sides. Referring to photo, lay doll hair on head and backstitch it with flesh-color yarn. Braid if desired.

Arms

Using dpn and body yarn, pick up and k 20 sts around armhole, k 37 rnds. Cut yarn, leaving a long end. Thread end in tapestry needle and draw yarn through loops. Stuff arm, pull end tight, and fasten off securely. Rep for 2nd arm.

Embroider eyes with blue, mouth with pink and eyebrows with brown.

Knute's Clothes

Pants

Using dpn and waste yarn, cast on 32 sts. Join without twisting, k 1 rnd with waste yarn. Change to black, k 5 rnds. P 1 rnd (turning rnd), k 60 rnds. Rep for 2nd pant leg.

Join pant legs as legs of body, creating a 2-st crotch. (68 sts)

Pm evenly spaced at left and right sides of pants. Inc 1 st on each side

of markers [every other rnd] 3 times. (80 sts)

K 24 rnds.

Waistband

P 1 rnd. K 5 rnds. P 1 rnd (turning ridge), k 5 rnds.

Fold waistband at turning ridge. Remove waste yarn and sew sts to inside of waistband. Before sewing last 3 or 4 sts, run elastic inside waistband casing. Cut elastic to desired length and secure ends. Sew down remaining sts.

Remove waste yarn from beg of pants legs. Turn hem to inside on turning ridge, and sew in place.

Sweater

Using waste yarn, cast on 88 sts. Join without twisting, k 1 rnd with waste yarn. Change to cream, k 6 rnds. P 1 rnd for turning ridge. K 1 rnd cream, 1 rnd maroon, 1 rnd cream, then work 3 rnds of pat from Chart A.

K 1 rnd cream, 1 rnd maroon, work 23 rnds of pat from Chart B.

Divide for front and back yokes

Back

Working pat in rows on 44 sts, work 22 rows. Place sts on holder.

Front

Place center 4 sts on holder.

Right yoke

Maintaining established pat throughout, work 12 rows on 20 sts. Shape neck edge by binding off 1 st at beg of each RS row 5 times. (15 sts)

Rep for left yoke, reversing shaping.

Bind off front and back shoulder sts tog as follows: Hold needles containing shoulder sts parallel, WS tog; with 3rd needle, using maroon, k first st on front and back needles tog, *k next st on both needles tog, bind off 1 st, rep from * until all sts are worked, fasten off. Rep for 2nd shoulder.

Put 14 back neck sts on holder.

Sleeves

Using waste yarn, cast on 40 sts. Join without twisting, k 1 rnd with waste yarn. Change to cream and k 4 rnds. P 1 rnd (turning ridge), k 1 rnd cream, 1 rnd maroon, 1 rnd cream.

Next rnd: [K3 cream, k1 black] 10 times.

K 1 rnd cream, 1 rnd maroon, work 19 rnds of pat from Chart B. Change to maroon, k 4 rnds. Leave sts on needles.

With maroon, pick up and k 40 sts evenly spaced around sweater armhole. Beg at underarm, bind off sleeve and body sts tog as for shoulder seams. Rep for 2nd sleeve.

Front Placket

Using maroon, RS facing, beg at left shoulder, pick up and k 20 sts along left front, 4 sts from front holder, 20 sts along right front and 14 sts from back. (58 sts)

Join and work 6 rnds, dec 2 sts by cdd at bottom corners of placket, and at beg of neck shaping [every other rnd] 3 times. (34 sts)

P 1 rnd (turning ridge). K 6 rnds, inc 1 st on each side of same points as decs were worked [every other rnd] 3 times. (58 sts)

Fold hem along turning ridge and sew knit sts to inside of sweater to form placket.

Referring to photo for placement, secure four flat silver beads, each with a seed bead, to placket—two on each side. Use maroon yarn to make button loops between plackets.

Ragnhild's Clothes

Bloomers

Using waste yarn, cast on 30 sts. Join without twisting, k 1 rnd with waste yarn. Change to cream, k 3 rnds.

Rnd 4: [Yo, k2tog] 15 times. (picot rnd)

Rnds 5–7: Knit.

Rnd 8: [Yo, k1, k2tog] 8 times.

Rnds 9–11: Knit.

Rnd 12: Inc 2 sts evenly. (32 sts)

Place sts on holder. Rep for 2nd leg.

Join legs and shape top of bloomers same as top of Knute's pants. Remove waste yarn, turn hem in along picot rnd to create a picot edge. Sew sts to inside of leg.

Using tan, create a twisted cord. Run twisted cord through eyelet openings in legs.

Petticoat

Lace border

Cast on 7 sts.

Row 1: K3, yo, k2tog, [yo] twice, k2.

Row 2: K2, [k1, p1] in double yo, k2, yo, k2 tog, k1.

Row 3: K3, yo, k2tog, k4.

Row 4: Bind off 2 sts, k3, yo, k2tog, k1.

Rep [Rows 1–4] 40 times. Bind off all sts.

With cream, pick up and k 120 sts along straight edge of lace. Join, work 22 rnds in St st. Create a slit in skirt by working skirt back and forth from this point, working a 1-st garter st edge on each side of slit. Beg with a k row, work 8 rows of St st.

Shape top

Row 9: [K4, k2tog] across. (100 sts)

Row 10 and all WS rows: K1, p to last st, k1.

Row 11: [K3, k2tog] across. (80 sts)

Row 13: [K2, k2tog] across. (60 sts)

Row 15: Dec 12 sts evenly across. (48 sts)

Row 16: Rep Row 10.

Knit across, cast on 5 sts to make a waistband extension. Knit back (to create a purl ridge on RS). Work 3 rows in St st. K next WS row to create a turning ridge. Work 3

rows in St st. Turn hem to inside, folding on turning ridge. Sew sts to inside to create a waistband. Sew snap on waistband and extension.

Dress

Using tan, cast on 100 sts, join without twisting, p 1 rnd, k 1 rnd. Change to black, k 1 rnd, p 1 rnd, k 1 rnd. Change to maroon, k 1 rnd, p 1 rnd, k 1 rnd. Change to black, k 39 rnds.

Shape waist

Rnd 1: [K3, k2tog] around. (80 sts)

Rnds 2 and 3: Knit.

Rnd 4: [K2, k2tog] around. (60 sts)

Rnds 5 and 6: Knit.

Rnds 7–12: Work in k1, p1 ribbing.

Rnds 13 and 14: Knit.

Placket

Divide to work back and forth for placket. Pm for center front, k to marker, pick up and k 2 sts in tops of next 2 sts of front, turn and work in rows from this point. (62 sts)

Row 1: K2, p to last 2 sts, end k2.

Row 2: Knit.

Rows 3–11: Rep Rows 1 and 2, ending with Row 1.

Divide for underarms: 27 sts in back, 3 on holders for each underarm, 15 sts in right front, 14 sts in left front.

Sleeves

Using black, cast on 28 sts. Join without twisting, work in k1, p1 rib for 4 rnds. K 23 rnds, lay aside. Work 2nd sleeve.

Join sleeves to bodice

Place 3 sts at each sleeve underarm on holder. K across right front bodice to underarm, first sleeve, dress back, 2nd sleeve, then left front bodice, turn.

Row 1 (WS): K2, p to last 2 sts, end k2.

Row 2: [K to 1 st before underarm, cdd, k to 2 sts before end of sleeve, cdd] twice, k to end.

Rows 3–12: Rep Rows 1 and 2. (58 sts)

Work 4 rows of k1, p1 ribbing. Bind off in pat.

Lap right placket over left. Sew 5 black buttons evenly spaced on outside of right placket. Graft underarm sts tog.

Sweater

Cast on 74 sts using waste yarn. Working in rows, change to maroon and work 4 rows of St st. P 1 row (turning ridge). K 1 row maroon, p 1 row tan, k 1 row maroon.

Beg with a WS row, work Rows 1–17 of pat from Chart C. Work 1 row maroon, 1 row tan, 1 row maroon in St st.

Divide for front and back yokes

Place 2 sts at each underarm on holders, 34 sts for back, 18 sts for each front.

Back

Working on 34 back sts only, work 18 rows in St st and Chart D pat.

Shape neck

Place center 10 sts on holder. Continue to work in pat, binding off 1 st at neck edge [every other row] 3 times. Place 9 shoulder sts on holder. Rep for 2nd shoulder.

Front

Work 14 rows in St st and Chart D pat.

Shape neck

Place 5 sts at neck edge on holder, bind off 1 st at neck edge [every other row] 4 times. Place 9 shoulder sts on holder. Rep shaping on other side.

Referring to instructions for Knute's sweater, bind off front and back shoulder sts tog. Remove waste yarn from bottom edge of sweater, fold hem under along purl turn ridge, sew hem to inside of sweater.

Sleeves

Using waste yarn, cast on 32 sts. Join without twisting, k 1 rnd with waste yarn. Change to maroon and k 4 rnds. P 1 rnd for a turning ridge. K 2 rnds maroon, 1 rnd tan, 1 rnd maroon. Working in St st, work Rnds 1–3 from Chart E, k 1 rnd maroon, 1 rnd tan. Work 24 rnds of Chart D pat.

Complete sleeve by p 5 rnds maroon to create inside facing for sleeve top. Rep for 2nd sleeve.

Insert sleeve into armhole, graft 2 underarm sts to 2 sts from sleeve. Sew sleeve into place. Sew down inside sleeve facing. Rep for 2nd sleeve. Remove waste yarn, turn sleeve hem inside sleeve along purl ridge and sew hem in place.

Front and Neck Bands

Pick up and k 32 sts along right front band, work 3 rows in St st. P 1 row for turning ridge, work 3 rows of St st. Fold hem inward along purl ridge, sew hem to inside edge of sweater. Rep for left side of sweater.

Pick up and k 56 sts along neck edge and top edges of front bands. Work 3 rows in St st. P 1 turning ridge, work 3 rows of St st. Fold hem inward along purl ridge and sew in place.

Referring to photo, secure 5 flat silver beads each with a seed bead to right side of cardigan to create buttons. ❖

Rep
CHART A

COLOR KEY FOR A & B
☐ Cream
◇ Black

Rep
CHART B

COLOR KEY FOR C–E
☐ Maroon
◇ Black
✕ Tan

End **Rep** Beg
CHART C

End **Rep** Beg
CHART D

Rep
CHART E

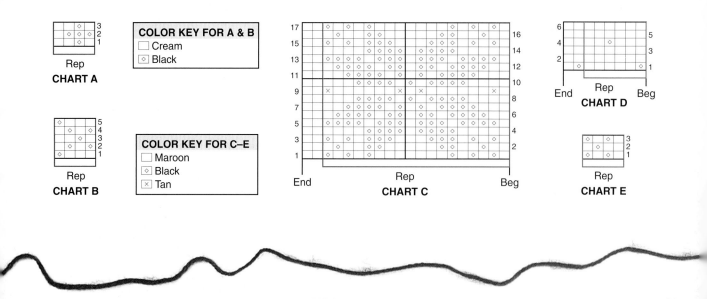

Garter-Stitch Doll Suit

Designs by Edie Eckman

Any doll will look stunning in this simple suit made with colorful blocks of garter stitch. It's a great way to use odd balls of yarn.

Skill Level

Beginner*

Size

Fits 18-inch doll

Materials

- Worsted weight 100 percent wool yarn: 85 yds each pink (A), violet (B), green (C); 40 yds gold (D)
- Size 7 (4.5mm) needles or size needed to obtain gauge
- Tapestry needle
- Size G/6 (4mm) crochet hook
- 3 (¾-inch) buttons

Gauge

20 sts and 40 rows = 4 inches/10cm in garter st

To save time, take time to check gauge.

Jacket

Back

With A, cast on 35 sts. K every row until back measures 5 inches, ending with a WS row. K12, join new strand of yarn and bind off center 11 sts, k12. Working both sides at once with separate yarns, work even until piece measures 5½ inches from beg. Bind off all sts.

Right Front

With B, cast on 20 sts. K every row until front measures 4½ inches from beg, ending with a WS row. Bind off 8 sts, k to end. Work even until piece measures 5½ inches from beg. Bind off all sts.

Left Front

With C, cast on 20 sts. K 1 inch, ending with a WS row.

Buttonhole row: K15, k2tog, yo, k3.

Work even, placing additional buttonhole rows when front measures 2½ inches and 4 inches from beg. Work even until piece measures 4½ inches from beg, ending with a RS row. Bind off 8 sts for front neck, k to end.

Work even until piece measures 5½ inches from beg. Bind off all sts.

Sleeves

With A, cast on 20 sts. K every row, inc 1 st each side [every 4th row] 7 times. (34 sts)

Work even until piece measures 3½ inches from beg. Bind off all sts. Rep with D for 2nd sleeve.

Finishing

Sew shoulder seams. Sew sleeves to sides of body. Sew side and underarm seams. Sew buttons opposite buttonholes.

Skirt

With D, cast on 38 sts. K 3 rows. With C, k 34 rows.

Dec row: K1, k2tog, k32, k2tog, k1. (36 sts)

K 3 rows.

Eyelet row: K3, *yo, k2tog, k2, rep from * across, end k1.

K 3 rows. Bind off all sts. Make 2nd piece with D and B.

Finishing

Sew side seams. With A, crochet a 12-inch ch. Weave ch through eyelets at waist and tie in a bow. ❖

Colorful Baby Blocks

Design by Elizabeth Mattfield

Square by square, block by block, use up your odd bits of yarn. Be sure to use yarns of a similar weight for each block.

Skill Level

Beginner*

Finished Size

Approximately 4 inches square

Materials

- Approximately 1½ oz assorted yarns of similar weights for each block
- Size 6 (4mm) needles or size needed to obtain gauge
- Tapestry needle
- Fiberfill or 4-inch square foam block

Gauge

20 sts = 4 inches/10cm in St st

Gauge is not critical to this project (unless cover has to fit snugly) but sts should be fairly firm.

Pattern Notes

This project is a good way to use up small amounts of yarns that are similar in weight. If it's important for the pieces to be exactly square and the same size, it's easiest to use several colors of the same yarn.

Six-Color Block

Sides

With color A, cast on 20 sts. *Work in St st for 4 inches. Work 1 row in reverse St st (k if next row should be a purl row, p if it should be a knit row).

Cut A, attach B, rep from *, cut B, attach C, rep from *, cut C, attach D, rep from *. Bind off all sts.

Ends

With E, *cast on 20 sts and work in St st for 4 inches, bind off all sts. With F, rep from *.

Finishing

Sew bound-off edge of side piece to cast on edge. Sew ends in place, matching corners to reverse St st ridges, and leaving 1 edge open. If using foam cube, you may need to leave 2 edges open to insert cube.

Stuff firmly, sew remaining edge.

Four-Color Block

With A, cast on 40 sts and work in St st for 4 inches, ending with a RS row.

Next row: Bind off 20 sts, knit across, forming a reverse St st ridge on RS. Cut A, attach B.

With B, work in St st for 4 inches, p last RS row. Cut B.

Next row: Attach C, p20, cast on 20 sts at end of row. (40 sts)

With C, work in St st for 4 inches, bind off 20 sts at beg of last row, p to end. (20 sts)

Cut C, attach D. Beg with a purl row, work in St st for 4 inches. Bind off all sts.

Referring to Fig. 1, fold on dotted lines, sew beg and end tog, then fold ends and sew all but 1 seam. Stuff firmly, then sew remaining seam. ❖

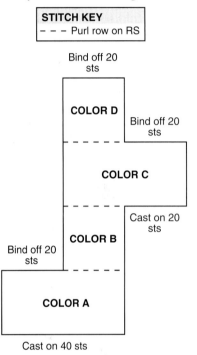

STITCH KEY
– – – Purl row on RS

Bind off 20 sts

COLOR D

Bind off 20 sts

COLOR C

COLOR B

Bind off 20 sts

Cast on 20 sts

COLOR A

Cast on 40 sts

FIG. 1

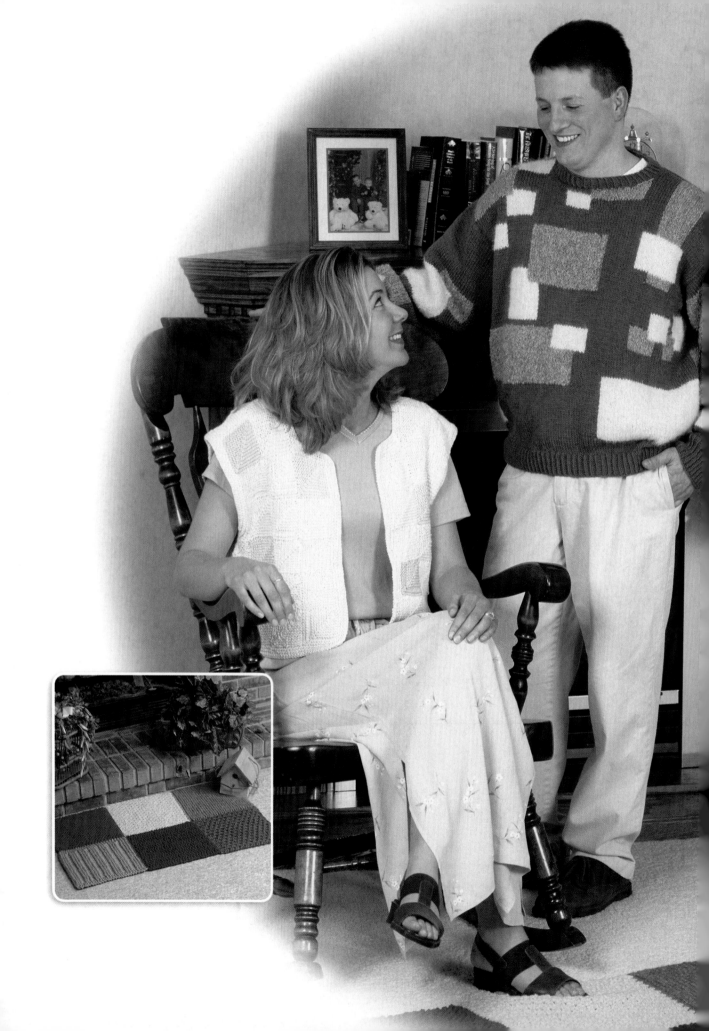

Knitted Samplers

Isn't it fun to try one of each kind! Choose your favorite colors and yarns from your stash. Use them to knit a variety of stitches which will create these beautiful sampler sweaters, afghans, rugs and vests!

Slip-Stitch Sampler Jacket

Design by Ann E. Smith

A shawl collar adds to the charm of this slip-stitch jacket using odd balls of yarn with a neutral shade as the main color.

Skill Level

Easy**

Sizes

Woman's extra-small (small, medium, large, extra-large) Instructions are given for smallest size, with larger sizes in parentheses. When only 1 number is given, it applies to all sizes.

Finished Measurements

Chest (buttoned): 37 (40½, 43¼, 46½, 49½) inches

Length: 24 (24½, 25, 25½, 26) inches

Materials

- Wool-Ease 80 percent acrylic/20 percent wool worsted weight yarn from Lion Brand Yarn (197 yds/3 oz per skein): 6 (7, 7, 8, 9) skeins fisherman #099 (MC), 1 (1, 2, 2, 2) skeins guava #133 (A), 1 (1, 1, 2, 2) skeins green heather #130 (B), 1 skein each lavender #143 (C), butterscotch #189 (D)
- Size 6 (4mm) needles
- Size 8 (5mm) needles or size needed to obtain gauge
- Stitch holders
- Tapestry needle
- 4 (1-inch) buttons
- 2 snaps

Gauge

20 sts and 44 rows = 4 inches/10cm in pat with larger needles

To save time, take time to check gauge.

Special Abbreviation

Sl 1p: With yarn on WS of fabric, sl 1 st purlwise.

Pattern Stitches

Band 1: Pat A (multiple of 2 sts + 1)

Row 1 (RS): With MC, k2, *sl 1p, k1, rep from * across, end sl 1p, k2.

Row 2: P1, *k1, p1, rep from * across.

Row 3: K1, *sl 1p, k1, rep from * across.

Row 4: K1, *p1, k1, rep from * across.

Rows 5–8: Rep Rows 1–4.

Band 2: Pat B (multiple of 4 sts + 1)

Row 1 (RS): With A, k4, sl 1p, *k3, sl 1p, rep from *, end k4.

Row 2: With A, k4, sl 1p, *k3, sl 1p, rep from *, end k4.

Row 3: With MC, k1, *sl 1p, k1, rep from * across.

Row 4: With MC, k1, *sl 1p, k1, rep from * across.

Rows 5–8: Rep Rows 1–4.

Band 3: With MC, rep Rows 1–8 of Pat A.

Band 4: Pat C (multiple of 4 sts + 1)

Row 1 (RS): With B, rep Row 1 of Pat A.

Row 2: With B, rep Row 2 of Pat A.

Rows 3 and 4: With MC, rep Rows 3 and 4 of Pat A.

Rows 5–8: Rep Rows 1–4.

Row 9: With C, rep Row 1 of Pat A.

Row 10: With C, rep Row 2 of Pat A.

Rows 11 and 12: With MC, rep Rows 3 and 4 of Pat A.

Rows 13–20: Rep Rows 1–8.

Band 5: With MC, rep Rows 1–8 of Pat A.

Band 6: Pat D (multiple of 4 sts + 1)

Row 1 (RS): With A, knit.

Row 2: With A, purl.

Row 3: With D, knit.

Row 4: With D, k1, * p3tog, do not sl sts off needle, yo, p same 3 sts tog again, k1, rep from * across.

Row 5: With A, knit.

Row 6: With A, purl.

Bands 1–6 make up 58-row body pat.

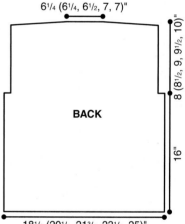

6¼ (6¼, 6½, 7, 7)"

8 (8½, 9, 9½, 10)"

16"

BACK

18½ (20¼, 21¾, 23½, 25)"

Back

Beg at lower edge with larger needles and MC, cast on 93 (101, 109, 117, 125) sts.

Set up row: K1, *p1, k1, rep from * across. Work 58 rows of body pat until piece measures approximately 16 inches from beg, ending with a WS row.

Shape armholes

Bind off 4 sts at beg of next 2 rows. Continue in pat on remaining 85 (93, 101, 109, 117) sts until piece measures approximately 24 (24½, 25, 25½, 26) inches from beg, ending with a WS row.

Shape shoulders and neck

Continuing in established pat, bind off [9 (10, 11, 12, 14) sts at each edge] twice, and [9 (11, 12, 13, 13) sts at each edge] once. Bind off remaining 31 (31, 33, 35, 35) sts for back neck.

Pocket Linings
Make 2

With larger needles and MC, cast on 21 sts. Beg with a purl row, work in St st to approximately 4 inches from beg, ending with a RS row. Place sts on a holder.

Right Front

Beg at lower edge with larger needles and MC, cast on 56 (60, 64, 68, 72) sts.

Set up row: K1, *p1, k1, rep from * to last 19 sts, end k19.

K 19 sts and place on a holder for buttonhole band. On remaining 37 (41, 45, 49, 53), beg body pat. Work even through completion of Row 4 of Pat D.

Join pocket

With A, k8 (10, 12, 14, 16), place next 21 sts on a holder, with WS of pocket lining facing, k21 from holder, k to end. With A, purl across.

Beg with Row 1 of Pat A, continue working 58-row pat until piece measures approximately 15½ (16, 16½, 17, 17½) inches from beg, ending with a WS row.

Shape neck

Dec 1 st at neck edge [every other row] 6 (6, 7, 8, 8) times.

At the same time, when piece measures approximately 16 inches from beg, ending with a RS row, shape armhole by binding off 4 sts at beg of next row. When neck decs are completed, continue in pat on remaining 27 (31, 34, 37, 41) sts until front measures approximately 24 (24½, 25, 25½, 26) inches from beg, ending with a RS row.

Shape shoulder

At armhole edge, bind off [9 (10, 11, 12, 14) sts] twice, then [9 (11, 12, 13, 13) sts] once.

Left Front

Beg at lower edge with larger needles and MC, cast on 56 (60, 64, 68, 72) sts.

Set up row: K20, *p1, k1, rep from * across.

Work body pat across first 37 (41, 45, 49, 53) sts, k19.

K 19 sts and place on a holder, continue pat across remaining sts. Work as for right front, reversing all shaping.

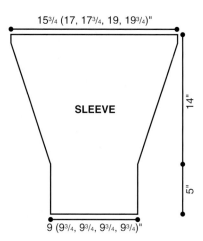

15¾ (17, 17¾, 19, 19¾)"

SLEEVE

14"

5"

9 (9¾, 9¾, 9¾, 9¾)"

Sleeves

Beg at lower edge with smaller needles and MC, cast on 45 (49, 49, 49, 49) sts.

Ribbing

Row 1 (WS): P1, *k1, p1, rep from * across.

Row 2: K1, *p1, k1, rep from * across.

Rep Rows 1 and 2 until cuff measures approximately 5 inches from beg, ending with a WS row.

Change to larger needles and beg body pat. Inc 1 st at each edge [every 4th row] 0 (0, 0, 0, 6) times, [every 6th row] 0 (3, 10, 23, 19) times, and [every 8th row] 17

(15, 10, 0, 0) times, working new sts into pat.

Continue to work in pat on 79 (85, 89, 95, 99) sts until piece measures approximately 19 inches from beg, ending with a WS row. Bind off all sts.

Finishing

Join shoulder seams. Set in sleeves, sewing bound off sts to sleeves sides for square armholes. Join underarm and side seams.

Left Front Band and Collar

With RS facing, return 19 sts from holder to smaller needle. With MC, continue in garter st until band fits along front edge to beg of neck shaping.

Shape collar

Inc 1 st at inside edge [every other row] 15 times, then [every 4th row] 15 times. Work even on 49 sts until collar fits along left front neck edge and to center back neck. Bind off all sts.

Sew band in place. Pm on band for 2 sets of buttons with first set 6 inches from lower edge and next set 6 inches from first neck shaping row.

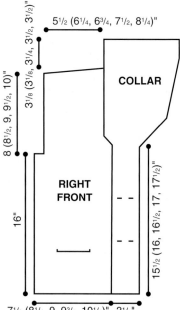

5½ (6¼, 6¾, 7½, 8¼)"

3⅛ (3⅛, 3¼, 3½, 3½)"

8 (8½, 9, 9½, 10)"

COLLAR

3⅛ (3⅛, 3¼, 3½, 3½)"

RIGHT FRONT

16"

15½ (16, 16½, 17, 17½)"

7½ (8¼, 9, 9¾, 10½)" 3½"

Right Front Band and Collar

Work to correspond to left band and collar, working buttonholes opposite markers as follows:

Buttonhole row (RS): K5, bind off 2 sts, k5, bind off 2 sts, k5.

On next row, k across and cast on 2 sts over each buttonhole. Complete as for left band.

Sew collar seam at center back neck. Fold collar in half to outside and sew back edge only to seam along RS of back neck. Fold again, matching to inside edge of garter stitch band. Tack in place at center back neck, along shoulders and at even intervals along neck edges to first neck shaping row. Sew buttons opposite buttonholes. Sew snaps onto inside edge of right front band and outside edge of left front band at lower side edges.

Pocket Edging

Sl sts from holder to smaller needles. With D, bind off knitwise. Sew pocket linings in place.

Lower Edging

With RS facing, using smaller needles and MC, pick up and k 1 st in each cast on st along lower edge. Bind off knitwise. ❖

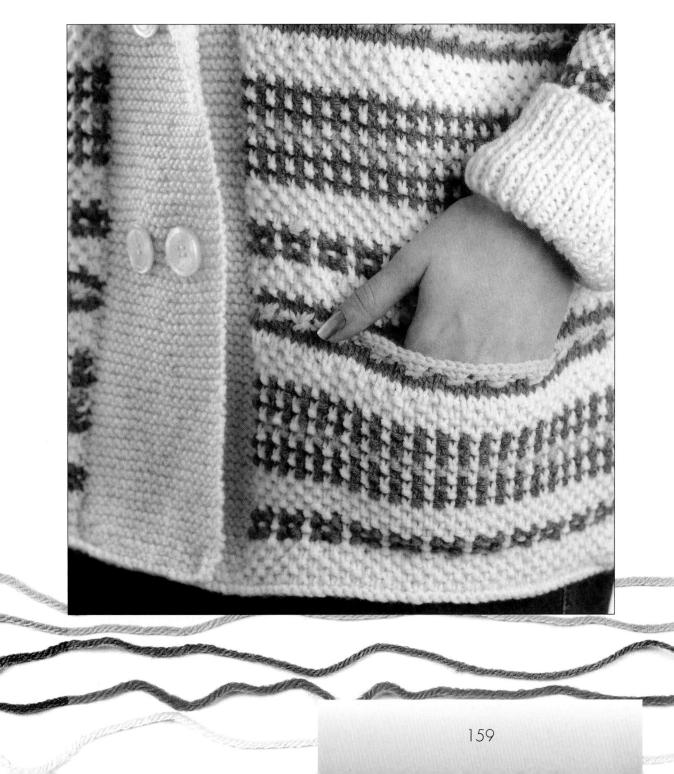

Summer Sampler Vest

Design by Edie Eckman

This vest is easy and fun to knit using a modular pattern that works for a variety of gauges and a mixture of yarns.

Skill Level

Intermediate***

Size

Woman's extra-small (small, medium, large, extra-large) All sizes are worked alike. Changes are made by varying gauge and number of sts in each square.

Finished Measurements

Chest: Approximately 36 (40, 44, 48, 52) inches

Materials

- A variety of sport and light worsted weight cotton and cotton-blend yarns in cream, ecru, off-white, in a variety of textures (optional): Approximately 900–1200 yards total, including about 190 yds of 1 yarn for borders
- Size 6 (4mm) or 7 (4.5mm) 16- and 24-inch circular needles or size needed for gauge and chosen yarn (see gauge instructions)
- 2 additional 24-inch or longer circular needles in same size or one size smaller
- Stitch markers
- Tapestry needle

Gauge

Work gauge swatch as follows: Using predominant yarn, complete 25-st Basic Square. Compare finished size of square to Fig. 1. If necessary, adjust number of sts and/or needle size and make additional gauge swatches until swatch measures desired dimension.

Special Abbreviations

Dd (double dec): Sl 1, k2tog, psso.

M1 (make 1): Inc by making a backward loop over right needle.

Pattern Notes

This is a modular pattern that works for a variety of gauges and a mixture of yarns. As long as the knitter uses yarns that are similar in weight, any slight inconsistencies in gauge will even out as the vest is assembled. If necessary, use 2 fine yarns held tog to obtain desired gauge.

Vest is not intended to meet in front.

Squares are worked back and forth on circular needles. Mark corner sts with removable st marker or safety pin.

All sizes are worked the same way; differences in size come from gauge and number of sts in each square. Refer to Fig. 1 for sizing.

After the Basic Square, each subsequent square is attached to previous ones without seams. The only seams are shoulder seams. As you knit, check to see that you are picking up sts correctly—all diagonals should be leaning the same way.

Instructions are given for neck, front and bottom bands to be worked in 1 piece on 4 circular needles, in rnds as with double points. Each band may be worked individually if enough circular needles are not available.

Choose yarns at random, keeping in mind that shiny or novelty yarns will draw the eye—watch placement of these yarns carefully to avoid highlighting portions of the body you may not want to feature!

For variety, switch yarns in the middle of a square, work stripes, or add an occasional purl row on the wrong side. Use no more than 2 purl rows (St st rows) on any 1 square to avoid distortion.

For a more prominent center double dec, sl next 2 sts tog as if to k2tog, k1, pass 2 sl sts over. On next row, purl center st.

Basic Square

Cast on 25 (27, 29) sts.

Row 1 and all WS rows: Knit.

Row 2: K11 (12, 13), dd, k11 (12, 13).

Row 4: K10 (11, 12), dd, k10 (11, 12).

Row 6: K9 (10, 11), dd, k9 (10, 11).

Continue working in this manner, dec 2 sts every other row until 3 sts remain, ending with a WS row.

Final row: Dd. Fasten off.

Vest Assembly

Work Basic Square (Square 1), using needle size and number of sts chosen after determining gauge.

Squares 2–5: Using a different yarn from that used in previous square, pick up and k 12 (13, 14) sts along top edge of previous square, cast on 13 (14, 15) sts at end of row. (25, 27, 29 sts)

Work Basic Square.

Square 6: Cast on 12 (13, 14) sts, pick up and k 1 st in bottom

If your square measures	Finished chest measurement	Finished length	Armhole length	Neck width
2¼"	36"	14⅝"	7⅞"	5¼"
2½"	40"	16¼"	8¾"	6"
2¾"	44"	17⅞"	9⅝"	6¾"
3"	48"	19½"	10½"	7½"
¾"	52"	21⅛"	11⅜"	8¼"

FIG. 1

right-hand corner of Square #1, and 12 (13, 14) sts along RH side of same square. (25, 27, 29 sts)

Work Basic Square.

Squares 7–10: Pick up and k 12 (13, 14) sts along top of previous square, 1 st in corner, and 12 (13, 14) sts along side of adjacent square. Work Basic Square.

Square 11: Work as for Square 2.

Referring to Fig. 2, continue working squares in this manner through Square 101.

Finishing

Fold vest with WS tog. Sew shoulder seams.

Armhole bands

Rnd 1: With RS facing, beg at center underarm, with 16-inch needle, pick up and k 1 st in each st to corner, 1 st in corner, 1 st in each ridge or st around armhole to corner, 1 st in corner, and 1 st in each st to beg.

Rnd 2: Purl.

Rnd 3: [K to 1 st before corner st, dd] twice, k to beg of rnd.

Rnds 4 and 5: Rep Rnds 2 and 3.

Rnd 6: Rep Rnd 2.

Bind off row: *Bind off to 1 st before corner st, dd, bind off that st, rep from * once, bind off remaining sts.

Neck, front and bottom border
(worked in 1 piece)

Rnd 1: With RS facing, beg at bottom edge under left armhole, pick up and k 1 st in each st across back and right front, 1 st in front corner; with 2nd needle, pick up and k 1 st in each ridge up right front, 1 st in corner, 1 st in each st, corner st and ridge to back center neck; with 3rd needle, continue to pick up and k 1 st in each st, corner st and ridge around neck, 1 st in corner, 1 st in each ridge down left front, 1 st in corner, and 1 st in each st to beg.

Rnd 2: Using 4th needle, purl sts from first needle. Use free needle to purl sts from next needle, and so on around to beg of rnd.

Rnd 3: [K to corner, M1, k corner st, M1] twice, [k to 1 st before corner, dd] 4 times, [k to corner, M1, k1, M1] twice, k to beg of rnd.

Rnds 4 and 5: Rep Rnds 2 and 3.

Rnd 6: Purl.

Bind off around first 2 corners, [bind off to 1 st before next corner, work dd, bind off resulting st] 4 times, bind off remaining sts. Fasten off securely. ❖

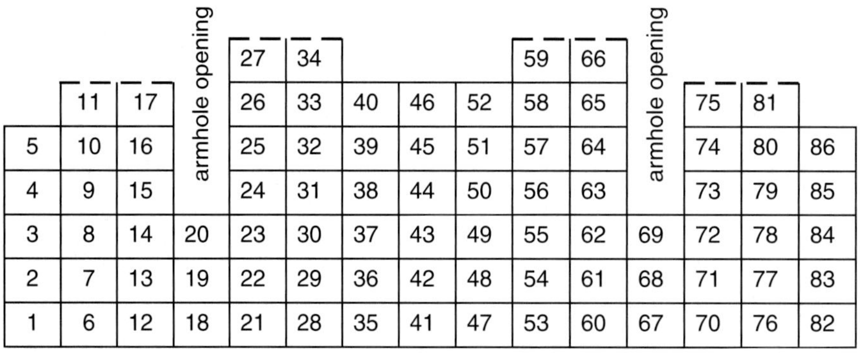

Dotted lines indicate shoulder seams

FIG. 2

Skill Level
Intermediate***

Size
Adult's small (medium, large)
Instructions are given for smallest size, with larger sizes in parentheses. When only 1 number is given, it applies to all sizes.

Finished Measurements
Chest: 42 (44, 46) inches

Armhole depth: 8½ (9, 9½) inches

Length to underarm: 14 (14, 16) inches

Materials
• Naturally Aspiring Aran 10-ply 60 percent New Zealand wool/40 percent alpaca worsted weight yarn from S.R. Kertzer (185 yds/100g per skein): 5 (5, 7) skeins #708 (MC)
• Naturally Café 10-ply 42 percent New Zealand wool/28 percent alpaca fleece/26 percent mohair/4 percent nylon bouclé yarn from S.R. Kertzer (85 yds/50g per ball): 3 balls #710 (A)
• Naturally Landscape 10-ply 95 percent New Zealand wool/5 percent poly binder novelty yarn from S.R. Kertzer (103 yds/50g per ball): 3 balls #803 (B)
• Size 3 (3.25mm) straight and 16-inch circular needles
• Size 6 (4mm) needles or size needed to obtain gauge
• Yarn bobbins
• Stitch holders
• Stitch markers

Gauge
20 sts and 26 rows = 4 inches/10cm in St st

To save time, take time to check gauge.

Pattern Stitch
1/1 Twisted Rib

Row 1 (RS): K1 tbl, *p1, k1 tbl, rep from* across.

Row 2: P1 tbl, *k1, p1 tbl, rep from * across.

Rep Rows 1 and 2 for pat.

Patchwork Pull
Design by Diane Zangl

This easy-fit pullover features a patchwork design, which is meant to use up odds and ends of various yarns.

Pattern Notes
Front and back are knit separately, then joined at shoulders. Sts are picked up around indented armhole and sleeves are worked downward—a good idea if yarn amounts are running short. K1, p1 ribbing finishes cuffs, lower edge and crew neckline.

St st is used throughout model shown, but patches could easily be patterned or textured to suit the knitter's fancy.

Wind separate bobbins or small balls of yarn for each color area.

To avoid holes when changing colors, always bring new color up from under old.

Back
With smaller needles and MC, cast on 97 (101, 105) sts. Work even in 1/1 twisted rib pat for 2 inches, ending with a WS row. Change to larger needles.

K 1 row, inc 8 (10, 10) sts evenly across. (105, 111, 115 sts)

Work even in St st for 9 (9, 13) rows. Referring to Chart A, work even in color pat until back measures 14 (14, 16) inches, ending with a WS row.

Shape underarm

Next row: Work 8 (10, 10) sts and sl to holder, work to last 8 (10, 10) sts and sl to 2nd holder. (89, 91, 95 sts)

Work even until armhole measures 8½ (9, 9½) inches, ending with a WS row.

Shape shoulders

Bind off 10 sts at beg of next 6 rows. Sl remaining 29 (31, 35) sts to holder for back neck.

Front
Work as for back until armhole measures 7½ inches, ending with a WS row.

Shape neck

Place center 21 (23, 27) sts on holder. Working on both sides of neck with separate balls of yarn, [dec 1 st at each neck edge every row] 4 times.

Work even until armhole measures same as for back.

Shape shoulders

Bind off at each arm edge [10 sts] 3 times.

Sew shoulder seams.

Neck band

With 16-inch circular needle and MC, pick up and k 80 (86, 100) sts around neckline, including sts on holders. Pm between first and last st. *[K1b, p1] around. Rep this rnd 5 more times. Bind off loosely in pat.

Sleeves
Sl sts from right back underarm to larger RH needle, join MC and pick up and k along straight edge of armhole, 1 st, pm, 83 (87, 93) sts, pm, 1 st, sl sts from 2nd underarm to LH needle.

Referring to Chart B for color placement and sizing, *sl 1 purlwise wyib, turn, p2tog tbl, p in color pat to marker, p2tog, sl 1 purlwise wyif, turn, k2tog, k in color pat to marker, ssk. Rep from * until all underarm sts have been worked.

Continuing in established pat [dec 1 st each end every 6th row] 15

(16, 17) times. (55, 57, 61 sts)

Work even until sleeve measures 17½ (18, 18½) inches, dec 4 sts on last row. Change to smaller needles.

Beg cuff

Work even in 1/1 twisted rib pat until cuff measures 2½ inches. Bind off in pat.

Finishing

Sew sleeve and body underarm seams. ❖

COLOR KEY
☐ MC
⊠ A
● B

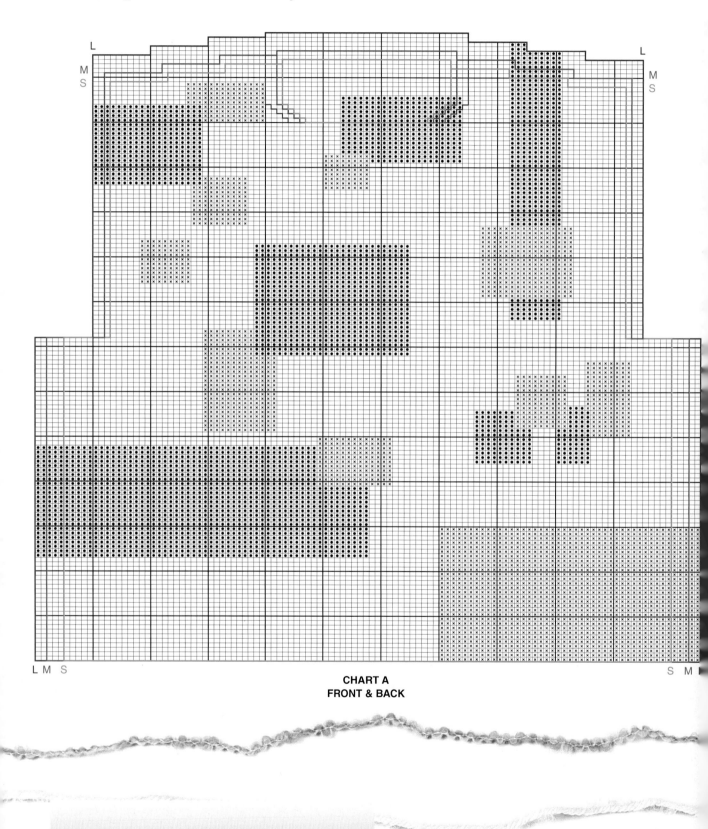

CHART A
FRONT & BACK

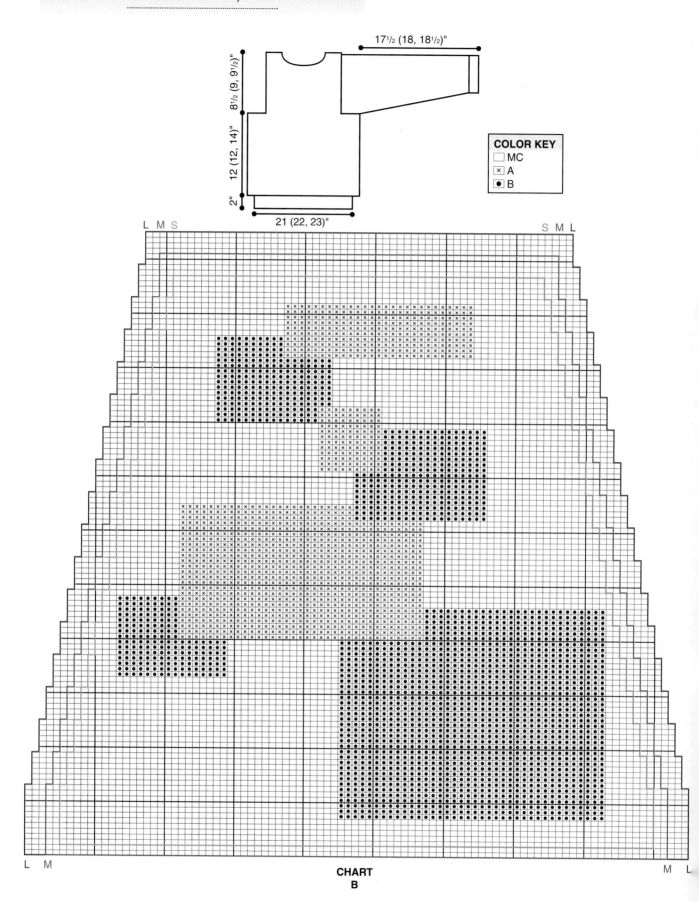

COLOR KEY
☐ MC
☒ A
● B

17½ (18, 18½)"

8½ (9, 9½)"

12 (12, 14)"

2"

21 (22, 23)"

L M S   S M L

L M   M L

**CHART
B**

Skill Level

Beginner*

Finished Size

Approximately 45 x 54 inches
(excluding fringe)

Materials

- Patons Décor 75 percent acrylic/
  25 percent wool worsted weight
  yarn from Spinrite Yarns (210
  yds/3½ oz per skein): 4 skeins
  each rich aqua #1612 (dark),
  aqua #1611 (medium), pale
  aqua #1610 (light)
- Size 7 (4.5mm) knitting needles
  or size needed to obtain gauge
- Tapestry needle
- Large crochet hook (to apply fringe)

Gauge

Each block measures approximately
3 inches square.

To save time, take time to check
gauge.

Special Abbreviations

K1b: Knit in back of st.

LT (left twist): Skip first st, knit
2nd st in back loop, then k
skipped st in front loop and sl
both sts from needle at once.

RT (right twist): Skip first st, knit
2nd st in front loop, then k
skipped st in front loop and sl
both sts from needle at once.

Pattern Notes

Afghan is made in 15 strips that
are joined tog after knitting
is completed.

To avoid weaving in so many tails,
when changing colors, leave an
8-inch tail for sewing.

Pattern Stitches

A. Rice Stitch

Row 1 (RS): Knit.

Row 2: Knit.

Row 3: K2, *p1, k1b, rep from *
across, end p1, k2.

Rows 4–21: Rep Rows 2 and 3.

Row 22: Knit.

B. Moss Stitch Zigzag

Row 1 (RS): Knit.

Row 2: K2, p11, k2.

Row 3: K4, p1, k1, p1, k8.

Row 4 and remaining WS rows:
K2, k the knit sts and p the purl
sts, end k2.

Row 5: K5, p1, k1, p1, k7.

Row 7: K6, p1, k1, p1, k6.

Row 9: K7, p1, k1, p1, k5.

Row 11: K8, p1, k1, p1, k4.

Row 13: Rep Row 9.

Row 15: Rep Row 7.

Row 17: Rep Row 5.

Row 19: Rep Row 3.

Row 21: K3, p1, k1, p1, k9.

Row 22: Rep Row 4.

C. Textured Stitch

Row 1 (RS): Knit.

Row 2: K5, p1, k3, p1, k5.

Row 3 and 4: Rep Rows 1 and 2.

Row 5: Knit.

Row 6: K3, p1, [k3, p1] twice, k3.

Rows 7 and 8: Rep Rows 5 and 6.

Rows 9–24: Rep Rows 1–8.

D. Garter Stitch Ladders

Row 1 (RS): Knit.

Row 2: K2, p11, k2.

Rows 3 and 4: Rep Rows 1 and 2.

Row 5: Knit.

Row 6: Knit.

Rows 7–18: Rep Rows 1–6.

Rows 19–22: Rep Rows 1–4.

E. Moss Stitch

Row 1 (RS): Knit.

Row 2: K3, [p1, k1] 4 times, p1, k3.

Row 3: K2, [p1, k1] 5 times, p1, k2.

Row 4: K2, [p1, k1] 5 times, p1, k2.

Row 5: K3, [p1, k1] 4 times, p1, k3.

Rows 6–21: Rep Rows 2–5.

Rows 22–24: Rep Rows 2–4.

F. Little Wave

Row 1 (RS): Knit.

Row 2: K2, p4, k2, p5, k2.

Row 3: K6, LT, k7.

Row 4: K2, p4, k1, p1, k1, p4, k2.

Row 5: K7, LT, k6.

Row 6: K2, p5, k2, p4, k2.

Row 7: Knit.

Row 8: Rep Row 6.

Row 9: K7, RT, k6.

Row 10: Rep Row 4.

Row 11: K6, RT, k7.

Row 12: Rep Row 2.

Gramma's Stitch Sampler Quilt

Design by Ann E. Smith

*Based on a quilt made by the
designer's grandmother, seven pattern
stitches and three colors combine for
an easy, but delightful afghan!*

Rows 13–20: Rep Rows 1–8.

G. Ridged Rib

Row 1 (RS): Knit.

Row 2: Knit.

Row 3: K2, [p1, k1] 5 times, p1, k2.

Row 4: K3, [p1, k1] 4 times, p1, k3.

Rows 5–24: Rep Rows 1–4.

Afghan
Strip 1
Make 6

Beg at lower edge with dark, cast on 15 sts, work Pat A. Change to light, work Pat B. Change to medium, work Pat C. Change to dark, work Pat D. Change to light, work Pat E. Change to medium, work Pat F. Change to dark, work Pat G. Change to light, work Pat A. Change to medium, work Pat B. Change to dark, work Pat C. Change to light, work Pat D. Change to medium, work Pat E. Change to dark, work Pat F. Change to light, work Pat G. Change to medium, work Pat A. Change to dark, work Pat B. Change to light, work Pat C. Change to medium, work Pat D. Bind off knitwise.

Strip 2
Make 5

Beg at lower edge with light, cast on 15 sts, work Pat A. Change to medium, work Pat B. Change to dark, work Pat C. Change to light, work Pat D. Change to medium, work Pat E. Change to dark, work Pat F. Change to light, work Pat G. Change to medium, work Pat A. Change to dark, work Pat B. Change to light, work Pat C. Change to medium, work Pat D. Change to dark, work Pat E. Change to light, work Pat F. Change to medium, work Pat G. Change to dark, work Pat A. Change to light, work Pat B. Change to medium, work Pat C. Change to dark, work work Pat D. Bind off knitwise.

Strip 3
Make 4

Beg at lower edge with medium, cast

on 15 sts, work Pat A. Change to dark, work Pat B. Change to light, work Pat C. Change to medium, work Pat D. Change to dark, work Pat E. Change to light, work Pat F. Change to medium, work Pat G. Change to dark, work Pat A. Change to light, work Pat B. Change to medium, work Pat C. Change to dark, work Pat D. Change to light, work Pat E. Change to medium, work Pat F. Change to dark, work Pat G. Change to light, work Pat A. Change to medium, work Pat B. Change to dark, work Pat C. Change to light, work Pat D. Bind off knitwise.

Finishing

Referring to Fig. 1, join panels tog using tails at the sides as follows:

Panel 1
Make 2

Working from right to left, join Strip 1, Strip 2 and Strip 3.

Panel 2
Make 1

Working from right to left, join Strip 1, Strip 2, Strip 1.

Panel 3
Make 2

Working from right to left, join Strip 3, Strip 2, Strip 1.

Working from right to left, join panels as follows: 1, 1, 2, 3, 3.

Fringe

Cut 18 (6-inch) strands of each color. Fold 3 strands of dark in half to form a loop. Insert a crochet hook from WS to RS and pull loop through corner of first dark square, take ends through loop and pull up to form a knot. Add 5 more dark fringes to dark square, then 6 light fringes to light square and 6 medium fringes to medium square. Matching colors, add 6 fringes to each square along each end of afghan. ❖

COLOR KEY
- Rich aqua
- Aqua
- Pale aqua

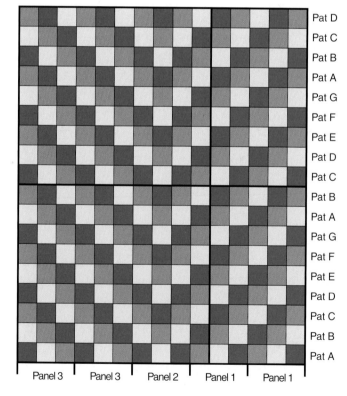

Panel 3 | Panel 3 | Panel 2 | Panel 1 | Panel 1

Pat D, Pat C, Pat B, Pat A, Pat G, Pat F, Pat E, Pat D, Pat C, Pat B, Pat A, Pat G, Pat F, Pat E, Pat D, Pat C, Pat B, Pat A

FIG. 1

Bulky Knit Rug

Design by Edie Eckman

Any weight of yarn can be used for this easy-to-knit rug. Just use several strands held together to obtain the correct gauge.

Skill Level

Beginner*

Finished Size

Approximately 24 x 36 inches

Materials

- 6 colors of yarn in bulky, worsted, DK or sport weight: approximately 4¾ oz for each square
- Size 15 (10mm) needles or size needed to obtain gauge
- Tapestry needle

Gauge

10 sts and 20 rows = 4 inches/10cm in garter st

Gauge is not critical to this project, but each combination of yarns should work to the same gauge.

Square 1

Cast on 30 sts. Knit every row until piece is square. Bind off all sts.

Rows 1 and 2: *K1, p1, rep from * across.

Rows 3 and 4: *P1, k1, rep from * across.

Rep Rows 1–4 for pat until piece is square. Bind off all sts.

Square 4

Cast on 30 sts.

Row 1: *K3, p3, rep from * across.

Row 2: *P3, k3, rep from * across.

Rep Rows 1 and 2 until piece is square. Bind off all sts.

Square 5

Cast on 3 sts. Knit 1 row.

Inc row: K in front and back of first st, k across.

Rep inc row every row until square measures 8½ inches long (or ½ diagonal measurement of other squares). Knit 1 row.

Dec row: K2tog, k across.

Rep dec row every row until 3 sts remain. Bind off.

Square 6

Cast on 30 sts.

Rows 1–6: Knit.

Row 7 (WS): K3, p24, k3.

Row 8: Knit.

Work [Rows 1–8] 6 times, rep Rows 1–5. Bind off all sts.

Finishing

Referring to Fig. 1, sew squares tog. ❖

Notes

Sample project was worked as follows:

Square 1

100 yds chunky weight acrylic/wool blend yarn, used single strand.

Square 2

300 yds worsted weight acrylic/wool blend yarn, 3 strands held tog.

Square 3

300 yds worsted weight acrylic yarn, 3 strands held tog.

Square 4

300 yds worsted weight wool yarn, 3 strands held tog.

Square 5

500 yds sport weight wool yarn, 5 strands held tog.

Square 6

400 yds DK weight acrylic/wool blend yarn, 4 strands held tog.

Square 2

Cast on 30 sts.

Row 1: K2, *p2, k2, rep from * across.

Rows 2 and 3: P2, *k2, p2, rep from * across.

Row 4: Rep Row 1.

Rep Rows 1–4 for pat until piece is square. Bind off all sts.

Square 3

Cast on 30 sts.

5	3	1	
6	4	2	24"

36"

FIG. 1

Textured Stripes Sampler Afghan

Design by Laura Polley

Use odd balls of soft, warm yarns to create this beautiful textured sampler afghan! This afghan would also be handsome stitched in a rainbow of colors.

STITCH & COLOR KEY

- ☐ K on RS, p on WS with CC1 (Natural)
- ⊟ P on RS, k on WS with CC1 (Natural)
- ■ K on RS, p on WS with CC2 (Brown)
- ⊟ P on RS, k on WS with CC2 (Brown)
- ▨ K on RS, p on WS with CC3 (Gray)
- ▨ P on RS, k on WS with CC3 (Gray)

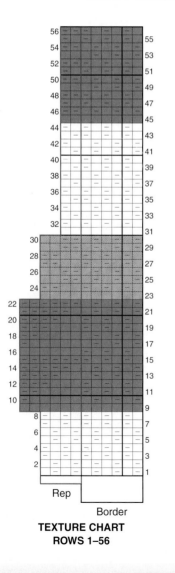

TEXTURE CHART ROWS 1–56

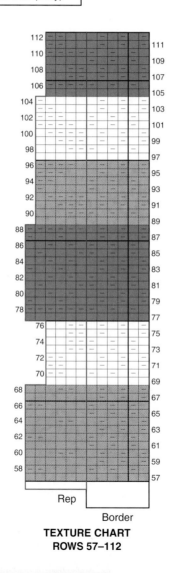

TEXTURE CHART ROWS 57–112

Skill Level

Intermediate***

Finished Size

Approximately 56 x 64 inches

Materials

- 8–14 different yarns (DK to heavy worsted weight) in various shades of off-white, cream and ivory (CC1's)
- 8–14 different yarns (DK to heavy worsted weight) in various shades of brown, tan and dark beige (CC2's)
- 8–14 different yarns (DK to heavy worsted weight) in various shades of grey (CC3's)
- Size 9 (5.5mm) 32-inch or longer circular needle or size needed to obtain gauge
- Tapestry needle

Gauge

18 sts = 4 inches/10cm in moss st (border pat)

To save time, take time to check gauge.

Pattern Notes

Each stripe of color is worked over 8, 10, 12 or 14 rows. Use yardage estimates to determine if you have enough of a particular yarn to work a given stripe.

8-row stripe: approximately 55 yds.

10-row stripe: approximately 70 yds.

12-row stripe: approximately 85 yds.

14-row stripe: approximately 100 yds.

Depending on the number and size of single skeins, you may choose to use a different yarn for every stripe, or use the same yarn for more than 1 stripe. Sample project used 36 different yarns, 7 of which were used more than once.

To work gauge swatch, using a worsted weight yarn, preferably a CC1, cast on 18 sts. Referring to chart, [work border pat (first 6 sts)] 3 times across. Work [Rows 1–8] twice. Piece should measure 4 inches from edge to edge.

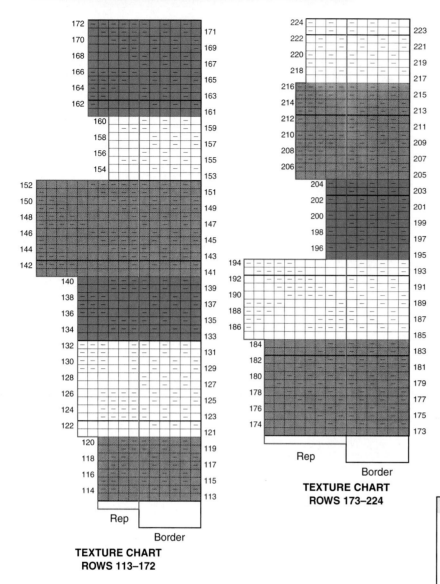

**TEXTURE CHART
ROWS 113–172**

**TEXTURE CHART
ROWS 173–224**

Row gauge is not uniform, as texture pats will affect it. While there will be some variation, finished length should be within 2–3 inches of the sample.

Circular needle is used to accommodate large number of sts. Do not join at end of row.

All color changes are made on a RS row to avoid color bumps.

St rep varies among the pats, but all divide evenly into 240-st center panel.

Afghan

Using same worsted weight CC1 used for swatch, cast on 252 sts.

Row 1 (RS): Reading chart from right to left, work first 6 sts from chart (border), work pat rep to last 6 sts, rep border across last 6 sts.

Row 2: Reading chart from left to right, first work border sts, work pat rep to last 6 sts, rep border across last 6 sts.

Work Rows 3–224 of chart pat as established, changing colors and yarns as indicated, then rep Rows 9–224 once. Bind off all sts in pat. ❖

STITCH & COLOR KEY
☐ K on RS, p on WS with CC1 (Natural)
⊟ P on RS, k on WS with CC1 (Natural)
■ K on RS, p on WS with CC2 (Brown)
▬ P on RS, k on WS with CC2 (Brown)
■ K on RS, p on WS with CC3 (Gray)
▬ P on RS, k on WS with CC3 (Gray)

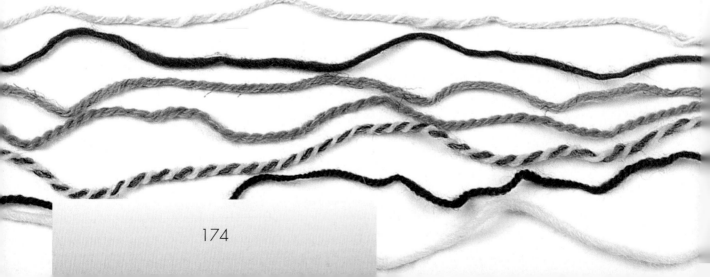

Special Thanks

We would like to thank the talented knitting designers whose work is featured in this collection.

Svetlana Avrakh
It's a Dog's Day, 36
Popsicle Stripes, 92

Kathie Ballard
Mock Cable Purse, 11
Easy Santa Ornament &
  Lapel Pin, 124

Dixie Butler
Side Cable Slippers, 19

Sue Childress
Baby's Car Seat Blanket, 12
Diamond Eyelet Purse, 43
Textured Blocks Scarf, 99

Edie Eckman
Rainbow Eyeglass Case, 27
Glitzy Clutch & Shoulder Bag, 28
Mohair Stripes Scarf & Pigtail Hat, 88
Mini Christmas Stocking Set, 126
Easter Basket & Eggs, 129
Glitzy Earrings, 132
Checkerboard Doll Pullover, 144
Garter-Stitch Doll Suit, 151
Summer Sampler Vest, 160
Bulky Knit Rug, 170

Diane Elliott
Little Lamb Ornament, 128

Frances Hughes
Smocked Ribbons Hat, 18
Face Cloth Quartet, 24

Rita Knudson
Catarina Kitt, Figure-Skating
  Gold Medalist, 44
A Norwegian Couple: Knute &
  Ragnhild, 146

Patsy Leatherbury
Summer Stripes Crop Tops, 89
Fiesta Grande Shawl, 114

Elizabeth Mattfield
Stretchy Headbands, 32
Striped Tiptop Hats, 84
Rugged Felted Stripes, 86
Colorful Baby Blocks, 152

Carolyn Pfeifer
One Skein Textured Pillow, 23
Patchwork Squares Afghan, 67
Fireside Warmer Afghan, 76

Laura Polley
Tie-Dye Cap, 14
Yarn Painting Cardigan, 52
Stained Glass Squares, 71
Peppermint Ice Cream Child's
  Sweater & Hat, 95
Textured Stripes Sampler Afghan, 172

Kathleen Sasser
Imitation Rag Rug, 80

Ann Smith
Nautical Vest, 116
Slip-Stitch Sampler Jacket, 156
Gramma's Stitch Sampler Quilt, 167

Kennita Tully
Silky Pink Evening Bag With Coin
  Purse, 30
Picnic Blanket & Pillow, 64
Color Splash Cardigan for the
  Family, 100
Sideways Knit Striped Cardigan, 104

Virginia Vaughn
Paparazzi Hat, 48
Checkered Socks, 50
Funky Hemmed Hat, 56
Ski Band Stripes, 81
A Touch of Color Hat & Scarf, 82

Barbara Venishnick
Winterfest Afghan, 78
Kaleidoscope Triangles Jacket, 110

Lois Young
Art Deco Place Mat, 22
Floral Table Runner &
  Coasters, 61
Misty Maples Pullover, 107

Thelma Young
Peek-a-Boo Holes Place Mat, 20
Fashion Doll Cheerleader Outfit, 133
Summer Dream Suit, 138

Diane Zangl
Toddler's Happy Hats, 8
Lacy Baby Bibs, 16
Kid's Color Pair, 58
Mini-Mitts & Hat Garland, 122
Patchwork Pull, 163

Standard Abbreviations

beg	begin(ning)
CC	contrast color
ch	chain
cn	cable needle
dec	decrease
dpn	double-pointed needle
g	gram(s)
inc	increase
k	knit
LH	left hand
MC	main color
oz	ounce(s)
p	purl
pat	pattern
pm	place marker
psso	pass slipped stitch over knit (or purl) stitch
rep	repeat
RH	right hand
rnd	round
RS	right side

sl	slip
ssk	slip, slip, knit (a left-slanting decrease): slip 2 stitches individually as if to knit to right-hand needle, reinsert tip of left needle and knit 2 stitches together through back loops
st(s)	stitch(es)
St st	Stockinette stitch
tbl	through back loops
tog	together
WS	wrong side
wyib	with yarn in back
wyif	with yarn in front
yo	yarn over
"	inch(es)
*	repeat instructions from asterisk as directed
[ ]	repeat instructions within brackets number of times stated

Buyer's Guide

Please check your local yarn shops first for featured yarns. If you are unable to find a product locally, contact the manufacturers listed below and ask where the closest retail source is in your area. Quickest results will be obtained by calling.

Bernat Yarns, Box 40, Listowel, Ontario N4W 3H3, Canada, (519) 291-3780

Berroco Inc., P.O. Box 367, Uxbridge, MA 01569-0367, (508) 278-2527

Brown Sheep Co., 100662 County Road 16, Mitchell, NE 69357, (308) 635-2198

Caron International, P.O. Box 222, Washington, NC 27889

Cascade Yarns, 2401 Utah Ave. S., Suite 505, Seattle, WA 98134, (800) 548-1048

Classic Elite Yarns, 300A Jackson St., Lowell, MA 01852, (800) 343-0308

Coats & Clark, P.O. Box 12229, Greenville, SC 29612-0229, (864) 877-8985

JCA/Reynolds Inc., 35 Scales Lane, Townsend, MA 01469-1094, (978) 597-8794

K1C2 Solutions for You, 2220 Eastman Ave. #105, Ventura CA 93003, (800) 607-2462

S.R. Kertzer Limited, 105A Winges Road, Woodbridge, Ontario, L4L 6C2 Canada, (800) 263-2354

Knitting Fever Inc., P.O. Box 502, Roosevelt, NY 11575, (516) 546-3600

Lion Brand Yarn Co., 34 W. 15th St., New York, NY 10011, (212) 243-8995

Lorna's Laces Yarns, P.O. Box 795, Somerset, CA 95684, (530) 626-4514

Patons Yarns, Box 40, Listowel, Ontario, N4W 3H3, Canada, (519) 291-3780

Plymouth Yarn Co Inc., P.O. Box 28, Bristol, PA 19007, (215) 788-0459

Tahki/Stacy Charles Inc., 1059 Manhattan Ave., Brooklyn, NY 11222, (718) 326-4433